POL MARTIN

LOVE AT FIRST BITE

Graphic Design
Pierre Leduc

Photographs by
Melissa du Fretay, Pol Martin (Ontario) Ltd. Studio

Coordinator
Josée Dugas

Props courtesy of WARES & WARES, Mississauga Home and Design Centre. Most merchandise available in store locations across Canada. Metropolitain Toronto, London, Calgary, Edmonton.

Published in Canada by
BRIMAR PUBLISHING INC.
8925, boulevard Saint-Laurent
Montréal, Canada H2N 1M5
Telephone: (514) 384-0776
Telex: 05-826756
Fax: (514) 384-0955

Published in the United States by
ECLAIR PUBLISHING INTERNATIONAL INC.
885 Third Avenue, Suite 2900
New York, NY 10022
Telephone: (212) 230-3266
Fax: (212) 230-3233

Legal Deposit: First Quarter 1990
Bibliothèque nationale du Québec
National Library of Canada

Library of Congress Cataloging-in-Publication Data
Martin, Pol
Love at First Bite
Includes index.
1. Cookery 1. Title
TX714.M375 1990 641.5-dc19 89-1218 CIP

ISBN 2-920845-65-9

Printed and bound in Canada

2088 A
1 2 3 4 5 6 7 8 9

TABLE OF CONTENTS

POL MARTIN: WORD OF MOUTH

Dear Friends,

Relax, experiment, enjoy—not the words you would expect to hear from a chef! Yet it is almost that simple to cook well and eat well. I have always believed that eating well, and enjoying it too, is within everyone's reach. Wonderful cuisine does not depend on an elaborately equipped kitchen or endless hours of preparation. All you need is a good chef's knife, a cutting board and a trusty frying pan. It's that simple!

I urge you to improvise, not to be afraid of your imagination. TRY is a key word in cooking, as in most things in life. Trial and error helps form our opinions and is often the best way to learn. Try substituting your favorite ingredients, or those that are freshest in your area. If a recipe calls for broccoli and you prefer cauliflower, try it with cauliflower. I'm not watching you through the pages, so feel free.

Eating is a constant concern in our society. How true it is that "We eat to live, but live to eat." I take great pleasure in eating, but I am the first to admit that eating properly takes a conscious effort. We want nutritionally balanced meals, and I provide nutritional data for every recipe. But the numbers do not always tell us what we want to hear. Cake is cake is cake. Take away the fattening ingredients and cake is no longer cake. My answer, for my body, is moderation and exercise. It works for me.

LOVE AT FIRST BITE is versatile and practical. I want you to use it as *the* cooking source that you can depend on. The recipes have been carefully written to be precise and informative. The accompanying photographs are a helpful visual reference and show the actual recipe when it was tested in my studio.

I really hope LOVE AT FIRST BITE becomes your best friend in the kitchen. I have had a great deal of fun creating it and am excited at the prospect of sharing these recipes with you.

Until we meet again, have fun . . . Bon appétit!

SOME TIPS AND HINTS FROM POL

"The art of cooking is essentially the understanding of techniques. Once you know the techniques, you can cook. Once you can cook, you can experiment."

- It is not necessary to follow a recipe to the letter. What is important is to follow the techniques used in a recipe.

- If you heat the pan before adding oil, you will need less oil.

- Using alcohol can give a special extra flavor. Reducing the liquid over high heat will evaporate the alcohol while leaving the flavor.

- Choose the freshest produce available, making substitutions if need be. For example, if green peppers look better than red peppers, then buy the green ones.

- Wonderful meals can be made with inexpensive cuts of meat (Lamb Shoulder Stew, for example) if the proper cooking technique is used.

- One good quality knife is better than 3 or 4 inexpensive ones.

- Cooking should be a fun adventure for the entire family. All children should learn the basics as soon as they are able.

- With the proper guidance, good cooking is very simple. The more fun you have in the kitchen, the more you will want to try. The more you practice, the better you will become. So have fun, my friends!

SUPER STARTERS

A bite here, a taste there—teasers to set the mood of your menu

Julienne of Vegetable Soup

serves 4

2 tbsp	(*30 ml*) butter
1	onion, finely chopped
3	carrots, pared and cut into fine julienne
½	turnip, peeled and cut into fine julienne
5 cups	(*1.2 L*) beef stock, heated
1 tsp	(*5 ml*) chopped fresh parsley
	salt and pepper

Heat butter in large saucepan over low heat. Add onion and cover; cook 5 minutes.

Add carrots and turnip; mix well and season. Cover and continue cooking 10 minutes.

Pour in beef stock, mix well and simmer soup 5 to 6 minutes.

Sprinkle with parsley and serve.

This soup is an ideal start to a fine luncheon.

1 serving *114 calories* *13 g carbohydrate*
2 g protein *6 g fat* *2.7 g fiber*

Cream of Turnip Royale

serves 4

3 tbsp	(*45 ml*) butter
½	onion, chopped
2	celery stalks, thinly sliced
2	potatoes, peeled, halved and thinly sliced
½	large turnip, peeled and sliced
½	seedless cucumber, thinly sliced
1 tbsp	(*15 ml*) chopped fresh parsley
1 tsp	(*5 ml*) marjoram
5 cups	(*1.2 L*) chicken stock, heated
3 tbsp	(*45 ml*) heavy cream
	salt and pepper

Melt butter in large saucepan over low heat. Add onion and celery; cover and cook 5 minutes.

Add remaining vegetables and season with salt and pepper. Sprinkle in parsley and marjoram; mix well. Cover and continue cooking 5 minutes.

Pour in chicken stock and bring to boil. Reduce heat to medium and cook, partly covered, 25 to 30 minutes or until vegetables are done.

Purée soup in food processor, mix in cream and serve. If desired, decorate portions by swirling a little extra cream into soup with fork.

1 serving	*161 calories*	*9 g carbohydrate*
2 g protein	*13 g fat*	*1.5 g fiber*

Cream of Mushroom with Yellow Pepper

serves 4

3 tbsp	(*45 ml*) butter
1	shallot, finely chopped
1 lb	(*500 g*) fresh mushrooms, cleaned* and sliced
1	yellow pepper, thinly sliced
½ tsp	(*2 ml*) tarragon
4 tbsp	(*60 ml*) flour
4½ cups	(*1.1 L*) chicken stock, heated
¼ cup	(*50 ml*) heavy cream
	salt and pepper
dash	paprika

Heat butter in large saucepan over low heat. Add shallot, mushrooms, yellow pepper and tarragon; mix well. Cover and cook 8 to 10 minutes.

Stir in flour until well incorporated. Cook 2 to 3 minutes, uncovered, over low heat.

Pour in chicken stock, mix well with whisk and correct seasoning. Pour in cream and bring to boil.

Cook soup, partly covered, 18 to 20 minutes over medium heat. Sprinkle with paprika before serving.

This soup will keep for 2 days if covered with buttered waxed paper and refrigerated

* *Remember to clean mushrooms without using water. Use of soft brush or cloth.*

1 serving	*194 calories*	*13 g carbohydrate*
4 g protein	*14 g fat*	*3.6 fiber*

Wintery Clam Chowder

serves 4

3 tbsp	(*45 ml*) butter
2	onions, diced small
1	celery stalk, diced small
3 tbsp	(*45 ml*) flour
4 cups	(*1 L*) fish stock, heated
3	potatoes, peeled and diced small
¼ cup	(*50 ml*) heavy cream
5 oz	(*142 g*) can baby clams
	juice from clams
	salt and pepper
pinch	celery seeds
pinch	thyme
dash	paprika
dash	ginger

Melt butter in large saucepan. Add onions and celery; cover and cook 2 minutes over medium heat.

Mix in flour until well incorporated. Cook 3 minutes, uncovered, over low heat.

Pour in fish stock and juice from clams; season and mix well. Add all seasonings and bring to boil.

Stir in potatoes, bring to boil again and reduce heat to medium. Cook 20 to 25 minutes, uncovered, stirring frequently.

Pour in cream and add clams to soup. Mix and cook 4 minutes over low heat. Do not allow liquid to boil.

Serve in large soup tureen.

1 serving	*266 calories*	*27 g carbohydrate*
8 g protein	*14 g fat*	*3.3 g fiber*

Cream of Pepper Soup

serves 4

3 tbsp	(*45 ml*) butter
½	onion, finely chopped
1	celery stalk, diced
1	yellow pepper, diced
1	red pepper, diced
1 tbsp	(*15 ml*) chopped fresh parsley
½ tsp	(*2 ml*) chervil
4 tbsp	(*60 ml*) flour
4½ cups	(*1.1 L*) chicken stock, heated
3 tbsp	(*45 ml*) heavy cream
	salt and pepper
dash	paprika

Heat butter in large saucepan over low heat. Add onion, cover and cook 4 minutes.

Stir in celery, cover and continue cooking 5 to 6 minutes.

Add yellow and red peppers, season and add parsley, chervil and paprika. Cover and cook 5 to 6 minutes over medium heat.

Mix in flour until well incorporated. Cook 3 minutes, uncovered, over low heat.

Pour in chicken stock, correct seasoning and mix well. Bring to boil; reduce heat to medium and cook soup, partly covered, 20 minutes.

Purée soup in food processor, incorporate cream and serve.

1 serving	*165 calories*	*10 g carbohydrate*
2 g protein	*13 g fat*	*1.1 g fiber*

1. After cooking onion for 4 minutes, add celery and continue cooking, covered, 5 to 6 minutes over low heat.

2. Add yellow and red peppers, season and add parsley, chervil and paprika. Cover and cook 5 to 6 minutes over medium heat.

3. Mix in flour until well incorporated. This will help to thicken soup.

4. After flour has cooked for several minutes, pour in chicken stock, correct seasoning and mix well. Bring to boil and finish cooking.

Classic Vichyssoise

serves 4

3	leeks, white part of stalk only
1 tbsp	(*15 ml*) butter
1	onion, thinly sliced
5	medium-large potatoes, peeled and thinly sliced
¼ tsp	(*1 ml*) thyme
½ tsp	(*2 ml*) marjoram
1	bay leaf
5 cups	(*1.2 L*) chicken stock, heated
¼ cup	(*50 ml*) heavy cream
	salt and pepper

It is important to wash leeks properly. Slit the stalk of the leek lengthwise, leaving ½ in. (*1.2 cm*) of uncut leek at the base to keep the leaves intact. Make another slit in the same manner to further free the leaves for a thorough washing. You will discover traces of sand and dirt deep inside that might otherwise have gone unnoticed. Slice cleaned leeks and set aside.

Melt butter in large saucepan over low heat. Add leeks and onion; cover and cook 10 minutes.

Add potatoes and season well with salt and pepper. Sprinkle in all seasonings and stir well. Cover and continue cooking 12 minutes.

Pour in chicken stock and bring to boil. Cook soup, partly covered, 30 minutes over medium heat.

Purée soup in food processor. Transfer to bowl and set aside to cool. Then chill in refrigerator.

When ready to serve, incorporate cream. You can also serve this soup warm, if desired.

1 serving	*276 calories*	*46 g carbohydrate*
5 g protein	*8 g fat*	*5.8 g fiber*

Lemony Cream of Broccoli Soup

serves 4

5 cups	(*1.2 L*) water
2	lemons, halved
3 tbsp	(*45 ml*) butter
½	onion, chopped
1	head broccoli, separated into flowerets and well washed in warm water
3 tbsp	(*45 ml*) flour
¼ cup	(*50 ml*) heavy cream
	salt and pepper

Pour water into saucepan. Drop in lemon halves and season with salt; bring to boil and continue boiling for 15 minutes.

Meanwhile, heat butter in large saucepan. Add onion, cover and cook 4 to 5 minutes over low heat.

Add broccoli and season well. Cover and continue cooking 7 to 8 minutes.

Mix in flour until well incorporated. Cover and continue cooking 2 minutes.

Remove lemon halves from boiling water and discard. Slowly incorporate liquid to broccoli in saucepan while stirring with wooden spoon.

Season well and stir in cream; bring to boil. Reduce heat to low and cook soup, partly covered, for 20 minutes.

Purée soup in food processor and serve.

1 serving *210 calories* *15 g carbohydrate*
6 g protein *14 g fat* *6.6 g fiber*

Curried Apple Soup

serves 4

3 tbsp	(*45 ml*) butter
½	onion, chopped
1	celery stalk, chopped
4	large apples, peeled, cored and thinly sliced
2 tbsp	(*30 ml*) curry powder
3 tbsp	(*45 ml*) flour
4 cups	(*1 L*) chicken stock, heated
2 tbsp	(*30 ml*) heavy cream
	salt and pepper

Melt butter in large saucepan over low heat. Add onion, cover and cook 5 minutes.

Add celery; continue cooking, covered, 3 to 4 minutes.

Mix in apples and sprinkle in curry powder. Stir well, cover and cook 5 minutes over medium-low heat.

Mix in flour until well incorporated. Cover and continue cooking 2 minutes over low heat.

Pour in chicken stock, mix well and bring to boil. Cook soup, partly covered, 15 minutes over low heat.

Transfer contents to food processor and blend no more than 15 seconds. Incorporate cream, season lightly if needed and serve.

1 serving *220 calories* *27 g carbohydrate*
1 g protein *12 g fat* *3.5 g fiber*

Hearty Vegetable Soup

serves 4

2 tbsp	(*30 ml*) butter
2	large carrots, pared and diced small
2	celery stalks, diced small
2	small onions, cubed small
½	turnip, peeled and diced small
2	potatoes, peeled and diced small
1 tsp	(*5 ml*) sweet basil
½ tsp	(*2 ml*) chervil
¼ tsp	(*1 ml*) thyme
¼ cup	(*50 ml*) dry white wine
5 cups	(*1.2 L*) chicken stock, heated
1 cup	(*250 ml*) fresh green peas
½ cup	(*125 ml*) grated Gruyère cheese
	salt and pepper

Melt butter in large saucepan over medium heat. Add carrots, celery, onions, turnip and potatoes; cover and cook 8 minutes.

Sprinkle in all seasonings; pour in wine and chicken stock. Mix well and correct seasoning. Cover and continue cooking 30 minutes.

Add peas; cover and cook another 8 minutes.

Mix in cheese and serve at once. Accompany with slices of fresh French bread, if desired.

1 serving	*292 calories*	*35 g carbohydrate*
11 g protein	*12 g fat*	*6.3 g fiber*

Baked White Wine and Onion Soup

serves 4

2 tbsp	(*30 ml*) butter
4–5	medium onions, thinly sliced
½ cup	(*125 ml*) dry white wine
4 cups	(*1 L*) beef stock, heated
1	bay leaf
¼ tsp	(*1 ml*) thyme
¼ tsp	(*1 ml*) marjoram
4	rounds toasted French bread
1 cup	(*250 ml*) grated Gruyère cheese
	salt and pepper

Melt butter in large, deep skillet. When hot, add onions and cook, uncovered, 30 minutes over medium-low heat. Stir 7 or 8 times during cooking.

Pour in wine and mix well. Cook over medium heat to reduce wine by half (about 3 to 4 minutes).

Pour in beef stock, mix well and add bay leaf and all seasonings. Mix well and cook, uncovered, 35 minutes over low heat.

Preheat oven to 450° F (*240 °C*).

Ladle soup into individual onion-soup bowls. Cover with toasted rounds of bread and top with grated cheese. Bake about 15 minutes or until cheese is nicely melted and bubbly brown. Serve.

1 serving	*319 calories*	*22 g carbohydrate*
15 g protein	*19 g fat*	*2.9 g fiber*

1. Begin cooking sliced onions in hot butter in large, deep skillet. Stir 7 or 8 times during the 30 minutes of cooking to help brown onions evenly.

2. After 30 minutes, onions should be nicely browned and tender.

3. Add wine and continue cooking to reduce liquid by half.

4. Add beef stock, bay leaf and all seasonings. Simmer over low heat for 35 minutes to marry all the flavors.

Clam-Stuffed Artichoke Bottoms

serves 4

2 tbsp	(*30 ml*) butter
2	green onions, chopped
6	large fresh mushroom caps, cleaned and chopped
2 tbsp	(*30 ml*) flour
1 cup	(*250 ml*) milk
5 oz	(*142 g*) can clams, drained
8	artichoke bottoms, heated
½ cup	(*125 ml*) grated cheese of your choice
	salt and pepper
pinch	nutmeg
pinch	paprika

Melt butter in skillet over medium heat. Add green onions and mushrooms; season well. Cover and cook 5 minutes.

Mix in flour until well incorporated. Cook 1 minute, uncovered. Pour in milk, mix thoroughly and season with nutmeg and paprika. Continue cooking 5 minutes over low heat.

Mix in clams, cover and cook 2 to 3 minutes over very low heat.

Stuff artichoke bottoms and top with cheese. Sprinkle with more paprika if desired. Broil 3 minutes in oven.

Serve on paper doilies.

1 serving	*246 calories*	*15 g carbohydrate*
15 g protein	*14 g fat*	*1.5 g fiber*

Pickled Mushroom Caps

serves 4

3 tbsp	(*45 ml*) olive oil
3	garlic cloves, smashed and chopped
1	onion, chopped
1 lb	(*500 g*) small fresh mushroom caps, well cleaned
¼ tsp	(*1 ml*) thyme
½ tsp	(*2 ml*) marjoram
1 tsp	(*5 ml*) tarragon
1	bay leaf
3	parsley sprigs
1	slice lemon, halved
1 cup	(*250 ml*) dry white wine
2 tbsp	(*30 ml*) wine vinegar
	salt and pepper

Heat oil in saucepan over medium heat. Add garlic and onion; cook 4 to 5 minutes, stirring several times.

Mix in mushroom caps and season with salt and pepper. Sprinkle in all seasonings, bay leaf, parsley and lemon. Mix well and add wine and vinegar; cover and cook 10 minutes over medium heat.

Remove cover and let mushrooms cool in saucepan.

Serve with other tasty starters.

1 serving	*156 calories*	*9 g carbohydrate*
3 g protein	*12 g fat*	*3.7 g fiber*

Vegetable-Stuffed Artichoke Bottoms

serves 4

2 tbsp	(*30 ml*) vegetable oil
1	shallot, chopped
1	zucchini, diced small
¼	eggplant, peeled and diced small
4½ oz	(*127 g*) can crabmeat, well drained
1 cup	(*250 ml*) grated mozzarella cheese
14 oz	(*400 ml*) canned artichoke bottoms
2 tbsp	(*30 ml*) breadcrumbs
	salt and pepper
	butter

Heat oil in large skillet over medium heat. Add shallot, zucchini and eggplant; season well. Cover and cook 10 to 12 minutes.

Mix in crabmeat and season well; continue cooking 4 to 5 minutes.

Stir in cheese and finish cooking another 2 minutes.

Meanwhile, warm artichoke bottoms in ovenproof baking dish with a bit of butter.

Stuff artichoke bottoms with vegetable mixture and top each with breadcrumbs. Broil in oven 1 to 2 minutes or until browned.

Serve at once.

1 serving	*300 calories*	*14 g carbohydrate*
16 g protein	*20 g fat*	*2.4 g fiber*

Broiled Stuffed Mushroom Caps

serves 4

2 tbsp	(*30 ml*) olive oil
16	large fresh mushroom caps, cleaned
2 tbsp	(*30 ml*) butter
3	shallots, finely chopped
3 tbsp	(*45 ml*) chopped fresh parsley
16	canned snails, rinsed and drained
1 tbsp	(*15 ml*) green peppercorns, smashed
2 tbsp	(*30 ml*) breadcrumbs
	salt and pepper
	lemon slices

Heat oil in frying pan over medium-high heat. Add mushroom caps and season; cook 2 to 3 minutes each side. Remove mushrooms from pan and set aside on ovenproof platter.

Add butter to pan. Cook shallots, parsley, snails and peppercorns 2 to 3 minutes over high heat. During cooking, season well with pepper but do not add salt.

Fill mushroom caps with mixture and sprinkle with breadcrumbs. Broil 2 to 3 minutes or until browned.

Serve with lemon slices.

1 serving *128 calories* *9 g carbohydrate*
5 g protein *8 g fat* *3.2 g fiber*

Adventurous Eggplant Sandwiches

serves 4

8	¼-in. (*0.65-cm*) thick slices eggplant
1 cup	(*250 ml*) seasoned flour
¼ tsp	(*1 ml*) paprika
2	eggs
1 cup	(*250 ml*) milk
3 tbsp	(*45 ml*) peanut oil
1 tbsp	(*15 ml*) butter
¼ lb	(*125 g*) fresh mushrooms, cleaned and chopped
1	shallot, chopped
1 tsp	(*5 ml*) chopped fresh parsley
1 tsp	(*5 ml*) flour
5 oz	(*142 g*) can crabmeat, well drained and finely chopped
½ cup	(*125 ml*) heavy cream
½ cup	(*125 ml*) grated Gruyère cheese
	salt and pepper

Dredge eggplant slices in flour; season with paprika and set aside.

Place eggs and milk in bowl; whisk well and season. Dip eggplant slices in mixture and set aside.

Heat peanut oil in large frying pan and cook eggplant slices 3 to 4 minutes each side, seasoning when turning over. It is best to do this in several batches or use more than one pan. When all eggplant slices have been browned, remove from pan and place 4 on ovenproof platter; set others aside on a plate.

Melt butter in saucepan over medium-low heat. Add mushrooms, shallot and parsley; cover and cook 3 to 4 minutes.

Mix in 1 tsp (*5 ml*) flour until incorporated; cook 1 minute, uncovered. Stir in crabmeat and season well. Continue cooking 2 to 3 minutes.

Pour in cream, correct seasoning and cook 4 to 5 minutes. Add half of cheese, mix well and cook 2 minutes.

Divide half of crabmeat mixture onto 4 eggplant slices on ovenproof platter. Close sandwiches with other eggplant slices and top with remaining filling.

Sprinkle with remaining cheese, adding more if needed, and broil 5 to 6 minutes in oven.

Serve with plenty of napkins.

1 serving	*544 calories*	*33 g carbohydrate*
22 g protein	*36 g fat*	*2.3 g fiber*

1. Dredge eggplant slices in seasoned flour; sprinkle with paprika, adding more if desired.

2. Dip slices in mixture of egg and milk to coat thoroughly.

3. Cook eggplant slices in hot peanut oil for 3 to 4 minutes each side. It is important not to overcrowd pan; the best method is to cook them in several batches.

4. Have bottom slices ready on ovenproof platter and top with some of crabmeat filling. Close sandwich with other eggplant slice and prepare to top with more filling and remaining cheese before broiling.

Avocado Shades of Green

serves 4

10	fresh asparagus stems, cleaned
2	canned hearts of palm, drained and diced
6–8	pitted black olives, chopped
1 tbsp	(*15 ml*) chopped fresh parsley
4 tbsp	(*60 ml*) mayonnaise
½ cup	(*125 ml*) frozen green peas, cooked
2 tbsp	(*30 ml*) pickled hot banana peppers, chopped
2	ripe avocados,* halved, pitted and basted with lemon juice
	few drops lemon juice
	few drops Pickapeppa sauce**
	salt and pepper
	lettuce leaves or bean sprouts

Cook asparagus (pare if not spring variety) in salted boiling water until tender. Drain and set aside.

Mix hearts of palm, olives and parsley together in bowl. Dice asparagus and add to bowl, mixing well.

Spoon in mayonnaise and sprinkle with lemon juice; mix until well incorporated.

Add Pickapeppa sauce, season well and mix again. Stir in green peas and pickled banana peppers; mix again.

Arrange avocado halves on serving platter with several leaves of lettuce or bean sprouts. This attractive finishing touch will complete the shades of green.

Spoon filling into shells and serve.

** It might be tricky to find 2 perfectly ripe avocados, so plan ahead and let them ripen at home. Leave them on the counter in a brown paper bag and check them each day for ripeness. As soon as they yield easily to the slightest pressure from your finger they are ready to be turned into "shades of green."*

*** Pickapeppa sauce is a hot pepper sauce from Jamaica.*

1 serving	*332 calories*	*15 g carbohydrate*
5 g protein	*28 g fat*	*6.0 g fiber*

Green Pepper and Roast Beef Salad

serves 4

4	¼-in. (*0.65-cm*) thick slices roast beef, cut into strips
1	shallot, chopped
1 tbsp	(*15 ml*) chopped fresh parsley
½	red pepper, cut into strips
1	green pepper, cut into strips
2 tbsp	(*30 ml*) wine vinegar
1 tbsp	(*15 ml*) Dijon mustard
2 tbsp	(*30 ml*) olive oil
¼ tsp	(*1 ml*) tarragon
	few drops hot pepper sauce
	salt and pepper
	romaine lettuce leaves, well washed and dried

Place beef strips, shallot, parsley and peppers in bowl; toss together.

Add vinegar and mustard; mix well.

Pour in oil and mix; season to taste. Add tarragon and hot pepper sauce; mix very well. Correct seasoning.

Arrange lettuce leaves on serving platter and add salad. Accompany with a variety of vegetables such as sliced tomatoes, green onions and marinated mushrooms.

1 serving	*253 calories*	*2 g carbohydrate*
32 g protein	*13 g fat*	*0.5 g fiber*

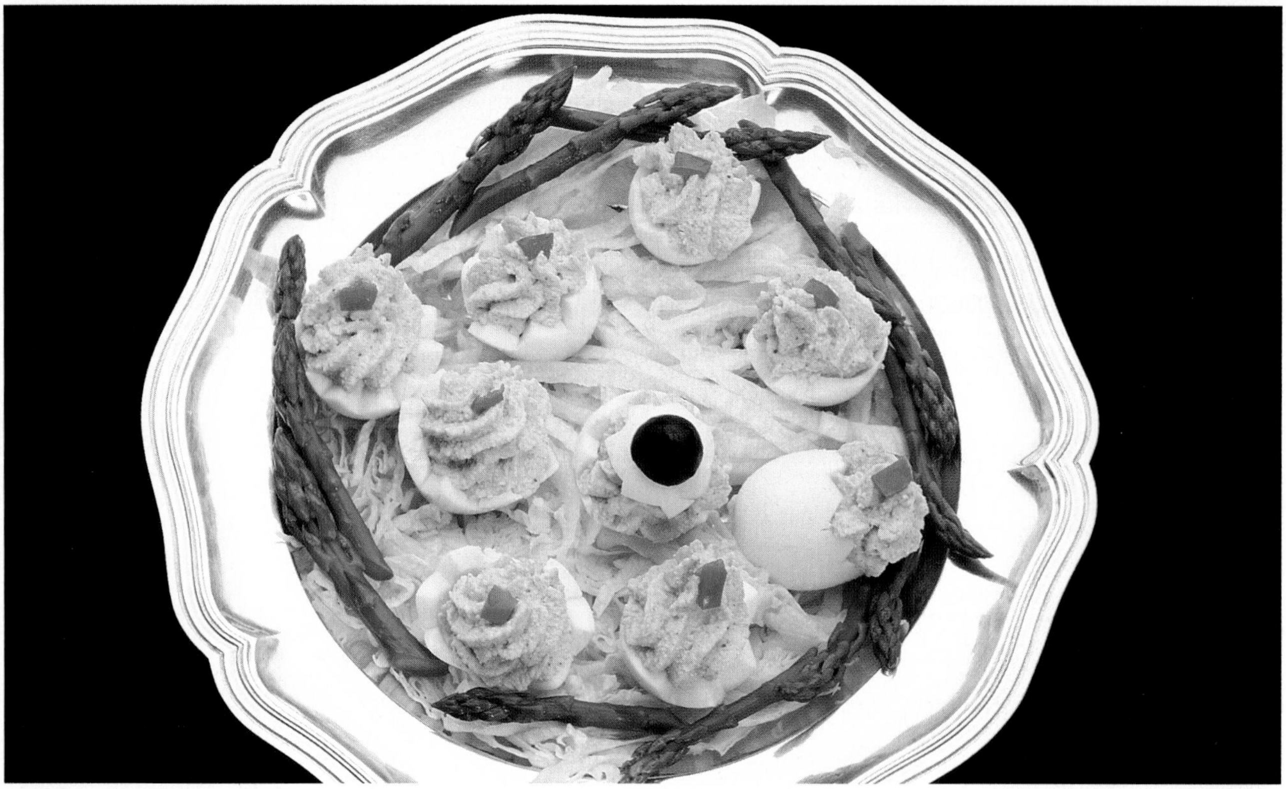

Curried Stuffed Eggs

serves 4

10	hard-boiled eggs
3 tbsp	(*45 ml*) mayonnaise
1 tbsp	(*15 ml*) curry powder
1 tbsp	(*15 ml*) Dijon mustard
dash	paprika
	salt and pepper
	few drops Pickapeppa sauce
	tiny pieces pimento for decoration
	shredded lettuce

Using small sharp knife, cut around middle of 8 eggs in a zigzag design. Carefully pry whites apart and remove yolks. Cut remaining 2 eggs in half.

Place all yolks from 10 eggs into wire sieve. Also add the whites from the plainly cut eggs. Force through into bowl.

Mix in mayonnaise, curry powder, mustard and paprika. Season with salt, pepper and Pickapeppa sauce; mix well until smooth.

Spoon mixture into pastry bag fitted with star nozzle and stuff decoratively cut egg whites. Decorate with pimento.

Arrange some shredded lettuce on serving platter and place eggs on top. Serve.

1 serving	*258 calories*	*0 g carbohydrate*
15 g protein	*22 g fat*	*0.1 g fiber*

Stuffed Hard-Boiled Eggs

serves 4–6

12	hard-boiled eggs, peeled
1 tbsp	(*15 ml*) Dijon mustard
3 tbsp	(*45 ml*) mayonnaise
¼ tsp	(*1 ml*) lemon juice
6	canned bamboo shoots, cut into ¼-in. (*0.65-cm*) lengths
¼ cup	(*50 ml*) vinaigrette
1 tsp	(*5 ml*) chopped fresh parsley
	salt and pepper
	paprika to taste
	sliced black olives

Carefully slice eggs in half lengthwise. Remove cooked yolks and force through wire sieve into bowl. This method will eliminate any lumps in the stuffing.

Add mustard and mayonnaise to egg yolks and mix well until thoroughly incorporated. Taste and add more mayonnaise, if desired.

Sprinkle in lemon juice and season well; mix again. Spoon mixture into pastry bag fitted with star nozzle and stuff egg whites.

Arrange stuffed eggs on attractive platter or bed of shredded lettuce. Sprinkle with paprika to taste and decorate with black olives.

In a small bowl, toss sliced bamboo shoots with vinaigrette and serve alongside eggs. Sprinkle with parsley.

If desired, cover eggs with plastic wrap and refrigerate up to 6 hours before serving.

1 serving	*259 calories*	*3 g carbohydrate*
13 g protein	*23 g fat*	*0.4 g fiber*

Irresistible Deep-Fried Camembert Wedges

serves 4

2	7-oz (*200-g*) Camembert cheeses, chilled
1 cup	(*250 ml*) seasoned flour
1 tsp	(*5 ml*) olive oil
3	beaten eggs
2 cups	(*500 ml*) breadcrumbs
	peanut oil for frying

Scrape off some of rind from cheese and cut each round into triangular wedges. Dredge in flour.

Add oil to beaten eggs, mixing well, and carefully dip pieces of cheese in mixture.

Dredge moistened cheese in flour again; then dip in beaten egg mixture again.

Finish by coating in breadcrumbs. Place all wedges on plate and transfer to freezer for 10 minutes.

Meanwhile, preheat plenty of peanut oil in electric deep-fryer set at 375°F (*190°C*).

Deep-fry cheese wedges in hot oil about 2 minutes or until golden brown. Drain on paper towels before serving. If desired, accompany with raspberry sauce (available in gourmet shops).

1 serving	*913 calories*	*65 g carbohydrate*
35 g protein	*57 g fat*	*3.0 g fiber*

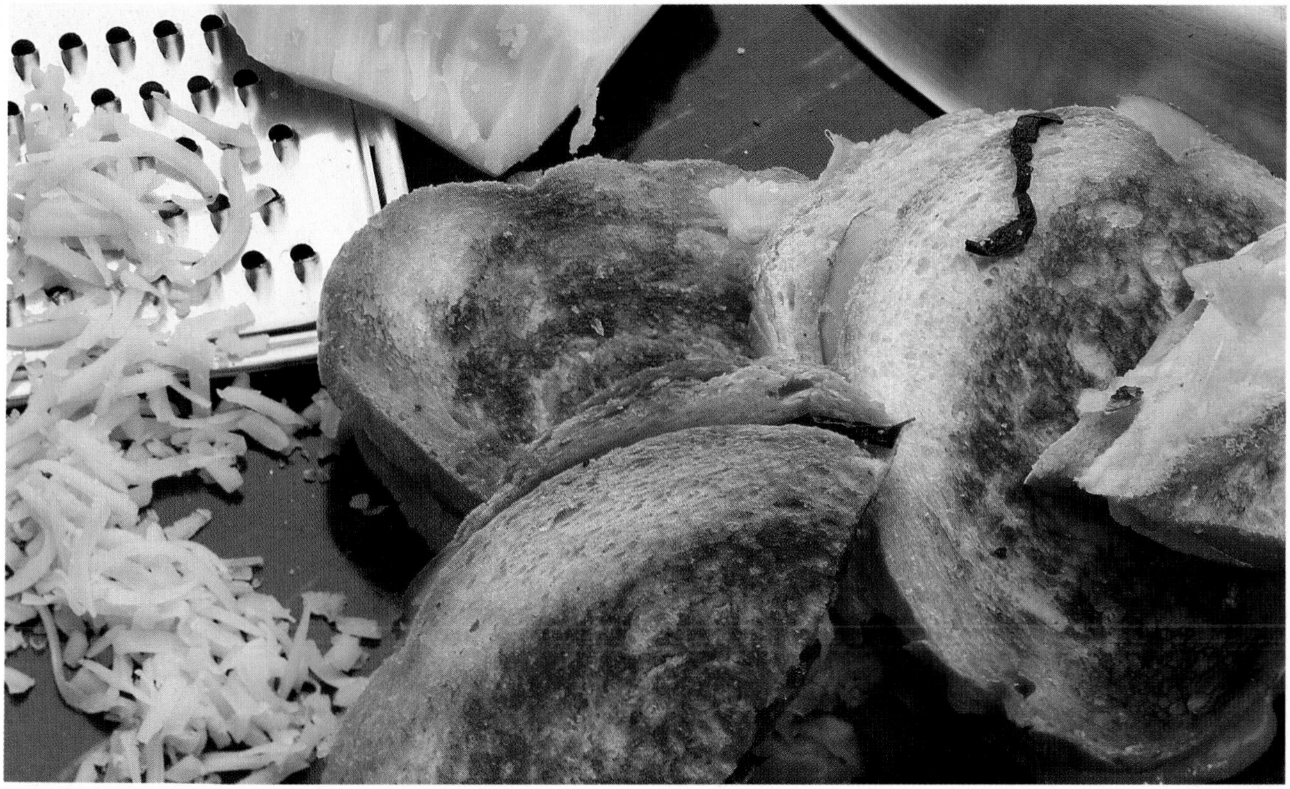

Croque-Monsieur New York Style

serves 4

3 tbsp	(*45 ml*) butter
1	small green pepper, halved and thinly sliced
8	thin slices French bread
8	slices Gruyère cheese
4	slices Black Forest ham
	freshly ground pepper

Heat 1 tbsp (*15 ml*) butter in small saucepan. Add green pepper and cover; cook 15 minutes over low heat.

Arrange slices of bread on cutting board to form sandwiches. Begin by covering bottom slice with piece of cheese generously seasoned with pepper.

Divide cooked green pepper among sandwiches and top with slice of ham. Cover with second piece of cheese and close sandwiches.

Place nonstick pan (two may be necessary) over medium-high heat. Spread 1 tbsp (*15 ml*) butter over one side of sandwiches, and when pan is hot add them, buttered side down.

Cook first side about 3 to 4 minutes or until golden brown. Meanwhile butter other side of bread.

Turn sandwiches over, continue cooking until nicely browned and serve. Slice in half, in sticks or in triangles.

1 serving	*472 calories*	*18 g carbohydrate*
28 g protein	*32 g fat*	*1.0 g fiber*

Bruschetta

serves 4

2 tbsp	(*30 ml*) vegetable oil
½	green pepper, chopped
1	onion, chopped
2	garlic cloves, smashed and chopped
¼ cup	(*50 ml*) dry white wine
28 oz	(*796 ml*) can tomatoes, drained and chopped
½ tsp	(*2 ml*) basil
1	fresh French baguette
1 tbsp	(*15 ml*) tomato paste
1½ cups	(*375 ml*) grated Gruyère cheese
pinch	thyme
dash	paprika
	salt and pepper

Heat oil in large skillet over medium-high heat. Add green pepper, onion and garlic; cook 3 to 4 minutes.

Pour in wine and cook 3 to 4 minutes over high heat.

Add tomatoes and all seasonings. Cook 15 minutes over high heat, stirring several times.

Meanwhile, slice bread into 2 pieces lengthwise and cut each half into 4 equal pieces. Toast on both sides in oven.

Add tomato paste to cooking tomato mixture; continue cooking 3 to 4 minutes over medium heat.

Stir in cheese, correct seasoning and spread over toasted bread. Broil 1 minute or so in oven; serve at once.

1 serving *610 calories* *57 g carbohydrate*
28 g protein *30 g fat* *4.5 g fiber*

1. Cook green pepper, onion and garlic in hot oil for 3 to 4 minutes over medium-high heat.

2. Add wine and cook 3 to 4 minutes over high heat to reduce liquid by about half.

3. Add tomatoes and all seasonings. Cook 15 minutes over high heat.

4. Add cheese and spread over toasted French bread.

Crusty Italian Sausage Bites

serves 4

1 tbsp	(*15 ml*) olive oil
1	onion, chopped
1	garlic clove, smashed and chopped
¾ lb	(*375 g*) Italian sausage, sliced
14 oz	(*400 ml*) canned tomato sauce
1	French baguette, sliced thick and toasted
1 cup	(*250 ml*) grated Gruyère cheese
	salt and pepper
	few drops Pickapeppa sauce

Heat oil in skillet over medium heat. Add onion and garlic; cook 4 minutes.

Add sausage slices, season well and continue cooking 7 to 8 minutes.

Pour in tomato sauce, correct seasoning and cook another 6 to 8 minutes.

Transfer contents to food processor and blend. Spread mixture over slices of toasted bread and place on ovenproof platter.

Top with cheese, sprinkle with Pickapeppa sauce and broil in oven until bubbly and lightly browned.

Serve at once with cool drinks.

1 serving	*706 calories*	*56 g carbohydrate*
35 g protein	*38 g fat*	*3.4 g fiber*

Cream Cheese Canapés

serves 8–10

½	celery stalk, diced small
1	shallot, chopped
4½ oz	(*127 g*) can crabmeat, well drained
12	pitted black olives
8 oz	(*250 g*) cream cheese
2 tbsp	(*30 ml*) plain yogurt
	few drops Pickapeppa sauce
	few drops Tabasco sauce
	salt and pepper

Place celery, shallot, crabmeat, olives and cream cheese in food processor. Blend 1 minute.

Add Pickapeppa sauce and Tabasco sauce; blend again 20 seconds.

Add yogurt, salt and pepper; blend to combine. Pour into bowl, cover and chill 1 hour.

Spread over crackers or toasted bread, or serve as dip for fresh vegetables.

1 serving	*110 calories*	*1 g carbohydrate*
4 g protein	*10 g fat*	*0.2 g fiber*

Aioli

serves 4–6

6	garlic cloves, peeled
2	egg yolks
¾ cup	(*175 ml*) olive oil
	salt and pepper
	cayenne pepper to taste
	few drops hot pepper sauce
	few drops lemon juice
	toasted French bread

Place garlic cloves in mortar and season with salt, pepper and cayenne pepper. Grind with pestle until garlic becomes almost paste-like.

Add egg yolks and continue mixing and grinding with pestle until well combined.

Begin adding oil very slowly, preferably drop by drop, while mixing constantly with pestle. The oil must incorporate perfectly to obtain a silky smooth aioli sauce.

Season with hot pepper sauce and lemon juice to taste. Mix again.

Serve aioli on slices of toasted French bread or, if preferred, on thick, crunchy crackers. Not surprisingly, aioli is very hot and spicy, so it is best served with a cool drink.

1 serving *414 calories* *30 g carbohydrate*
6 g protein *30 g fat* *1.4 g fiber*

1. Preparing aioli really requires a mortar and pestle. If you don't have one you might consider it a worthwhile investment. It will come in handy for other recipes as well.

2. Grind seasoned garlic cloves with pestle until paste-like.

3. Add egg yolks and continue mixing and grinding until well combined and smooth.

4. Incorporating the oil takes some patience as it must be added very slowly to ensure that the sauce does not separate. Be sure to mix constantly while adding the oil drop by drop.

Cheesy Deep-Fried Potato Peel

serves 4–6

4	baked potatoes
½ cup	(*125 ml*) grated Cheddar or your choice of cheese
	salt and pepper

Preheat plenty of peanut oil in electric deep-fryer set at 375°F (*190°C*).

Slice potatoes in half lengthwise and scoop out most of flesh, which can be reserved for use in other recipes.

Cut remaining potato skins into smaller pieces suitable for finger eating. Deep-fry 5 to 6 minutes or adjust time depending on how much potato flesh is left on peel.

Drain well on paper towels and transfer peel to ovenproof plate. Top with cheese and season; broil 2 minutes to melt cheese and serve at once.

This recipe is sure to be a winner when served to "tide them over" during ball season.

1 serving *160 calories* *11 g carbohydrate*
4 g protein *11 g fat* *1.0 g fiber*

Potato-Skin Crowd Pleaser

serves 4–6

2 tbsp	(*30 ml*) bacon fat
1	onion, thinly sliced
1	green pepper, thinly sliced
12	large fresh mushrooms, cleaned and thinly sliced
5	baked potatoes, halved lengthwise
5	slices crisp cooked bacon, chopped
1 cup	(*250 ml*) grated cheese (mozzarella or Cheddar or both, if desired)
	salt and freshly ground pepper

Heat bacon fat in saucepan. Add onion, green pepper and mushrooms; season well. Cook 5 to 6 minutes over medium heat.

Mix well and continue cooking another 8 minutes over low heat.

Meanwhile, scoop out about ¾ of potato flesh from each half. Reserve for use in other recipes. Arrange skins on large serving platter and warm in oven if not already hot.

Fill potatoes with vegetable mixture and top with bacon and your choice of cheese; season well.

Broil 5 to 6 minutes in oven until cheese is bubbly. Serve as halves or cut into slices for a larger group of people.

1 serving	*414 calories*	*30 g carbohydrate*
6 g protein	*30 g fat*	*1.4 g fiber*

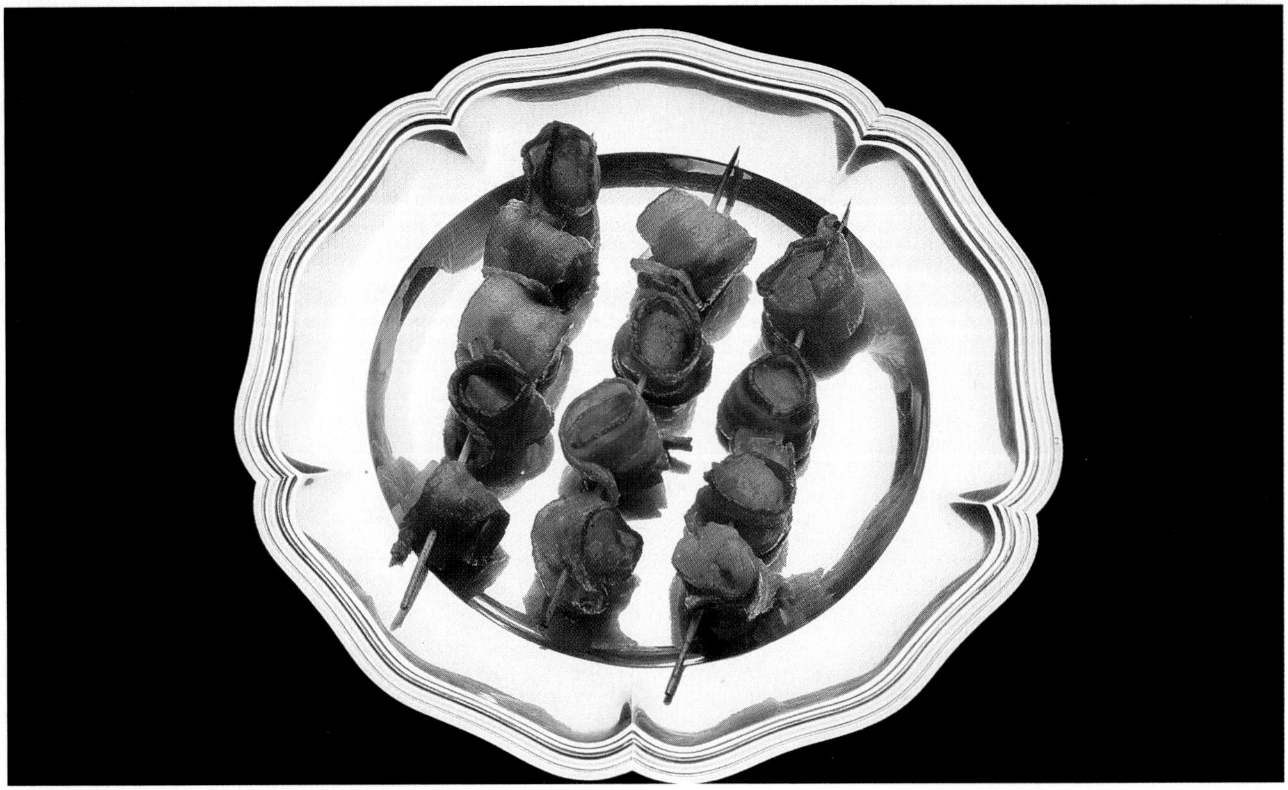

Bacon-Wrapped Pineapple on Skewers

serves 4

14 oz	(*398 ml*) can large pineapple chunks, drained
½ cup	(*125 ml*) your favorite barbecue sauce
1 tsp	(*5 ml*) teriyaki sauce
¼ cup	(*50 ml*) honey
8	slices bacon, precooked 3 minutes
	pepper

Place pineapple chunks in bowl. Add barbecue sauce, teriyaki sauce and honey; season with pepper. Marinate 15 minutes.

Cut bacon slices in half and use each half to wrap a piece of pineapple. Carefully thread on wooden skewers.

Broil 1 to 2 minutes. Serve with cocktail sauce.

1 serving *203 calories* *30 g carbohydrate*
5 g protein *7 g fat* *0.8 g fiber*

Ham Cones with Vegetable Aspic

serves 4

1	celery stalk, diced small
1	carrot, pared and diced small
1	potato, peeled and diced small
½ cup	(*125 ml*) frozen sweet green peas
½	zucchini, diced small
10 oz	(*300 ml*) canned beef consommé
¼ oz	(*7 g*) envelope unflavored gelatine
¼ cup	(*50 ml*) boiling water
2 tbsp	(*30 ml*) mayonnaise
8	thin slices cooked ham
	shredded lettuce

Cook vegetables in salted boiling water for 8 to 10 minutes or until tender.

Meanwhile, heat consommé in small saucepan. Dilute gelatine in ¼ cup (*50 ml*) boiling water and add to consommé; cook 2 minutes, stirring frequently. Remove and chill.

Drain vegetables, cool under running water and drain again. Pat dry with paper towel.

Place vegetables in mixing bowl, add mayonnaise and stir to incorporate.

Pour ¼ cup (*50 ml*) of cooled consommé mixture into bowl containing vegetables; mix very well.

Cupping ham slices in hand, roll into cone shapes and secure with toothpick. Fill with vegetable mixture.

Carefully place cones on stainless-steel wire rack set over large plate or cookie sheet. Brush cones with consommé gelatine mixture and place in refrigerator for 15 minutes.

Baste cones again; chill another 15 minutes.

Repeat above procedure. Be sure to place the consommé gelatine mixture back in the refrigerator each time.

Serve cones on chilled serving platter on bed of shredded fresh lettuce. If desired, decorate with cubed pieces of leftover consommé gelatine.

1 serving	*201 calories*	*12 g carbohydrate*
18 g protein	*9 g fat*	*4.7 g fiber*

Chicken Fingers in Beer Batter

serves 4

1 cup	(*250 ml*) flour
1 cup	(*250 ml*) beer
½ cup	(*125 ml*) water
1	egg yolk
1	egg white, beaten stiff
1	whole chicken breast, skinned, boned and cut in large strips
	salt
	few drops Worcestershire sauce
	few drops hot sauce
	peanut oil for frying

Place flour in bowl. Add salt, mix and pour in beer. Whisk well and pour in water; whisk again until smooth.

Incorporate egg yolk; then incorporate beaten egg white. Whisk again until well blended and refrigerate batter 2 hours before using.

Preheat plenty of peanut oil in electric deep-fryer set at 375°F (*190°C*).

Place chicken strips in bowl and marinate in Worcestershire and hot sauces for about 10 minutes while oil is heating.

Dip chicken in batter and deep-fry about 7 to 8 minutes or according to thickness of strips.

Drain on paper towels before serving and accompany with dipping sauce.

1 serving	*345 calories*	*29 g carbohydrate*
19 g protein	*15 g fat*	*1.2 g fiber*

Last-Minute Appetizer

serves 4

1	small cantaloupe
1	avocado
8	slices prosciutto
	salt and pepper
	lemon juice

Cut cantaloupe in half across the width; scoop out and discard seeds and fibers. Cut halves into 4 equal slices, remove skins, season and set aside.

Cut avocado in half lengthwise and carefully pry halves apart, twisting slightly if needed. Remove pit with the help of small knife. Peel fruit and slice each half into 4 equal pieces; immediately brush with lemon juice to prevent discoloring.

Pair slice of cantaloupe with slice of avocado; wrap with slice of prosciutto. Secure bundles with toothpicks.

Serve on pretty glass plates.

1 serving *186 calories* *15 g carbohydrate*
9 g protein *10 g fat* *2.4 g fiber*

Baked Chicken Wings

serves 4

12	large chicken wings
1 tbsp	(*15 ml*) olive oil
2 tbsp	(*30 ml*) honey
2 tbsp	(*30 ml*) soy sauce
2	garlic cloves, smashed and chopped
2 tbsp	(*30 ml*) breadcrumbs
	juice ¼ lemon
	salt and pepper

Snip off tips from wings and cut each into 2 pieces. Place in large bowl and add oil, honey, soy sauce, garlic and lemon juice. Season well and toss; marinate 1 hour.

Preheat oven to 450°F (*240°C*).

Thread wings on skewers and place on cookie sheet. Bake 10 minutes.

Turn skewers over and continue baking another 8 minutes.

Change oven setting to broil.

Sprinkle breadcrumbs over wings and broil 5 minutes. Serve.

1 serving *209 calories* *12 g carbohydrate*
20 g protein *9 g fat* *0.1 g fiber*

Buffalo Style Deep-Fried Wings

serves 4

2 lb	(*900 g*) chicken wings
2 cups	(*500 ml*) seasoned flour
3	beaten eggs
1 tsp	(*5 ml*) vegetable oil
2 cups	(*500 ml*) seasoned breadcrumbs
	salt and pepper
	paprika to taste
	peanut oil for frying

Preheat plenty of peanut oil in electric deep-fryer set at 375°F (*190°C*).

Snip off tips from wings and cut each into two. Parboil 10 to 12 minutes. Drain well.

Dredge wings in flour. Dip wings in beaten eggs mixed with vegetable oil; then coat with breadcrumbs. Season with salt, pepper and paprika.

Deep-fry 5 to 6 minutes or until golden brown. Serve with your favorite hot, spicy sauce.

1 serving *282 calories* *23 g carbohydrate*
18 g protein *13 g fat* *1.1 g fiber*

Chicken Liver Pâté

serves 4

1 lb	(*500 g*) chicken livers, cleaned
2 tbsp	(*30 ml*) butter
2	onions, chopped
2	garlic cloves, smashed and chopped
1	celery stalk, chopped
½ tsp	(*2 ml*) savory
1 tsp	(*5 ml*) chervil
½ tsp	(*2 ml*) grated lemon rind
¼ cup	(*50 ml*) dry white wine
2 tbsp	(*30 ml*) cognac
4 tbsp	(*60 ml*) sour cream
pinch	thyme
	salt and pepper

Slice chicken livers in half and remove fat; set aside.

Melt butter in large skillet over medium heat. Cook onions, garlic and celery, covered, 4 to 5 minutes.

Add livers and all seasonings. Stir in lemon rind; cover and cook 15 minutes over medium heat. Stir occasionally during cooking process.

Pour in wine and cognac; cover and continue cooking 5 to 6 minutes.

Transfer mixture to food processor and blend until well incorporated and smooth.

Add sour cream and continue mixing several minutes. Pour into serving bowl and chill overnight.

Serve on toasted French bread or on crackers. Accompany with various condiments.

1 serving	*262 calories*	*8 g carbohydrate*
26 g protein	*14 g fat*	*1.3 g fiber*

1. Clean chicken livers and slice in half to remove fat.

2. Cook onions, garlic and celery in hot butter, covered, for 4 to 5 minutes.

3. Add livers and all seasonings. Stir in lemon rind and continue cooking, covered, 15 minutes.

4. Pour in wine, then cognac; resume cooking.

Chicken Spiced with Apple in Pastry

serves 4

2 tbsp	(*30 ml*)	butter
1		celery stalk, diced
2		apples, peeled, cored and diced large
3 tbsp	(*45 ml*)	flour
¼ tsp	(*1 ml*)	paprika
2 cups	(*500 ml*)	chicken stock, heated
2		whole chicken breasts, cooked and skinned, diced large
2 tbsp	(*30 ml*)	sour cream
4		cooked vol-au-vent shells,* hot
		salt and pepper
		chopped walnuts

Melt butter in skillet over low heat. Add celery and apples; cover and cook 5 minutes.

Stir in flour until well incorporated. Season and sprinkle in paprika. Cook 2 minutes, uncovered, over low heat.

Pour in chicken stock and bring to boil. Cook, uncovered, 8 to 10 minutes over medium heat.

Mix in cooked chicken and simmer 2 minutes to heat. Mix in sour cream and spoon mixture into pastry shells. Sprinkle with nuts and serve.

* *Commercial frozen pastry dough is quite suitable for this recipe.*

1 serving	*565 calories*	*35 g carbohydrate*
32 g protein	*33 g fat*	*2.2 g fiber*

Cold Chicken Salad

serves 2

½	cantaloupe, flesh scooped out into balls
1	whole chicken breast, cooked, skinned and diced large
1 tsp	(*5 ml*) cumin
½	shallot, chopped
1	celery stalk, diced
1 tbsp	(*15 ml*) chutney
1 tbsp	(*15 ml*) mayonnaise
1 tbsp	(*15 ml*) sour cream
	salt and pepper
	few drops lemon juice

Toss together cantaloupe balls, chicken, cumin, shallot, celery and chutney; season well.

Add mayonnaise and sour cream; mix until evenly coated.

Sprinkle in lemon juice and accompany with lettuce leaves, if desired.

1 serving	*258 calories*	*14 g carbohydrate*
28 g protein	*10 g fat*	*1.9 g fiber*

Lobster Coquilles in Tomato Sauce

serves 4

2 tbsp	(*30 ml*) butter
2	garlic cloves, smashed and chopped
2	shallots, chopped
1 lb	(*500 g*) canned frozen lobster meat, thawed and drained
28 oz	(*796 ml*) can tomatoes, drained and chopped
1 tsp	(*5 ml*) oregano
½ cup	(*125 ml*) grated mozzarella cheese
	salt and pepper

Melt butter in skillet over low heat. Add garlic and shallots and cook 2 to 3 minutes.

Mix in lobster meat and cook 2 to 3 minutes over high heat. Remove lobster and set aside.

Add tomatoes and oregano to pan; season well. Cook 8 to 10 minutes over medium heat.

Return lobster to sauce, stir and add cheese. Cook 2 minutes; then transfer to individual scallop dishes. Serve at once.

1 serving *269 calories* *9 g carbohydrate*
29 g protein *13 g fat* *1.7 g fiber*

Lobster in Cream Sauce on Toast

serves 4

2 tbsp	(*30 ml*) butter
1	shallot, chopped
1	green pepper, diced small
1	zucchini, diced small
1 lb	(*500 g*) canned frozen lobster meat, thawed and drained
3 tbsp	(*45 ml*) flour
1½ cups	(*375 ml*) chicken stock, heated
¼ cup	(*50 ml*) heavy cream
	salt and pepper
dash	paprika
	toasted bread

Melt butter in skillet over medium-low heat. Add shallot, green pepper and zucchini; cover and cook 8 minutes.

Stir in lobster and season well; sprinkle in paprika. Cook 3 minutes, uncovered. Remove lobster and set aside.

Add flour to vegetables in pan and mix until well incorporated. Cook 2 minutes over low heat.

Pour in chicken stock, mix and bring to boil. Cook 4 to 5 minutes over medium-low heat.

Add cream, stir and correct seasoning. Cook 2 to 3 minutes over low heat. Return lobster to sauce, stir and spoon over toasted bread.

1 serving	*342 calories*	*26 g carbohydrate*
28 g protein	*14 g fat*	*2.4 g fiber*

Escargots with Garlic Butter *

serves 4

½ lb	(*250 g*) unsalted butter
1 tbsp	(*15 ml*) chopped fresh parsley
3	garlic cloves, smashed and chopped
3	shallots, chopped
24	snail shells
24	canned snails, well washed and drained
	salt and pepper
	few drops Tabasco sauce
	few drops Worcestershire sauce
	juice ¼ lemon

Place butter, parsley, garlic and shallots in food processor. Season with salt and blend until well combined.

Add Tabasco sauce, Worcestershire sauce, ground pepper and lemon juice. Blend again and set aside.

Preheat oven to 400°F (*200°C*) and have ready four escargot dishes, tongs and forks.

Place a small bit of garlic butter in each shell and add a snail. Cover snail with more butter until it is level with top of shell. Place shells in escargot dishes; place dishes on cookie sheet and cook 3 minutes in oven.

Change oven setting to broil and set snails on oven rack about 6 in. (*15 cm*) from top element. Broil 2 to 3 minutes or until butter is hot and bubbly.

It is essential that snails be served immediately. They are usually accompanied by thick slices of fresh French bread. (This recipe is not exactly a dieter's dream!)

* *Should you need garlic butter for another recipe or just want to have some on hand, feel free to double the ingredients. Garlic butter freezes very well if shaped in a cylindrical tube and wrapped tightly in foil.*

1 serving	*453 calories*	*0 g carbohydrate*
3 g protein	*49 g fat*	*0 g fiber*

1. Garlic butter is easy to make with the help of a food processor. It can also be prepared by hand if you are willing to exert the necessary muscle power.

2. Add the garlic and shallots to the butter and parsley already in bowl of food processor.

3. Season with salt and blend until well combined.

4. Add Tabasco sauce, Worcestershire sauce, ground pepper and lemon juice. Blend again for a few seconds. Then set aside until ready to use.

Elegant Asparagus with Vinaigrette

serves 4

2	large bunches fresh asparagus
1 tbsp	(*15 ml*) Dijon mustard
1	egg yolk
3 tbsp	(*45 ml*) white wine vinegar
½ cup	(*125 ml*) olive oil
2 tbsp	(*30 ml*) heavy cream
1 tsp	(*5 ml*) green peppercorns, smashed
	salt and pepper
	few drops hot pepper sauce

Slice off 1 in. (*2.5 cm*) of stalk from base of asparagus. Pare and wash thoroughly to remove all traces of sand.

Cook asparagus in salted boiling water for 7 to 8 minutes. Cool under cold running water and drain well; set aside.

Place mustard in bowl. Add egg yolk and vinegar; whisk together. Season well.

Incorporate oil in thin stream while whisking constantly. Pour in cream, mixing constantly with electric beater.

Add smashed peppercorns, mix well and season with hot pepper sauce.

To serve, pour vinaigrette into gravy boat or an attractive bowl. Gather asparagus in a neat pile and place between folds of napkin, which will absorb any excess moisture.

Guests should help themselves to several asparagus at a time and dip them in vinaigrette.

1 serving *337 calories* *6 g carbohydrate*
4 g protein *33 g fat* *2.0 g fiber*

Bacon and Onion Quiche

serves 4

5	slices crisp cooked bacon
2	onions, thinly sliced and cooked
1 tbsp	(*15 ml*) chopped fresh parsley
1 cup	(*250 ml*) grated Gruyère cheese
1	egg
2	egg yolks
1 cup	(*250 ml*) heavy cream
	pie dough
	freshly ground pepper
pinch	paprika
pinch	nutmeg

Preheat oven to 375 °F (*190 °C*). Roll out dough on floured surface and line 9-in. (*23-cm*) quiche mold. Prick bottom of dough with fork and let rest 1 hour.

Arrange bacon slices in bottom of pie shell. Cover with cooked onions and sprinkle with parsley. Add half of cheese and season with pepper.

Place whole egg and additional yolks in bowl. Pour in cream and add paprika and nutmeg; beat with whisk.

Pour egg mixture into pie shell and top with remaining cheese. Place quiche on cookie sheet and bake 35 minutes in oven.

Let stand several minutes before slicing.

1 serving	*662 calories*	*23 g carbohydrate*
21 g protein	*54 g fat*	*1.2 g fiber*

Eggplant Quiche

serves 4

2 tbsp	(*30 ml*) vegetable oil
1	eggplant, peeled and diced
2	garlic cloves, smashed and chopped
1	zucchini, diced
1 cup	(*250 ml*) canned tomatoes, drained and chopped
½ tsp	(*2 ml*) tarragon
1 tbsp	(*15 ml*) sweet basil
1 cup	(*250 ml*) grated Emmenthal cheese
1	egg
2	egg yolks
1 cup	(*250 ml*) heavy cream
	pie dough
	salt and black pepper
pinch	nutmeg
pinch	cayenne pepper

Preheat oven to 375°F (*190°C*). Roll out dough on floured surface and line 9-in. (*23-cm*) quiche mold. Prick bottom of dough with fork and let rest 1 hour.

Meanwhile, heat oil in skillet over medium heat. Add eggplant, garlic and zucchini; season well. Cook 15 minutes.

Stir in tomatoes and continue cooking another 15 to 20 minutes.

Add tarragon and basil; mix in ½ cup (*125 ml*) of cheese. Cook 2 minutes and correct seasoning.

Pour filling into pie shell and set quiche on cookie sheet.

Place whole egg and additional yolks in bowl. Add nutmeg, cayenne pepper, salt and black pepper to taste. Pour in cream and whisk well.

Pour egg mixture into pie shell and carefully mix with fork to help liquid drain to bottom.

Top with remaining cheese and bake 35 minutes in oven.

Let stand several minutes before slicing.

1 serving	*685 calories*	*24 g carbohydrate*
19 g protein	*57 g fat*	*2.6 g fiber*

1. Cook eggplant, garlic and zucchini in hot oil for 15 minutes over medium heat.

2. Stir in tomatoes and continue cooking another 15 to 20 minutes.

3. Add seasonings and half of cheese; mix well and continue cooking another 2 minutes.

4. Fill oven-ready quiche crust with mixture and prepare to bake in oven.

Blue Cheese Dip

serves 4

1/3 lb	(*150 g*) blue cheese
12	pitted black olives
1 tbsp	(*15 ml*) sour cream
1/4 tsp	(*1 ml*) paprika
2 tbsp	(*30 ml*) chutney
	salt and pepper
	celery stalks, well washed and cut into 3 pieces

Blend cheese and olives together in food processor for about 1 minute.

Add sour cream and continue blending until combined. Season and sprinkle in paprika.

Add chutney and blend again until smooth. Pour dip into bowl; cover and chill 2 hours.

Spoon dip into pastry bag fitted with star nozzle. Stuff celery stalks, or other vegetables if desired. Serve.

1 serving *186 calories* *6 g carbohydrate*
9 g protein *14 g fat* *1.9 g fiber*

RISE AND SHINE

A glorious celebration to start the day

Mixed Fruit Salad in Cantaloupe Shells

serves 2

1	cantaloupe
1½ cups	(*375 ml*) cubed watermelon
1	orange, peeled and sectioned
½ cup	(*125 ml*) mixed green and purple seedless grapes
¼ cup	(*50 ml*) Lamb's light rum
2 tbsp	(*30 ml*) chopped walnuts
	juice 1 lime

Cut cantaloupe in half using small knife in zigzag cutting motion. Remove seeds and discard. Remove most of flesh and chop; place in bowl.

Add remaining fruits to bowl containing cantaloupe; sprinkle in rum and mix well. Marinate 15 to 20 minutes.

Sprinkle with lime juice, toss and spoon back into shells. Top with nuts and serve.

1 serving *329 calories* *50 g carbohydrate*
5 g protein *6 g fat* *6.1 g. fiber*

Kiwi Salad with Raspberry Sauce

serves 4

1½ cups	*(375 ml)*	fresh raspberries, washed
2 tbsp	*(30 ml)*	sugar
¼ cup	*(50 ml)*	peach flavored Jazz vodka
4		kiwis, peeled and sliced

Drain raspberries well and place in saucepan with sugar and half of vodka. Cover and cook 6 to 8 minutes over medium heat.

Transfer mixture to food processor; blend. Set aside to cool.

Meanwhile, place kiwi slices in bowl and marinate in remaining vodka for 15 minutes.

When ready to serve, spoon kiwi slices into dessert bowls and top with raspberry sauce. If desired, garnish with whipped cream.

1 serving	*131 calories*	*23 g carbohydrate*
1 g protein	*1 g fat*	*3.6 g fiber*

Grapefruit Salad

serves 4

2	large grapefruit, halved
2	large seedless oranges, halved
½ cup	(*125 ml*) mixed green and purple seedless grapes
1 cup	(*250 ml*) strawberries, washed, hulled and halved
1 tbsp	(*15 ml*) sugar
	juice 1 orange
	juice 1 lemon

Using paring knife, cut along inside of grapefruit shell to remove entire half in one piece. Set shells aside and section fruit as shown in technique; place in bowl.

Section oranges in same way as grapefruit and add to bowl. Toss in remaining fruit and sugar. Sprinkle in fruit juices and mix lightly.

Spoon fruit back into shells and serve with croissants for a quick, satisfying breakfast.

1 serving *132 calories* *31 g carbohydrate*
2 g protein *0 g fat* *3.3 fiber*

1. Using paring knife, cut along inside of grapefruit shell to remove entire half in one piece.

2. Spoon out any remaining flesh or juice from shells and discard; set shells aside. Take whole grapefruit halves that have been removed and section fruit as shown in picture 4.

3. Remove rind from oranges using a knife. Try to avoid cutting off too much of the flesh.

4. Section fruit by cutting on either side of the casing supporting the segments.

Broiled Pears in Egg Sauce

serves 4

4	egg yolks
½ cup	(*125 ml*) granulated sugar
1½ cups	(*375 ml*) hot milk
2 tbsp	(*30 ml*) peach flavored Jazz vodka
4	poached pears
2 tbsp	(*30 ml*) brown sugar
	fresh berries for decoration

Place egg yolks and granulated sugar in stainless-steel bowl; beat together well.

Whisk in milk until well incorporated. Place bowl over saucepan containing hot water. Cook over medium heat, stirring constantly until cream coats back of wooden spoon.

Mix in vodka and set aside to cool.

Place drained poached pears in baking dish. Pour in cooked cream and sprinkle with brown sugar. Broil 1 minute in oven.

Decorate with fresh berries and serve.

1 serving	*344 calories*	*61 g carbohydrate*
7 g protein	*8 g fat*	*2.9 fiber*

Strawberries in Red Wine

serves 4

2½ cups (*625 ml*) strawberries, washed and hulled
2 tbsp (*30 ml*) sugar
1 cup (*250 ml*) dry red wine
½ cup (*125 ml*) whipped cream

Make sure that strawberries are well drained and place in bowl. Sprinkle in sugar and toss gently.

Pour in wine and marinate 2 hours on counter.

Drain strawberries, transfer to clean bowl and decorate with whipped cream.

1 serving	*114 calories*	*14 g carbohydrate*
1 g protein	*6 g fat*	*2.2 g fiber*

Purée of Fruit

serves 4

1 tbsp	(*15 ml*) butter
3	apples, peeled, cored and sliced
2 tbsp	(*30 ml*) maple syrup
1 tsp	(*5 ml*) cinnamon
½ cup	(*125 ml*) sultana raisins
1 cup	(*250 ml*) heavy cream, whipped
	juice ½ orange
	fresh blackberries for decoration

Melt butter in saucepan over medium heat. Add apples, maple syrup, cinnamon and orange juice; cook 6 minutes, stirring occasionally.

Mix in raisins and continue cooking 3 to 4 minutes.

Transfer contents to food processor and blend until puréed. Set aside to cool.

When ready to serve, fold whipped cream into fruit mixture and spoon into dessert bowls. Decorate with fresh berries.

1 serving	*397 calories*	*41 g carbohydrate*
2 g protein	*25 g fat*	*3.5 g fiber*

Watermelon Salad in Pineapple Boats

serves 2

1	fresh ripe pineapple
1 cup	(*250 ml*) chopped seeded watermelon
2 tbsp	(*30 ml*) seedless golden raisins
1 tsp	(*5 ml*) your favorite liqueur

Slice pineapple in half legthwise using sharp knife. Separate halves and remove center core from each. Decoratively cut flesh in zigzag pattern to make room for fruit filling.

Chop some of pineapple and place in bowl with watermelon and raisins. Sprinkle in liqueur and toss; let stand 15 minutes.

Fill pineapple boats with fruit filling and serve chilled.

1 serving *173 calories* *39 g carbohydrate*
2 g protein *1 g fat* *3.9 g fiber*

Poached Pears in Light Syrup

serves 4

1 cup	(*250 ml*) granulated sugar
2 cups	(*500 ml*) water
4	pears, cored and peeled
2 tbsp	(*30 ml*) brown sugar
1 tsp	(*5 ml*) butter
1 tsp	(*5 ml*) cinnamon
½ cup	(*125 ml*) orange juice
2 tbsp	(*30 ml*) chopped walnuts
	juice 1 lime
	rind 1 orange and 1 lime, cut into julienne

Place granulated sugar, water and lime juice in small saucepan. Bring to boil over high head and continue cooking 3 minutes. Do not stir.

Meanwhile, place pears, brown sugar, butter and fruit rinds in another saucepan. Sprinkle in cinnamon and add orange juice.

Pour in syrup and cook 10 to 12 minutes over medium heat.

Remove saucepan from heat and let pears cool in syrup mixture.

Serve cold with chopped walnuts.

1 serving 292 calories 62 g carbohydrate
2 g protein 4 g fat 3.2 g fiber

1. Peel and core pears neatly to enhance their final appearance.

2. While syrup is being made, place pears in another saucepan.

3. Add brown sugar and butter; sprinkle in julienned fruit rinds.

4. Add cinnamon, orange juice and syrup. Cook 10 to 12 minutes over medium heat.

Healthy Banana-Nut Muffins

serves 6–8

1 cup	(*250 ml*) all-purpose flour
1 cup	(*250 ml*) whole-wheat flour
¾ cup	(*175 ml*) brown sugar
½ cup	(*125 ml*) chopped walnuts
2 tsp	(*10 ml*) baking powder
1 tsp	(*5 ml*) cinnamon
½ tsp	(*2 ml*) salt
2	medium bananas, mashed
2	large eggs
1 cup	(*250 ml*) milk
⅓ cup	(*75 ml*) vegetable oil

Preheat oven to 400°F (*200°C*).

Mix both flours with brown sugar and walnuts. Stir in baking powder, cinnamon and salt.

Place mashed bananas in separate bowl and add eggs, milk and oil; mix until well combined.

Add wet ingredients to dry, mixing just until moistened. Spoon into lightly greased muffin tins and bake 15 to 20 minutes depending on size.

Check that muffins are done before removing from oven. Cool on wire racks several minutes before serving.

1 serving	*307 calories*	*53 g carbohydrate*
8 g protein	*7 g fat*	*3.6 g fiber*

Eggs en Cocotte

serves 4

4	large eggs
1 cup	(*250 ml*) heavy cream
	salt and pepper

Preheat oven to 250°F (*180°C*).

Have ready deep ovenproof tray filled with 1 in. (*2.5 cm*) hot water.

Break eggs into cocotte dishes and divide cream among them. Season and set in tray; bake 10 to 12 minutes in oven.

Serve with toast and jam.

1 serving	*288 calories*	*2 g carbohydrate*
7 g protein	*28 g fat*	*0 g fiber*

Asparagus Wrapped in Ham with Hollandaise Sauce

serves 4

2 bunches fresh asparagus, pared, base trimmed
8 slices Virginia ham, heated
1½ cups (*375 ml*) hot Hollandaise sauce *

Preheat oven to 375 °F (*190 °C*).

Cook asparagus in plenty of salted boiling water for 7 to 8 minutes or until tender. Drain well.

Divide asparagus into 8 bundles and wrap each bundle with slice of ham; place in baking dish.

Pour sauce over bundles and bake 3 minutes. Serve.

* *See Poached Eggs with Hollandaise Sauce, page 93.*

1 serving	*595 calories*	*6 g carbohydrate*
19 g protein	*55 g fat*	*2.0 g fiber*

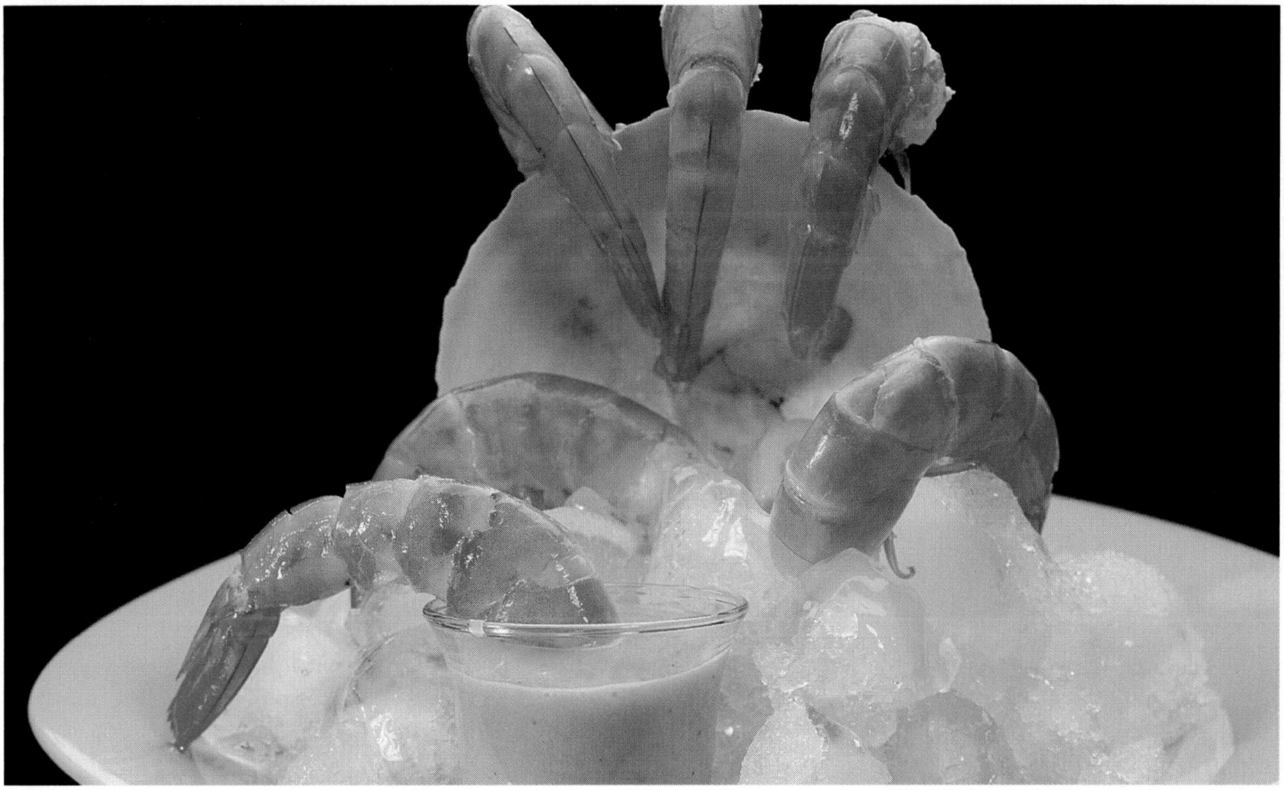

Shrimp Rouille

serves 4

16	jumbo shrimp, washed
6	cloves garlic, peeled
1	egg yolk
1 tbsp	(*15 ml*) tomato paste
½ cup	(*125 ml*) green olive oil
	few drops lemon juice
	salt and pepper
	few drops Tabasco sauce

Place shrimp in saucepan with enough cold water to cover. Bring to boil. Immediately remove from heat and let stand 2 to 3 minutes on counter.

Cool shrimp in cold running water. Drain well, peel and devein. Set aside.

Place garlic cloves in small saucepan with 1 cup (*250 ml*) water; bring to boil and continue cooking 8 minutes.

Drain well and place cloves in mortar; mash with pestle.

Add egg yolk and tomato paste; mix well. Incorporate oil in thin stream while mixing constantly with pestle.

Season with lemon juice, salt, pepper and Tabasco sauce.

Serve sauce with cooked shrimp.

1 serving	*384 calories*	*1 g carbohydrate*
23 g protein	*32 g fat*	*0 g fiber*

Two-in-One

serves 4

1½ cups (*375 ml*) all-purpose flour, sifted
3 tbsp (*45 ml*) brown sugar
¼ tsp (*1 ml*) salt
1 cup (*250 ml*) milk
1 cup (*250 ml*) hot water
12 large eggs
3 tbsp (*45 ml*) melted butter
2 tbsp (*30 ml*) butter
12 slices crisp cooked bacon
pure maple syrup

Sift flour, brown sugar and salt into large bowl. Whisk in milk until well incorporated; then whisk in water.

Add 4 eggs and whisk until smooth. Pour through wire sieve into clean bowl and whisk in melted butter. Cover with plastic wrap, touching surface, and chill 1 hour.*

Make crepes following technique of Allumettes, page 99.

From the stack of crepes you have just prepared, take 12 and place them in oven to keep hot. Refrigerate or freeze remaining crepes for later use.

Heat 1 tbsp (*15 ml*) butter in each of 2 large nonstick frying pans over medium heat.

Add 4 eggs to each pan; cover and cook 4 to 5 minutes over low heat or until done to taste. The whites should be soft and moist.

Meanwhile, arrange 3 crepes per person on dinner plates, slightly overlapping but also covering most of plate.

When eggs are ready, carefully place 2 on each plate over crepes and partly cover whites with sides of crepe. Arrange bacon around plate and moisten with maple syrup. Serve at once.

* *The batter can be made the night before, if preferred.*

1 serving	*875 calories*	*96 g carbohydrate*
26 g protein	*43 g fat*	*1.8 g fiber*

1. Sift flour, brown sugar and salt into large bowl.

2. Whisk in milk until well incorporated; then whisk in water.

3. Add 4 eggs and whisk well until smooth.

4. Pour batter through wire sieve into clean bowl and whisk in butter. Cover with plastic wrap, touching surface, and chill 1 hour.

Baked Eggs

serves 4

2 tbsp	(*30 ml*) butter
8	large eggs
	salt and pepper

Preheat over to 350°F (*180°C*).

Divide butter into 4 individual ovenproof egg dishes and place in oven to melt.

Break 2 eggs into each dish and season well. Bake 12 to 15 minutes.

Serve with small rounds of toast.

1 serving	*201 calories*	*0 g carbohydrate*
12 g protein	*17 g fat*	*0 g fiber*

Home-Style Hash Browns and Sausages

serves 4

8	breakfast-style pork sausage links
4	potatoes, boiled in skins *
2 tbsp	(*30 ml*) butter
2	shallots, chopped
1 tbsp	(*15 ml*) chopped fresh parsley
1 tsp	(*5 ml*) chopped fresh chives
	salt and pepper
	nutmeg to taste

Prepare sausage links for broiling by first cooking them in boiling water for 3 minutes. This technique will remove some of the fat. Drain well and set aside.

Peel potatoes and chop. Heat butter in cast-iron frying pan (or substitute if not available). Add potatoes and cook 20 minutes over low heat, stirring occasionally.

Meanwhile, broil sausages in oven until skins are crisp and insides thoroughly cooked.

Add remaining ingredients to potatoes; mix thoroughly. Cook another 3 to 4 minutes.

Serve sausages with hash browns and accompany with your favorite style of eggs.

* *Do not overcook potatoes. For this recipe they are better if still a little firm.*

1 serving *462 calories* *52 g carbohydrate*
14 g protein *22 g fat* *2.5 g fiber*

Eggplant Baked Eggs

serves 2

2 tbsp	(*30 ml*) butter
1	green onion, chopped
½	small onion, chopped
1	garlic clove, smashed and chopped
½	eggplant, peeled and diced
1 tsp	(*5 ml*) chopped fresh parsley
½ tsp	(*2 ml*) oregano
¼ tsp	(*1 ml*) thyme
1	ripe tomato, cored and chopped
½ cup	(*125 ml*) grated Monterey Jack cheese
2 tsp	(*10 ml*) melted butter
4	eggs
	salt and pepper
pinch	sugar
	slices toasted French baguette

Melt 2 tbsp (*30 ml*) butter in skillet over medium heat. Add both onions and garlic; cook 3 minutes.

Stir in eggplant, parsley, oregano and thyme; mix well. Season, cover and cook 15 minutes, stirring frequently.

Add tomato and sugar; correct seasoning and mix well. Cover and continue cooking 10 minutes.

Meanwhile preheat oven to 350°F (*180°C*).

Add cheese to eggplant mixture, mix well and cook 1 to 2 minutes. Set aside.

Divide melted butter between two individual oven-proof egg dishes. Place in oven for several minutes to heat.

Cover bottom of dishes with eggplant mixture and return to oven 5 to 6 minutes.

Break 2 eggs into each dish over eggplant and season well. Bake 12 to 15 minutes.

Serve with toast.

1 serving	*494 calories*	*16 g carbohydrate*
22 g protein	*38 g fat*	*2.5 g fiber*

Scrambled Eggs with Cheese

serves 4

6	large eggs
2 tbsp	(*30 ml*) light cream
2 tbsp	(*30 ml*) chopped fresh chives
1 cup	(*250 ml*) grated well-aged white Cheddar cheese
2 tbsp	(*30 ml*) butter
	salt and pepper
dash	paprika

Beat eggs with cream, chives and cheese, using fork. Season well.

Heat butter in large nonstick frying pan over medium-high heat.

When butter is bubbling, pour in eggs and cook 15 seconds without stirring. Stir gently with wooden spoon to give eggs shape; let cook another 15 seconds without stirring.

Monitor heat carefully—if heat is too high eggs will become rubbery.

When eggs are cooked but still soft and moist, immediately remove from stove, sprinkle with paprika and serve. Accompany with slices of raisin bread and fresh fruit.

1 serving	*310 calories*	*2 g carbohydrate*
17 g protein	*26 g fat*	*0 g fiber*

Scrambled Mushroom Eggs on Quarter Loaves

serves 4

2 tbsp	(*30 ml*) butter
½	Spanish onion, thinly sliced
½ lb	(*250 g*) fresh mushrooms, cleaned and sliced
6	large eggs
½ tsp	(*2 ml*) celery seeds
1	French baguette
	salt and pepper
pinch	paprika
pinch	nutmeg

Heat butter in nonstick frying pan over low heat. Add onion and cook 8 to 10 minutes or until soft.

Add mushrooms and all seasonings; continue cooking 3 to 4 minutes over medium heat.

Beat eggs with fork, pour into pan with mushrooms and proceed to scramble.

Meanwhile, cut baguette in half and then cut each piece into two again lengthwise, for a total of 4 pieces. Toast lightly in oven set at broil.

Serve scrambled eggs over quarter loaves.

1 serving	*429 calories*	*51 g carbohydrate*
18 g protein	*17 g fat*	*4.3 g fiber*

Scrambled Eggs à la Française

serves 6–8

8	large eggs
¼ cup	(*50 ml*) light cream
½ cup	(*125 ml*) grated Swiss cheese
2 tbsp	(*30 ml*) butter
	salt and pepper

Beat eggs with cream and cheese, using fork. Season with pepper.

Place stainless-steel bowl over saucepan containing 3 cups (*750 ml*) boiling water set over medium heat.

Add butter to bowl and let melt. Pour in beaten egg mixture and whisk gently and constantly until eggs are softly scrambled. If you stop stirring, eggs will probably stick to bowl.

Serve, buffet style, with Rösti Potatoes (page 104) or Home-Style Hash Browns and Sausages (page 77).

1 serving — 144 calories — 0 g carbohydrate
9 g protein — 12 g fat — 0 g fiber

Soft-Boiled Eggs in Crepe Bundles

serves 4

4	**large eggs, at room temperature**
8	**crepes***
½ cup	**(*125 ml*) grated well-aged white Cheddar cheese**
	salt and pepper

Using spoon, carefully immerse eggs in saucepan filled with gently boiling water. Boil 5 minutes.

Remove eggs from water and quickly cool in cold water for 1 minute only.

Carefully peel shells and set each egg on 2 stacked crepes. Wrap into bundles and place in baking dish.

Sprinkle with cheese and broil 2 minutes. Serve at once. Have salt and pepper at table for seasoning.

* *See Crepes Stuffed with Veal, page 240.*

1 serving	*436 calories*	*35 g carbohydrate*
20 g protein	*24 g fat*	*1.4 g fiber*

1. Using spoon, carefully immerse eggs in saucepan filled with gently boiling water. Boil 5 minutes.

2. Remove eggs from water and quickly cool in cold water for 1 minute only—just long enough to stop cooking process.

3. Carefully peel shells and set each egg on 2 stacked crepes. Finish recipe as directed.

4. A properly cooked soft-boiled egg should have a runny yolk similar to this one.

Soft-Boiled Eggs

serves 4

4 large eggs
4 slices toasted bread, cut into sticks

Have eggs ready at room temperature. Bring plenty of water to boil in saucepan.

Add eggs and boil 3 to 4 minutes or a little longer, depending on your taste.

Remove eggs from water and place in eggcups. Carefully slice off top of each egg and serve with toast.

1 serving *118 calories* *8 g carbohydrate*
8 g protein *6 g fat* *0.4 g fiber*

Soft-Boiled Eggs with Mushroom Garnish

serves 2

4	large eggs, at room temperature
2 tbsp	(*30 ml*) butter
½ lb	(*250 g*) fresh mushrooms, cleaned and sliced
3	shallots, chopped
1 tbsp	(*15 ml*) chopped fresh chives
1	garlic clove, smashed and chopped
½ cup	(*125 ml*) grated Emmenthal cheese
	salt and pepper

Using spoon, carefully immerse eggs in saucepan filled with gently boiling water. Boil 5 minutes.

Remove eggs from water and quickly cool in cold water for 1 minute only.

Carefully peel shells and set 2 eggs in each individual egg plate. Set aside.

Heat butter in large frying pan over medium-high heat. Add remaining ingredients except cheese and cook 3 to 4 minutes.

Spoon mushroom garnish over eggs, season and top with cheese. Broil in oven until melted.

1 serving *465 calories* *6 g carbohydrate*
27 g protein *37 g fat* *3.1 g fiber*

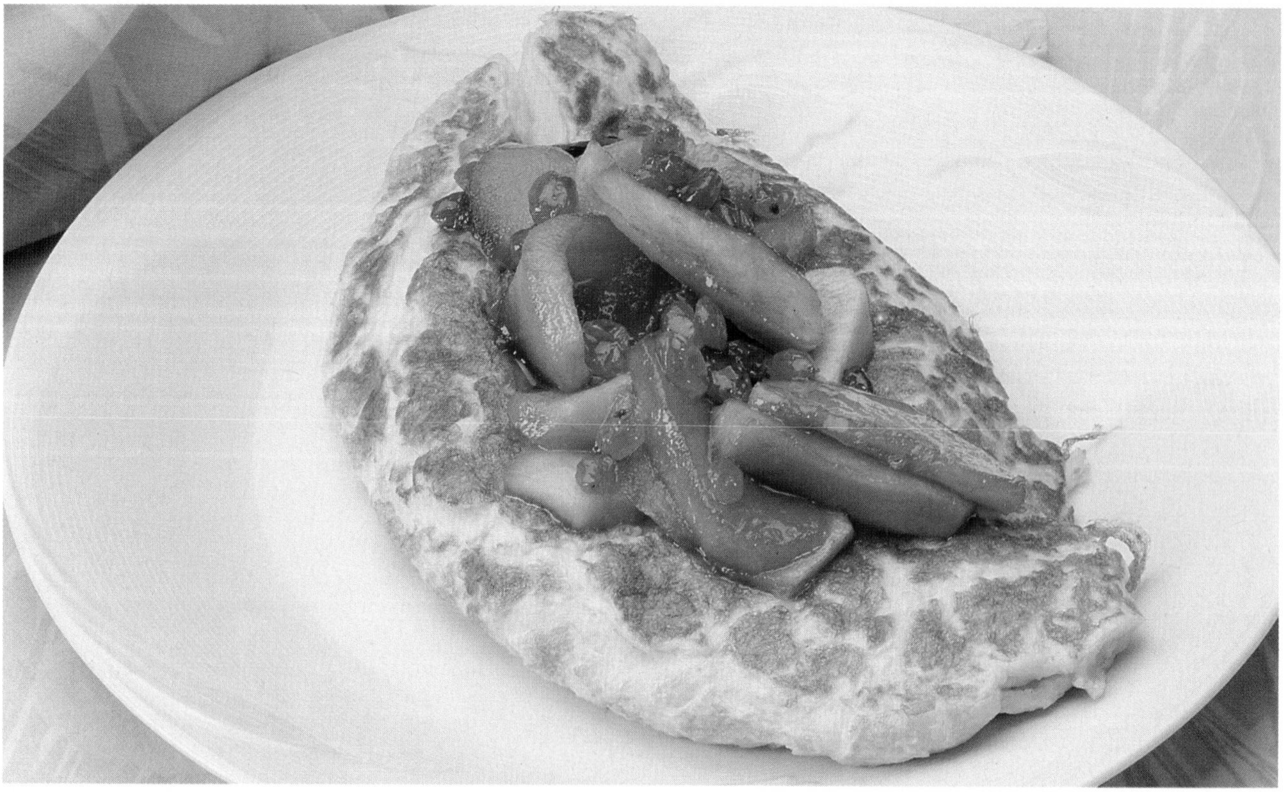

Apple-Raisin Omelet

serves 2

2 tbsp	(*30 ml*) butter
2	apples, peeled, cored, quartered and sliced
2 tbsp	(*30 ml*) brown sugar
2 tbsp	(*30 ml*) sultana raisins
1 tbsp	(*15 ml*) plum jelly
4	large eggs
2 tbsp	(*30 ml*) light cream
1 tbsp	(*15 ml*) granulated sugar

Preheat oven to 250°F (*120°C*).

Heat 1 tbsp (*15 ml*) butter in nonstick frying pan. Cook apples and brown sugar, covered, 4 minutes over medium heat.

Stir in raisins and continue cooking 2 minutes. Add jelly, mix well and finish cooking 3 to 4 minutes, uncovered. Transfer to ovenproof dish and keep hot in oven.

Heat remaining butter in nonstick frying pan over medium-high heat. Meanwhile, beat eggs and cream together with fork.

Pour eggs into hot butter and let cook 30 seconds without stirring.

Gently stir middle of omelet to help eggs set. Continue cooking 30 seconds or until eggs have taken shape but are still soft. Then, using spatula, start rolling omelet from right to left while tilting pan in direction of roll. Sprinkle sugar on underside of omelet to glaze.

Turn omelet out onto heated platter and slit middle as shown on facing page. Stuff with some of apple mixture and spoon remainder over omelet. Slice and serve.

1 serving	*481 calories*	*51 g carbohydrate*
13 g protein	*25 g fat*	*3.4 g fiber*

1. Cook apples and brown sugar, covered, in nonstick frying pan 4 minutes over medium heat.

2. Stir in raisins and continue cooking 2 minutes.

3. Add plum jelly, mix well and finish cooking 3 to 4 minutes, uncovered.

4. Once omelet is made, slit middle with knife and stuff with some of apple mixture. Spoon remaining mixture over omelet.

Strawberry Omelet

serves 2

1 cup	(*250 ml*) strawberries, washed and hulled
3 tbsp	(*45 ml*) sugar
1 tbsp	(*15 ml*) very finely chopped lemon rind
4	large eggs
2 tbsp	(*30 ml*) light cream
1 tbsp	(*15 ml*) butter
	fresh strawberries for decoration

Place strawberries, sugar and lemon rind in saucepan. Cook 3 to 4 minutes over medium heat, stirring once.

Transfer contents to food processor; blend until puréed. Set aside.

Beat eggs with cream in small bowl. Heat butter in medium-size nonstick frying pan over medium heat.

Increase heat to medium-high and pour in eggs; let cook 30 seconds without stirring.

Gently stir middle of omelet to help eggs set. Continue cooking 30 seconds, or until eggs have taken shape but are still soft.

Spoon 4 tbsp (*60 ml*) of strawberry sauce over eggs and begin rolling omelet from right to left using spatula, tilting pan in direction of roll.

Turn omelet out onto heated platter and serve with remaining sauce. Decorate with fresh strawberries.

1 serving	*327 calories*	*26 g carbohydrate*
13 g protein	*19 g fat*	*2.2 g fiber*

Flat Vegetable Omelet

serves 4

2 tbsp	(*30 ml*) butter
1	medium onion, sliced
½ lb	(*250 g*) fresh mushrooms, cleaned and halved
1 tsp	(*5 ml*) tarragon
1 cup	(*250 ml*) canned tomatoes, drained and chopped
6	beaten eggs
½ cup	(*125 ml*) grated Gruyère cheese
	salt and pepper

Heat butter in large nonstick frying pan over high heat. Add onion, mushrooms and tarragon; season well. Cook 5 minutes.

Add tomatoes and season well; continue cooking 5 to 6 minutes.

Pour in eggs and let cook 15 seconds without stirring.

Gently stir middle of omelet to help eggs set; cook another 15 seconds or so without stirring.

Sprinkle in cheese and finish cooking in oven at broil for 2 to 3 minutes.

Slice and serve.

1 serving	*243 calories*	*10 g carbohydrate*
17 g protein	*15 g fat*	*2.7 g fiber*

Cold Omelet with Tangy Vinaigrette

serves 2

6	large eggs
1 tbsp	(*15 ml*) chopped fresh parsley
1 tsp	(*5 ml*) chopped fresh chives
2 tbsp	(*30 ml*) light cream
2 tbsp	(*30 ml*) butter
1 tbsp	(*15 ml*) Dijon mustard
1	garlic clove, peeled and blanched 3 minutes in boiling water, then mashed
3 tbsp	(*45 ml*) white wine vinegar
½ cup	(*125 ml*) green olive oil
	few drops Tabasco sauce
	salt and pepper

Beat eggs with fork and season. Mix in parsley, chives and cream.

Heat butter in medium-size nonstick frying pan over medium heat. When hot, increase heat to medium-high and pour in eggs; let cook 1 minute without stirring.

Gently stir middle of omelet to help eggs set and continue cooking 1 to 2 minutes or until eggs have taken shape but are still soft.

Using spatula, start to roll omelet from right side of pan towards left, tilting pan in direction of roll.

Turn omelet out onto serving platter; set aside until cold.

Place all remaining ingredients in small bowl; vigorously whisk together and immediately pour over cold omelet. Serve with crackers if desired.

1 serving	*867 calories*	*3 g carbohydrate*
19 g protein	*87 g fat*	*0.2 g fiber*

Banana-Filled Omelet

serves 2

3 tbsp	(*45 ml*) butter
2	bananas, sliced
2 tbsp	(*30 ml*) brown sugar
4	large eggs
¼ cup	(*50 ml*) milk or light cream
2 tbsp	(*30 ml*) rum

Heat 1 tbsp (*15 ml*) butter in small frying pan over medium heat. Add bananas and brown sugar; cook 2 to 3 minutes. Set aside.

Beat eggs with milk and rum; set aside.

Heat remaining butter in nonstick frying pan over medium-high heat. When hot, pour in eggs and let cook 30 seconds without stirring.

Gently stir middle of omelet to help eggs set. Continue cooking 30 seconds or until eggs have taken shape but are still soft.

Spread half of bananas over eggs and begin rolling omelet from right to left using spatula, tilting pan in direction of roll.

Turn nicely browned omelet out onto heated platter and decorate with remaining bananas.

1 serving	*509 calories*	*37 g carbohydrate*
14 g protein	*30 g fat*	*3.9 g fiber*

Western Omelet

serves 2

2 tbsp	(*30 ml*) butter
½	onion, chopped
1	green onion, chopped
½	green pepper, chopped
½ cup	(*125 ml*) leftover cooked ham, diced
4	eggs
	salt and pepper

Heat butter in medium-size nonstick frying pan over medium heat. Add vegetables and ham; cook 4 minutes. Season well.

Beat eggs with fork and season. Increase heat to medium-high and pour eggs over vegetables. Let cook 1 minute without stirring.

Gently stir middle of omelet to help eggs set. Continue cooking 1 to 2 minutes, or until eggs have taken shape but are still soft. Then, using spatula, start to roll omelet from the right side towards the left, tilting pan in direction of roll.

Keep heat on while you are rolling to finish cooking eggs—the underside should be nicely browned. When omelet is rolled to far edge of pan, position plate against edge and turn frying pan upside-down, spilling omelet out onto plate. This technique takes some practice, but once you have acquired the skill all your omelets will be perfectly shaped.

Slice omelet and serve at once.

1 serving	*321 calories*	*4 g carbohydrate*
20 g protein	*25 g fat*	*0.7 g fiber*

Poached Eggs with Hollandaise Sauce

serves 4

2	egg yolks
2 tbsp	(*30 ml*) cold water
1 cup	(*250 ml*) clarified butter
4	small slices toasted bread
4	slices Black Forest ham, heated
4	hot poached eggs
	few drops lemon juice
	sald and pepper

Place egg yolks in stainless-steel bowl. Add water and set bowl over saucepan containing 3 cups (*750 ml*) hot water. Do not place over heat.

Whisk egg yolks until very thick. Then incorporate clarified butter in thin stream while whisking constantly.

Add few drops lemon juice and season to taste.

Arrange plates with toasted bread covered with ham and topped with poached egg. Pour sauce over and serve immediately.

1 serving	*602 calories*	*8 g carbohydrate*
12 g protein	*58 g fat*	*0.4 g fiber*

Cheese Soufflé

serves 4

1¼ cups (*300 ml*) grated Gruyère, Emmenthal or mozzarella cheese
4 tbsp (*60 ml*) butter
4 tbsp (*60 ml*) flour
1¼ cups (*300 ml*) cold milk
4 egg yolks, room temperature
5 egg whites, beaten stiff at room temperature
salt and pepper
extra butter for mold

Preheat oven to 375 °F (*190 °C*). Butter 6-cup (*1.5-L*) soufflé mold; sprinkle sides and bottom with cheese.

Melt butter in saucepan over very low heat. Mix in flour using wooden spoon and cook 3 to 4 minutes.

Pour in half of milk and stir 2 minutes over medium heat. Gradually add remaining milk while stirring constantly to make smooth paste.

Add salt and slowly bring to boil, stirring constantly until mixture starts to adhere slightly to pan. This should take about 3 to 4 minutes. Remove from heat and let cool slightly.

Add egg yolks, one by one, mixing with wooden spoon between additions. Add cheese and pepper.

Incorporate large spoonful of beaten egg white to yolk mixture. Then pour yolks into bowl containing whites. Use spatula to fold together until batter is an even color.

Pour batter into mold and run thumb around inside edge, about ½ in. (*1.2 cm*) deep into batter. This will form an extra little top. Bake 35 minutes.

1 serving	*455 calories*	*11 g carbohydrate*
24 g protein	*35 g fat*	*0.3 g fiber*

1. Prepare soufflé mold by greasing well with butter and sprinkling sides and bottom with grated cheese; set aside.

2. Melt butter in saucepan over low heat. Mix in flour and incorporate, using wooden spoon. Cook 3 to 4 minutes over very low heat.

3. Pour half of milk into saucepan and stir several minutes while cooking over medium heat. Continue incorporating milk a little at a time, stirring to make smooth paste.

4. When time, add egg yolks one by one, mixing well with wooden spoon between additions. Notice that saucepan has been removed from heat.

Potato Soufflé

serves 4

¼ cup	(*50 ml*) grated mozzarella cheese
1 lb	(*500 g*) white potatoes, peeled
3 tbsp	(*45 ml*) butter
¼ tsp	(*1 ml*) nutmeg
½ cup	(*125 ml*) light cream, heated
4	egg yolks, room temperature
6	egg whites, room temperature
	salt and pepper
dash	paprika
dash	savory
dash	cayenne pepper
	extra butter for mold

Preheat oven to 375°F (*190°C*).

Prepare 6-cup (*1.5-L*) soufflé mold by greasing well with butter and sprinkling sides and bottom with mozzarella cheese; set aside.

Cut potatoes into small pieces to decrease cooking time and place in saucepan filled with water; season with salt. Boil until just cooked—do not overcook!

Drain potatoes well and return to saucepan. Place over low heat and dry several minutes. Purée through potato ricer or food mill into large bowl.

Stir in butter until well incorporated. Add all seasonings and mix well. Pour in cream and incorporate. Mixture should have consistency of mashed potatoes.

Using wooden spoon, beat in all egg yolks at the same time. Set bowl aside.

Beat egg whites until stiff, using copper bowl if available, and spoon a bit of white into egg yolk mixture. Incorporate well.

Fold egg yolk mixture into egg whites, using rubber spatula to incorporate evenly. Rotate bowl while folding and continue until no trace of white is left.

Pour batter into mold and run thumb around inside edge, about ½ in. (*1.2 cm*) deep into batter. This will form an extra little top. Bake 35 minutes.

1 serving	*296 calories*	*18 g carbohydrate*
11 g protein	*20 g fat*	*2.4 g fiber*

Crepe Bouchées

serves 6–8

3 tbsp	(*45 ml*) butter
2	shallots, finely chopped
¼ lb	(*125 g*) fresh mushroom caps, cleaned and finely chopped
1 tbsp	(*15 ml*) finely chopped fresh parsley
1 tsp	(*5 ml*) herbes de Provence
2 tbsp	(*30 ml*) flour
1½ cups	(*375 ml*) milk
½ cup	(*125 ml*) grated Gruyère cheese
8	crepes *
	few drops Tabasco sauce
dash	paprika
	salt and pepper
	several large oranges (optional)

Heat butter in skillet over medium heat. Cook shallots, mushroom caps and seasonings, including herbs, 3 to 4 minutes to evaporate moisture from mushrooms.

Season well and stir in flour. Mix and continue cooking 2 minutes over low heat.

Pour in milk while mixing with wooden spoon. Increase heat to medium-low and season. Continue cooking 3 to 4 minutes or until smooth.

Add cheese and mix well. Remove sauce from heat and set aside to cool.

Spread mushroom mixture over each crepe, covering whole surface. Roll loosely and place on plate; cover lightly with plastic wrap. Chill 2 hours.

Slice crepe rolls into pieces about 1 in. (*2.5 cm*) long. Serve cold or, if preferred, warm several minutes in oven at broil.

Use oranges for creative presentation, if desired.

* *See Crepes Stuffed with Veal, page 240.*

1 serving	*121 calories*	*5 g carbohydrate*
5 g protein	*9 g fat*	*0.5 g fiber*

Crêpes Savoyardes

serves 4

8	crepes *
8	thin slices Black Forest ham
8	thin slices Gruyère cheese or 1½ cups (*375 ml*) grated cheese
2 tbsp	(*30 ml*) melted butter
dash	paprika
	pepper

Preheat oven to 350°F (*180°C*).

Stack ham and cheese on each crepe. Season with paprika and pepper lightly. Roll and place in baking dish.

Baste crepes with melted butter and bake 10 to 15 minutes in oven.

* *See Crepes Stuffed with Veal, page 240.*

1 serving	*560 calories*	*50 g carbohydrate*
27 g protein	*28 g fat*	*1.4 g fiber*

Allumettes

serves 6–8

1½ cups (*375 ml*) all-purpose flour
¼ tsp (*1 ml*) salt
1 cup (*250 ml*) cold milk
3 eggs
1 cup (*250 ml*) beer
3 tbsp (*45 ml*) melted butter
your favorite jam
granulated sugar

Place flour and salt in large bowl. Whisk in milk. Add eggs; mix very well.

Mix in beer until batter is smooth. Strain batter and stir in butter. Cover with sheet of plastic wrap touching surface; chill 1 hour.

Lightly butter crepe pan and place over high heat. Mix batter well. When butter is hot, pour in small ladle of batter. Tilt pan and rotate, causing batter to cover bottom of pan. Cook 1 minute over medium-high heat until underside is lightly browned.

Turn crepe over; cook 30 seconds. Stack crepes on plate as they are cooked and monitor heat. Grease pan if needed.

To serve, spread opened crepe with jam. Roll and place on ovenproof platter; sprinkle with granulated sugar. Broil 3 minutes.

1 serving *295 calories* *50 g carbohydrate*
6 g protein *7 g fat* *1.1 g fiber*

Croque-Madame

serves 4

8	thick slices Farmer's bread, toasted
4	slices Italian ham
1 cup	(*250 ml*) grated Gruyère cheese
1 cup	(*250 ml*) white sauce,* heated
	salt and pepper

Arrange 4 slices of bread on large ovenproof platter. Cover each with slice of ham and top with ½ cup (*125 ml*) cheese. Season well.

Close sandwiches with remaining bread and spoon white sauce over each.

Top with remaining cheese and broil 5 to 6 minutes in oven until bubbly and light brown.

Slice and serve.

* *See Poached Salmon with Egg Sauce, page 338.*

1 serving	*476 calories*	*39 g carbohydrate*
26 g protein	*24 g fat*	*1.6 g fiber*

1. Arrange 4 slices of bread on large ovenproof platter and cover each with ham.

2. Top with grated cheese, reserving half. Be sure to season well.

3. Close sandwiches with remaining bread.

4. Spoon white sauce over each sandwich; sprinkle with remaining cheese before broiling in oven.

Apple-Raisin Sauté for French Toast

serves 4

2 tbsp	(*30 ml*) butter
3	apples, peeled, cored, quartered and sliced
½ cup	(*125 ml*) sultana raisins
¼ tsp	(*1 ml*) cinnamon
2 tbsp	(*30 ml*) maple syrup
dash	nutmeg

Heat butter in frying pan over medium heat. Add apples, raisins, cinnamon and nutmeg; mix well. Cook 8 to 10 minutes.

Stir in maple syrup and continue cooking another 5 minutes.

Serve with French toast, pancakes or eggs.

1 serving *206 calories* *37 g carbohydrate*
1 g protein *6 g fat* *3.4 g fiber*

Delicious French Toast

serves 4

5	large eggs
¼ cup	(*50 ml*) light cream
1 tbsp	(*15 ml*) honey
8	thick slices French bread, with crust
3 tbsp	(*45 ml*) butter
	strawberry jam
	confectioners' sugar

Preheat oven to 200°F (*100°C*).

Beat eggs with cream and honey in large bowl.

Dip 4 slices of bread into mixture to coat thoroughly; transfer to plate.

Heat half of butter in large nonstick frying pan. When hot, add first 4 pieces of bread. Cook over medium heat 2 minutes on each side or until nicely browned.

Transfer first batch to ovenproof platter and keep hot.

Repeat above procedure with remaining butter and slices of bread.

Serve with strawberry jam and sprinkle portions with a little confectioners' sugar.

1 serving	*483 calories*	*65 g carbohydrate*
13 g protein	*19 g fat*	*1.8 g fiber*

Rösti Potatoes

serves 4

4	large potatoes, boiled in skins *	
4	slices bacon, diced small	
2 tbsp	(*30 ml*) butter	
	salt and pepper	

Peel potatoes and grate into long, fine strands; set aside.

Cook bacon in large nonstick frying pan over medium heat until done. Discard bacon pieces, leaving fat in pan.

Quickly add grated potatoes to pan and cook 10 to 12 minutes over medium heat, stirring frequently. Season several times during cooking.

Using wide metal spatula, press potatoes down flat. Lift up corner and slip butter underneath. Continue cooking 6 to 7 minutes or until nicely browned on bottom.

To serve, flip over to show browned side.

* *Do not overcook potatoes.*

1 serving	*205 calories*	*27 g carbohydrate*
4 g protein	*9 g fat*	*2.7 g fiber*

1. Peel potatoes and grate into long, fine strands; set aside.

2. Cook bacon in large nonstick frying pan over medium heat until done. Discard bacon pieces, leaving fat in pan.

3. Quickly add grated potatoes to pan and cook 10 to 12 minutes over medium heat, stirring frequently. Season several times during cooking.

4. Using wide metal spatula, press potatoes down flat. Lift up corner and slip butter underneath. Continue cooking 6 to 7 minutes or until nicely browned on bottom.

Cottage Cheese Pancakes

serves 4

4	eggs, separated
1½ tbsp	(*25 ml*) sugar
4 tbsp	(*60 ml*) cottage cheese
¼ cup	(*50 ml*) all-purpose flour
2 tbsp	(*30 ml*) melted butter
	extra cottage cheese and maple syrup

Using electric mixer, beat egg whites in small bowl until quite foamy. Add sugar and continue beating until stiff.

Beat yolks in separate bowl and incorporate cheese; blend well.

Add flour to egg yolks; then incorporate beaten whites. Mix batter until quite smooth. Stir in melted butter.

Heat frying pan or griddle with thin film of oil. Cook pancakes over medium-high heat until nicely browned on both sides.

Serve with extra cheese and maple syrup.

1 serving *308 calories* *39 g carbohydrate*
11 g protein *12 g fat* *0.2 g fiber*

Cocoa and Whipped Cream

serves 2

1 cup	(*250 ml*) heavy cream, chilled
½ tsp	(*2 ml*) vanilla
1 tbsp	(*15 ml*) confectioners' sugar
4 tbsp	(*60 ml*) cocoa
4 tbsp	(*60 ml*) granulated sugar
2 cups	(*500 ml*) scalded milk, still hot
	grated mint-flavored chocolate

To make whipped cream, chill stainless-steel bowl in refrigerator. Pour cold cream and vanilla into bowl; beat with electric beater until peaks form.

Sprinkle in confectioners' sugar and incorporate, using rubber spatula. Set aside in refrigerator.

In another stainless-steel bowl, mix cocoa with granulated sugar. Gradually add milk while whisking constantly.

Pour cocoa into 2 large glasses. Top with whipped cream (use pastry bag for ease) and sprinkle each serving with a little grated chocolate.

1 serving	*778 calories*	*58 g carbohydrate*
15 g protein	*54 g fat*	*1.2 g fiber*

Bavarian Coffee

serves 4

4 oz	(*125 g*) semisweet chocolate
1½ cups	(*375 ml*) heavy cream, whipped
	strong hot black coffee for four
dash	cinnamon

Place chocolate in stainless-steel bowl placed over saucepan half-filled with hot water. Heat saucepan so that water is bubbling and melts chocolate.

Place hot coffee into pitcher and mix in melted chocolate. Pour into 4 Irish-coffee glasses or attractive mugs, being sure to leave at least 1 in. (*2.5 cm*) free for cream. Carefully spoon whipped cream into glasses so that it rests on liquid.

Sprinkle with cinnamon and serve at once.

1 serving	*518 calories*	*12 g carbohydrate*
5 g protein	*50 g fat*	*0.8 g fiber*

RUSH-HOUR COOKING I

Great-tasting recipes in the shortest possible time, thanks to the microwave

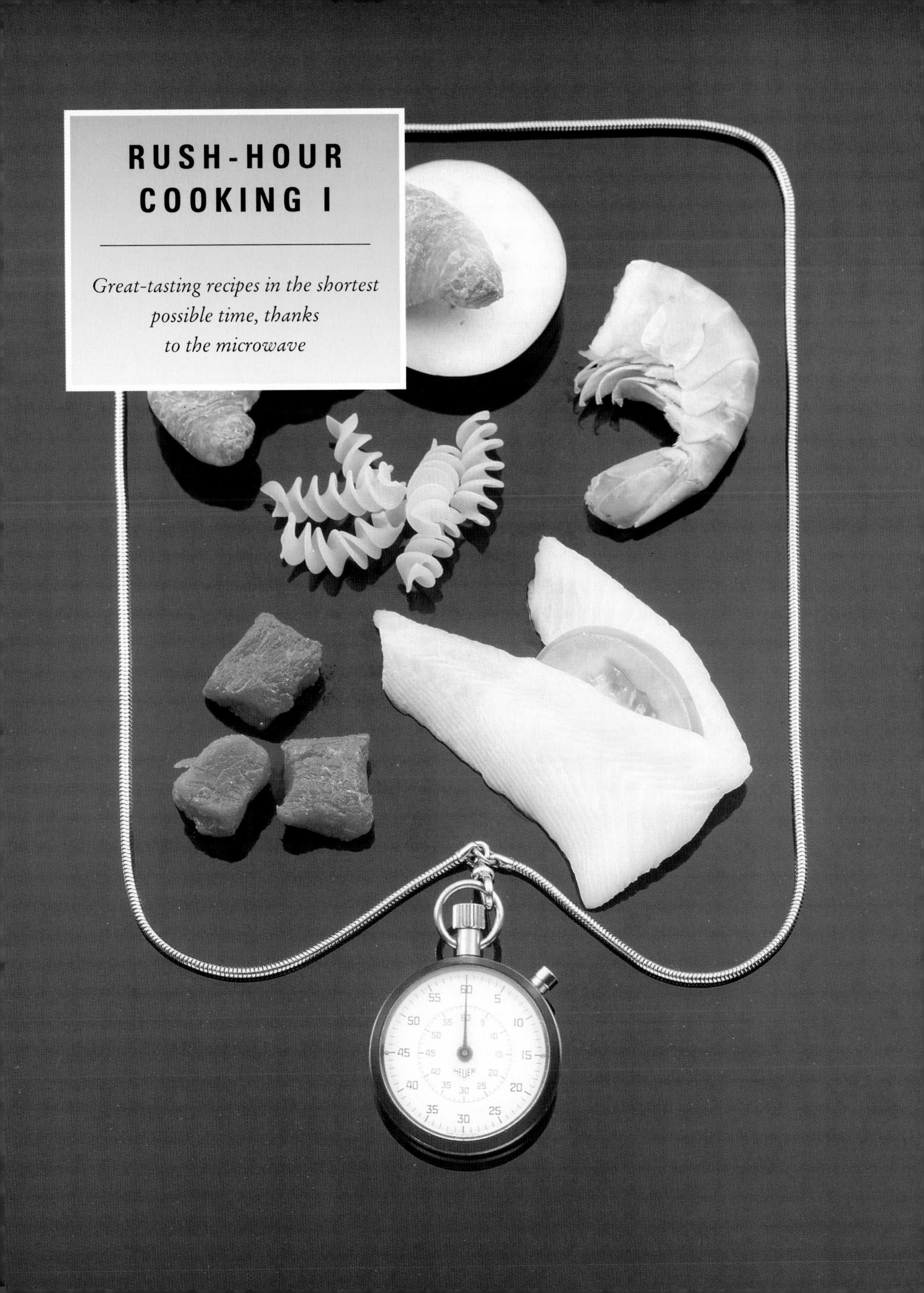

Hot Multi-Vegetable Salad

serves 4

Microwave setting: HIGH
Cooking time: 11 minutes

1 tbsp	(*15 ml*) vegetable oil
1	garlic clove, smashed and chopped
1	onion, cut into small sections
2	carrots, pared and thinly sliced
½	zucchini, thinly sliced
½	red pepper, sliced
1	green pepper, cut into cubes
1	celery stalk, sliced
12	snow pea pods, cleaned
2 tbsp	(*30 ml*) wine vinegar
3 tbsp	(*45 ml*) olive oil
	salt and pepper

Place vegetable oil, garlic, onion and carrots in 12-cup (*3-L*) casserole. Season, cover and microwave 3 minutes.

Add zucchini, red and green peppers, celery and pea pods; season well. Cover and microwave 8 minutes, stirring once during cooking.

Sprinkle vegetables with vinegar and olive oil; toss and serve hot. Accompany with fruit in season, if desired.

1 serving	*190 calories*	*13 g carbohydrate*
3 g protein	*14 g fat*	*4.9 g fiber*

Cocktail Meatballs with Chickpea Dip

serves 4–6

Microwave setting: HIGH
Cooking time: 15 minutes (preheating required)

1 tsp	(*5 ml*) vegetable oil
½	eggplant, peeled and diced
2	garlic cloves, smashed and chopped
19 oz	(*540 ml*) can chickpeas, drained
½	hot banana pepper, chopped
1 cup	(*250 ml*) canned tomatoes, drained
24	cocktail-size meatballs, made of sausage meat (raw)
2 tbsp	(*30 ml*) olive oil
1 tbsp	(*15 ml*) soy sauce
dash	paprika
	salt and pepper

Place vegetable oil, eggplant and garlic in 12-cup (*3-L*) casserole; season well. Cover and microwave 7 minutes.

Stir in chickpeas, hot banana pepper, tomatoes and paprika; correct seasoning. Microwave 6 minutes, uncovered.

Meanwhile, toss meatballs in mixture of olive oil and soy sauce; set aside.

Remove casserole from microwave and pour contents into food processor; blend to purée. Remove and transfer to serving bowls.

Place browning plate in microwave and preheat 10 minutes at HIGH.

When browning plate is ready, add meatballs and season; microwave 1 minute.

Turn meatballs over and continue microwaving 1 minute.

Serve meatballs using toothpicks; accompany with chickpea dip.

1 serving	*455 calories*	*27 g carbohydrate*
35 g protein	*23 g fat*	*5.9 g fiber*

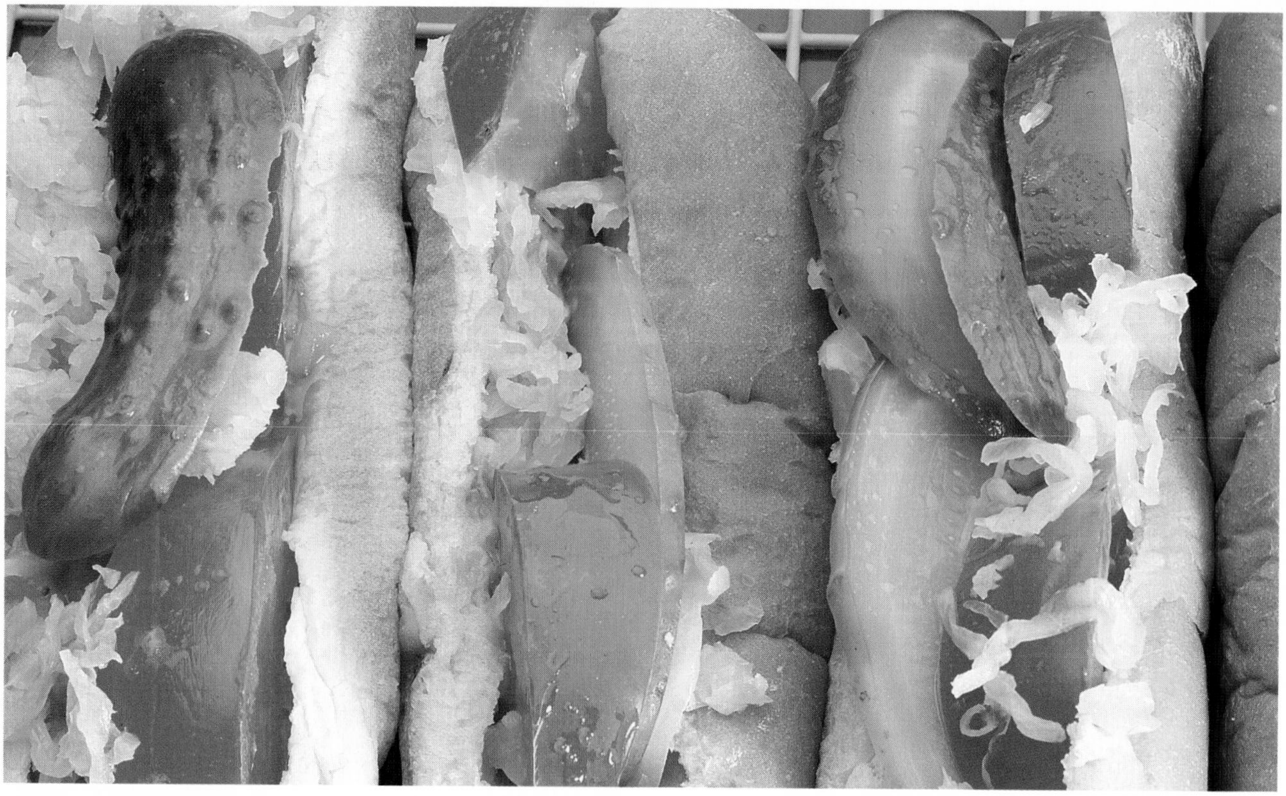

Sour Dogs

serves 4

Microwave setting: HIGH
Cooking time: 3 minutes

4	beef wieners
4	hot dog buns
1	tomato, cut into wedges
1 cup	(*250 ml*) sauerkraut, heated
2	large dill pickles, sliced
	various condiments

Place wieners in buns and wrap each in paper towel. Microwave 3 minutes.

Remove and garnish with tomato, sauerkraut and pickles. Top with your favorite condiments. Serve at once.

1 serving	*279 calories*	*26 g carbohydrate*
10 g protein	*15 g fat*	*3.2 g fiber*

Potato Cheese Pie

serves 4

Microwave settings: HIGH, MEDIUM-HIGH
Cooking time: 10 minutes

2 tbsp	(*30 ml*) butter
2	large shallots, finely chopped
4	large potatoes, boiled in skins, peeled and thinly sliced
4	thin slices Black Forest ham, cut into narrow strips
6	large eggs
1 cup	(*250 ml*) grated Swiss cheese
	salt and pepper
pinch	nutmeg

Place butter and shallots in 8-cup (*2-L*) glass pie plate. Microwave 2 minutes, uncovered, at HIGH.

Arrange potatoes in one layer in pie plate, overlapping slightly. Season with salt, pepper and nutmeg; top with strips of ham.

Beat eggs with fork and season; pour over ham and potatoes. Microwave 5 minutes, uncovered, at HIGH.

Sprinkle in cheese and finish microwaving 3 minutes, uncovered, at MEDIUM-HIGH.

Let stand 2 minutes before slicing. Serve with lettuce leaves and sliced tomatoes. This recipe makes an easy yet interesting lunch.

1 serving	*472 calories*	*27 g carbohydrate*
28 g protein	*28 g fat*	*4.1 g fiber*

Eggplant Munch Toast

serves 4

Microwave setting: HIGH
Cooking time: 25 minutes

1 tsp	(*5 ml*) olive oil
1	small onion, chopped
1	garlic clove, smashed and chopped
1	medium-size eggplant, peeled and thinly sliced
½	seedless cucumber, peeled and sliced
1	tomato, cut into wedges
1 tsp	(*5 ml*) oregano
6–8	slices toasted bread, cut in half
½ cup	(*125 ml*) grated Gruyère cheese
½ cup	(*125 ml*) grated Cheddar cheese
	salt and pepper
dash	paprika

Place oil, onion, garlic and eggplant in 12-cup (*3-L*) casserole. Season with salt, pepper and paprika; cover and microwave 10 minutes.

Add cucumber and tomato; season and add oregano. Microwave 15 minutes, uncovered.

Place pieces of bread on cookie sheet and spoon eggplant mixture on top. Sprinkle with both cheeses and broil in conventional oven for 1 to 2 minutes or until top is bubbly.

Serve as a nutritious lunch or as an early dinner before the show.

1 serving	*253 calories*	*21 g carbohydrate*
13 g protein	*13 g fat*	*2.6 g fiber*

1. Place oil, onion, garlic and eggplant in casserole. Season with salt, pepper and paprika; cover and microwave 10 minutes.

2. Add cucumber and tomato; season and add oregano. Microwave 15 minutes, uncovered.

3. Spoon eggplant mixture over pieces of bread set on cookie sheet.

4. Top with both cheeses and broil in conventional oven until bubbly.

Hot Dip for Seafood—California Style

serves 4

Microwave setting: HIGH
Cooking time: 5 minutes

½	seedless cucumber, peeled and diced
½	green pepper, diced
1½ cups	(*375 ml*) canned red kidney beans, drained
1 tsp	(*5 ml*) Pickapeppa sauce
2 tbsp	(*30 ml*) sour cream
	few drops Worcestershire sauce
	few drops Tabasco sauce
	salt and pepper
dash	paprika

Place cucumber, green pepper, kidney beans and Pickapeppa sauce in 12-cup (*3-L*) casserole. Add Worcestershire sauce, Tabasco sauce, salt, pepper and paprika. Mix well. Cover and microwave 5 minutes.

Transfer contents to food processor; blend until puréed. Mix in sour cream.

Spoon dip into serving bowl and serve with fresh-cooked seafood such as shrimp.

1 serving	*118 calories*	*19 g carbohydrate*
6 g protein	*2 g fat*	*6.8 g fiber*

Fresh Shrimp Salad

serves 4

Microwave setting: HIGH
Cooking time: 4 minutes

1 lb	*(500 g)* medium shrimp
½ cup	*(125 ml)* water
1	celery stalk, chopped
1	green pepper, chopped
2	large carrots, pared and grated
1 tbsp	*(15 ml)* chopped fresh parsley
4 tbsp	*(60 ml)* mayonnaise
	salt and pepper
	few drops Tabasco sauce
	few drops lemon juice

Place shrimp and water in 12-cup *(3-L)* casserole. Cover and microwave 4 minutes. Remove casserole from microwave and let stand 2 minutes on counter, covered.

Drain shrimp and cool under cold running water. Drain well, shell and devein.

Chop shrimp and place in large bowl. Add vegetables and parsley; season and mix well.

Mix in mayonnaise and remaining ingredients. Correct seasoning and serve on your choice of bread.

1 serving	*192 calories*	*5 g carbohydrate*
16 g protein	*12 g fat*	*1.5 g fiber*

Apple Spiced Chicken Salad in Croissants

serves 2

Microwave setting: MEDIUM-HIGH
Cooking time: 7 minutes

1 tbsp	(*15 ml*) butter
1	whole chicken breast, skinned, split into 2 and boned
1	celery stalk, sliced
1	celery stalk, diced small
1	red apple, peeled and diced small
¼	green pepper, diced small
1 tsp	(*5 ml*) curry powder
3 tbsp	(*45 ml*) mayonnaise
2	large fresh croissants
	salt and pepper
	paprika to taste
	few drops lemon juice

Place butter, chicken breast and sliced celery in 12-cup (*3-L*) casserole; season. Cover and microwave 7 minutes.

Turn chicken over. Cover casserole and let stand 3 minutes.

Drain chicken and chop; place in bowl. Add diced celery, apple and green pepper.

Sprinkle in curry powder and mix well. Incorporate mayonnaise and season with paprika and lemon juice. Correct seasoning.

Serve in opened croissants with fresh sliced tomatoes and wedges of apple, if desired.

1 serving	*626 calories*	*39 g carbohydrate*
32 g protein	*38 g fat*	*2.2 g fiber*

Crab Mix on Crusty Baguette

serves 4

Microwave setting: HIGH
Cooking time: 8 minutes

3 tbsp	(*45 ml*) butter
1	celery stalk, diced small
½	red pepper, diced small
½	zucchini, diced small
3 tbsp	(*45 ml*) flour
1½ cups	(*375 ml*) hot milk
7 oz	(*200 g*) can snow crab meat, well drained
1	French baguette, divided into 4 lengths, each halved and hollowed
	salt and pepper
pinch	nutmeg

Place butter, celery, red pepper and zucchini in 12-cup (*3-L*) casserole. Cover and microwave 3 minutes.

Mix in flour until well incorporated; season. Pour in milk, stir well and season again. Sprinkle in nutmeg. Microwave 4 minutes, uncovered, stirring once.

Mix in crab and microwave 1 minute, uncovered. Spoon into pieces of baguette and serve with light salad.

1 serving *382 calories* *45 g carbohydrate*
19 g protein *14 g fat* *2.6 g fiber*

Mushroom Scrambled Eggs on Toast

serves 4

Microwave setting: HIGH
Cooking time: 7 minutes 15 seconds

1 tbsp	(*15 ml*) butter
6	large fresh mushrooms, cleaned and sliced
1 tbsp	(*15 ml*) chopped fresh parsley
1	green onion, chopped
4	large eggs
¼ cup	(*50 ml*) milk
½ cup	(*125 ml*) grated Gruyère cheese
	salt and pepper
dash	paprika
	toasted bread
	crumbled cooked bacon

Place butter, mushrooms, parsley and green onion in 12-cup (*3-L*) casserole; cover and microwave 4 minutes.

Break eggs into bowl, add milk and beat with fork. Season with salt, pepper and paprika. Mix in cheese.

Pour eggs over mushrooms in casserole; microwave 2 minutes, uncovered.

Mix eggs well and continue microwaving 1 minute 15 seconds, uncovered.

Serve on toasted bread topped with bacon.

1 serving	*279 calories*	*11 g carbohydrate*
16 g protein	*19 g fat*	*1.4 g fiber*

1. Place butter, mushrooms, parsley and green onion in casserole. Cover and microwave 4 minutes.

2. Meanwhile, mix eggs with milk, using fork, and stir in grated cheese. Season well with salt, pepper and paprika.

3. Pour eggs over mushrooms in casserole; microwave 2 minutes, uncovered.

4. Mix eggs well and finish microwaving 1 minute 15 seconds, uncovered.

Smoked Salmon and Eggs

serves 4

Microwave setting: HIGH
Cooking time: 5 minutes

1 tbsp	(*15 ml*) butter
1	celery stalk, sliced
½	seedless cucumber, peeled, halved lengthwise and thinly sliced
4	cherry tomatoes, halved
1 tsp	(*5 ml*) curry powder
5	large eggs
4	slices smoked salmon
	salt and pepper

Place butter, celery, cucumber, cherry tomatoes and curry powder in 12-cup (*3-L*) casserole. Season with salt and pepper. Cover and microwave 2 minutes.

Beat eggs with fork and season; pour over vegetables but do not stir. Microwave 2 minutes, uncovered.

Mix well and continue microwaving 1 minute, uncovered.

Serve eggs with smoked salmon. Accompany with toast, if desired.

1 serving	*189 calories*	*3 g carbohydrate*
15 g protein	*13 g fat*	*0.7 g fiber*

Tomato Omelet

serves 2

Microwave setting: HIGH
Cooking time: 9 minutes

1 tbsp	(*15 ml*) butter	
4	large eggs	
1 tsp	(*5 ml*) chopped fresh parsley	
3	thick slices tomato	
2	thick slices Italian bread, toasted	
	salt and pepper	

Place butter in 8-cup (*2-L*) rectangular dish and microwave 2 minutes, uncovered.

Break eggs into bowl, add parsley and beat with fork.

Pour eggs into hot butter, arrange slices of tomato on top and season; microwave 4 minutes, uncovered.

Roll up cooked ends of omelet and continue microwaving 3 minutes.

Roll omelet and divide in half. Serve over toasted bread.

1 serving *294 calories* *18 g carbohydrate*
15 g protein *18 g fat* *1.3 g fiber*

Lunch-time Casserole

serves 4

Microwave settings: HIGH, MEDIUM-HIGH
Cooking time: 18 minutes

1 tbsp	(*15 ml*) butter
1	small onion, chopped
6	large fresh mushrooms, cleaned and sliced
1 tbsp	(*15 ml*) chopped fresh parsley
6	beef wieners, sliced on angle
1 tbsp	(*15 ml*) teriyaki sauce
2 cups	(*500 ml*) cooked long-grain rice
28 oz	(*796 ml*) can tomatoes, drained
1 cup	(*250 ml*) grated Cheddar cheese
	salt and pepper

Place button, onion, mushrooms and parsley in 12-cup (*3-L*) casserole. Cover and microwave 3 minutes at HIGH.

Mix in wieners and sprinkle in teriyaki sauce; mix again. Add rice, mix and season.

Arrange tomatoes over rice and season well with pepper. Sprinkle in cheese. Cover and microwave 15 minutes at MEDIUM-HIGH.

1 serving	*607 calories*	*42 g carbohydrate*
22 g protein	*39 g fat*	*4.0 g fiber*

1. Place butter, onion, mushrooms and parsley in casserole. Cover and microwave 3 minutes at HIGH.

2. Mix in wieners and sprinkle in teriyaki sauce; mix again.

3. Add rice, mix and season.

4. Arrange tomatoes over rice and season well with pepper. Sprinkle in cheese. Cover and microwave 15 minutes at MEDIUM-HIGH.

Cucumber Lemon Rice

serves 4

Microwave settings: HIGH, MEDIUM-HIGH
Cooking time: 7 minutes

2 tbsp	(*30 ml*) butter
1	celery stalk, thinly sliced
2	whole hearts of palm, sliced
¼	seedless cucumber, peeled and sliced on angle
1 tbsp	(*15 ml*) chopped fresh parsley
2½ cups	(*625 ml*) leftover cooked long-grain rice
12	pitted black olives, sliced
	chopped rind 1 lemon
dash	paprika
	salt and pepper

Place half of butter in 12-cup (*3-L*) casserole. Add celery, hearts of palm, cucumber, parsley and lemon rind. Cover and microwave 3 minutes at HIGH.

Mix in rice, olives and paprika; season well. Dot with remaining butter and finish microwaving 4 minutes, covered, at MEDIUM-HIGH.

Correct seasoning and serve.

1 serving *252 calories* *32 g carbohydrate*
4 g protein *12 g fat* *3.7 g fiber*

Chicken Livers, Apples and Artichokes

serves 2

Microwave settings: HIGH, MEDIUM-HIGH
Cooking time: 7 minutes (preheating required)

½ lb	(*250 g*) chicken livers, cleaned, fat removed
1 tbsp	(*15 ml*) chopped fresh parsley
½	small onion, chopped
1 tsp	(*5 ml*) vegetable oil
1 tsp	(*5 ml*) curry powder
1 tbsp	(*15 ml*) butter
2	artichoke hearts, halved
1	celery stalk, sliced
1	apple, cored, peeled, halved and sliced
1 cup	(*250 ml*) leftover cooked long-grain rice
	few drops Tabasco sauce
	few drops Pickapeppa sauce
	few drops lemon juice
	salt and pepper

Place livers, parsley, onion, vegetable oil, Tabasco sauce and Pickapeppa sauce in bowl; mix well. Mix in curry powder and set aside.

Place butter, artichoke hearts, celery and apple in 12-cup (*3-L*) casserole; sprinkle in lemon juice and season well. Cover and microwave 4 minutes at HIGH.

Mix in rice and microwave 1 minute, covered, at HIGH. Set casserole aside.

Place browning plate in microwave and preheat 10 minutes at HIGH.

When browning plate is ready, add chicken livers and microwave 1 minute at MEDIUM-HIGH.

Turn livers over and continue microwaving 1 minute at MEDIUM-HIGH.

Stir livers into vegetable mix in casserole and serve. If vegetables are too cold, reheat slightly.

1 serving	*430 calories*	*47 g carbohydrate*
29 g protein	*14 g fat*	*3.4 g fiber*

Curried Eggplant Sauce

serves 4

Microwave setting: HIGH
Cooking time: 33 minutes

1 tsp	(*5 ml*) vegetable oil
1	small onion, chopped
2	garlic cloves, smashed and chopped
1 tbsp	(*15 ml*) chopped fresh parsley
1 tsp	(*5 ml*) herbes de Provence
1	large eggplant, peeled and diced large
2 tbsp	(*30 ml*) curry powder
3 tbsp	(*45 ml*) flour
2 cups	(*500 ml*) chicken stock, heated
	salt and pepper
	raisins for decoration

Place oil, onion and garlic in 12-cup (*3-L*) casserole. Add parsley and herbes de Provence; cover and microwave 3 minutes.

Add eggplant and sprinkle in curry powder; mix well and season. Cover and microwave 15 minutes.

Mix eggplant, mashing with wooden spoon.

Mix in flour until well incorporated; then pour in chicken stock. Stir, correct seasoning and microwave 15 minutes, uncovered.

Serve sauce over white rice and decorate portions with raisins.

1 serving	*57 calories*	*10 g carbohydrate*
2 g protein	*1 g fat*	*1.9 g fiber*

1. Place oil, onion, garlic, parsley and herbes de Provence in casserole. Cover and microwave 3 minutes.

2. Add eggplant and sprinkle in curry powder; mix well and season. Cover and microwave another 15 minutes.

3. Mix eggplant, mashing with wooden spoon.

4. Mix in flour until well incorporated; then pour in chicken stock and finish microwaving.

White Herb Sauce for Pasta

serves 4

Microwave settings: HIGH, MEDIUM
Cooking time: 9 minutes 30 seconds

3 tbsp	(*45 ml*)	butter
3 tbsp	(*45 ml*)	flour
1½ cups	(*375 ml*)	hot milk
1 tsp	(*5 ml*)	chopped fresh mint
1 tsp	(*5 ml*)	chopped fresh parsley
½ tsp	(*2 ml*)	thyme
¼ cup	(*50 ml*)	finely grated Gruyère cheese
dash		nutmeg
		salt and pepper
		assortment of cooked sliced vegetables such as carrots or green beans (optional)

Place butter in 12-cup (*3-L*) casserole; microwave 30 seconds, uncovered, at HIGH. Mix in flour until well incorporated and microwave 1 minute, uncovered, at HIGH.

Pour in hot milk and whisk until smooth. Add all seasonings and microwave 6 minutes, uncovered, at HIGH, stirring 3 times during cooking.

Mix in cheese and microwave 2 minutes, uncovered, at MEDIUM.

Add vegetables, if desired, and let stand 1 minute before serving over hot pasta.

1 serving *197 calories* *13 g carbohydrate*
7 g protein *13 g fat* *1.4 g fiber*

Jumbo Pasta-Shell Salad

serves 4

Microwave setting: HIGH
Cooking time: 6 minutes

1 tsp	(*5 ml*) vegetable oil
2	whole hearts of palm, sliced
4	artichoke hearts, halved
½	red pepper, sliced
½	zucchini, halved lengthwise and sliced
12	snow pea pods, ends pared
1	shallot, sliced
1	garlic clove, smashed and chopped
4 cups	(*1 L*) cooked jumbo pasta shells *
1½ tbsp	(*25 ml*) olive oil
1 tbsp	(*15 ml*) wine vinegar
1 tbsp	(*15 ml*) chopped fresh parsley
1 cup	(*250 ml*) grated Cheddar cheese
	salt and pepper
	lemon juice

Place vegetable oil, hearts of palm, artichokes, red pepper, zucchini, pea pods, shallot and garlic in 12-cup (*3-L*) casserole. Season well and sprinkle with a few drops lemon juice. Cover and microwave 3 minutes.

Stir vegetables and add pasta shells. Sprinkle in olive oil, vinegar and a little more lemon juice. Add parsley and season; cover and microwave 3 minutes.

Transfer to serving plate or bowl, top with cheese and serve.

** It is best to cook the pasta shells a little past the "al dente" stage as they can be quite chewy, especially when served in a salad.*

1 serving — 410 calories — 46 g carbohydrate
16 g protein — 18 g fat — 4.6 g fiber

Spaghetti with Vegetable Cheddar Sauce

serves 4

Microwave setting: HIGH
Cooking time: 11 minutes

2½ tbsp	(*40 ml*) butter
2	green onions, chopped
4	large fresh mushrooms, cleaned and diced
3 tbsp	(*45 ml*) flour
2 cups	(*500 ml*) hot milk
1 cup	(*250 ml*) grated Cheddar cheese
4	portions cooked spaghetti, hot
4	slices cooked bacon, chopped
dash	paprika
	salt and pepper

Place butter, green onions and mushrooms in 12-cup (*3-L*) casserole. Cover and microwave 3 minutes.

Sprinkle in flour and paprika; incorporate well using wooden spoon.

Mix in ¾ of milk and microwave 3 minutes, uncovered, stirring halfway through.

Incorporate remaining milk, season and add cheese. Stir well and microwave 5 minutes, uncovered, stirring halfway through.

Pour sauce over portions of spaghetti and top with chopped bacon.

1 serving	*516 calories*	*54 g carbohydrate*
21 g protein	*24 g fat*	*2.7 g fiber*

1. Place butter, green onions and mushrooms in casserole. Cover and microwave 3 minutes.

2. Sprinkle in flour and paprika; incorporate using wooden spoon.

3. Mix in ¾ of milk and microwave 3 minutes, uncovered, stirring at halfway mark.

4. Incorporate remaining milk, season and add cheese. Stir well and finish microwaving 5 minutes, uncovered. Stir at halfway point.

Sausage and Bean Cheese Casserole

serves 4

Microwave settings: HIGH, MEDIUM
Cooking time: 14 minutes

1 tsp	(*5 ml*) olive oil
1	small onion, chopped
1	celery stalk, diced
1 lb	(*500 g*) lean ground beef
3	small smoked pork sausages, thinly sliced on angle
2 cups	(*500 ml*) tomato clam juice
19 oz	(*540 ml*) can red kidney beans, drained
3 tbsp	(*45 ml*) tomato paste
½ tsp	(*2 ml*) chopped fresh oregano
½ cup	(*125 ml*) grated Gruyère cheese
	salt and pepper
	few drops Pickapeppa sauce

Place oil, onion and celery in 12-cup (*3-L*) casserole. Cover and microwave 3 minutes at HIGH.

Mix in beef and sliced sausages; season and add Pickapeppa sauce. Cover and microwave 4 minutes at HIGH.

Pour in tomato clam juice, stir well and incorporate kidney beans and tomato paste. Add oregano and microwave 5 minutes, uncovered, at HIGH.

Incorporate grated cheese and finish microwaving 2 minutes, uncovered, at MEDIUM.

Serve over pasta and accompany with additional vegetables, if desired.

1 serving	*504 calories*	*12 g carbohydrate*
42 g protein	*32 g fat*	*1.4 g fiber*

Speedy Spaghetti with Smoked Salmon

serves 2

Microwave setting: HIGH
Cooking time: 3 minutes

2 tbsp	(*30 ml*) butter
½	zucchini, sliced
8	snow pea pods, ends pared
6	cherry tomatoes, halved
2	portions cooked spaghetti, still hot
4	thin slices smoked salmon, cut into small pieces
1 tbsp	(*15 ml*) chopped fresh parsley
	salt and pepper
	grated Parmesan cheese

Place half of butter in 12-cup (*3-L*) casserole. Add vegetables and season; cover and microwave 3 minutes.

Stir in hot spaghetti, smoked salmon, remaining butter and parsley; let stand 1 minute.

Top with grated cheese and serve.

1 serving	*398 calories*	*52 g carbohydrate*
25 g protein	*10 g fat*	*3.4 g fiber*

Clam Sauce for Linguine

serves 4

Microwave setting: HIGH
Cooking time: 13 minutes

3 tbsp	(*45 ml*) butter
1	onion, chopped
1 tbsp	(*15 ml*) chopped fresh parsley
1 tsp	(*5 ml*) fennel seeds
8	fresh mushrooms, cleaned and diced small
4 tbsp	(*60 ml*) flour
1 cup	(*250 ml*) chicken stock, heated
5 oz	(*142 g*) can baby clams, juice drained and reserved
2 tbsp	(*30 ml*) heavy cream
4	portions cooked linguine, hot
	salt and pepper
dash	paprika

Place butter, onion, parsley and fennel seeds in 12-cup (*3-L*) casserole. Cover and microwave 3 minutes.

Add mushrooms and season; continue microwaving 3 minutes, covered.

Sprinkle in flour and mix until well incorporated. Season with paprika.

Pour in chicken stock and reserved clam juice; microwave 7 minutes, uncovered, stirring twice during cooking time.

Mix in clams and incorporate cream; let stand, uncovered, on counter.

Spoon sauce over hot linguine and serve at once.

1 serving *377 calories* *52 g carbohydrate*
13 g protein *13 g fat* *3.1 g fiber*

1. Place butter, onion, parsley and fennel seeds in casserole. Cover and microwave 3 minutes.

2. Add mushrooms and season; continue microwaving 3 minutes, covered.

3. Mix in flour until well incorporated; season with paprika.

4. Pour in chicken stock and reserved clam juice; finish microwaving 7 minutes, uncovered. Stir sauce twice during cooking.

Fresh Mussel Sauce for Pasta

serves 4

Microwave setting: HIGH
Cooking time: 17 minutes

3 tbsp	(*45 ml*) butter
2	onions, cut into wedges
4	large fresh mushrooms, cleaned and quartered
1 tbsp	(*15 ml*) chopped fresh parsley
4 tbsp	(*60 ml*) flour
2 cups	(*500 ml*) milk, heated
2 lb	(*900 g*) fresh mussels, cleaned
1	lemon, quartered
¼ cup	(*50 ml*) dry white wine
dash	paprika
	salt and pepper
dash	nutmeg

Place butter, onions, mushrooms, parsley and paprika in 12-cup (*3-L*) casserole. Cover and microwave 3 minutes.

Mix in flour until well incorporated. Season.

Pour in milk, stirring well; sprinkle with nutmeg. Microwave 8 minutes, uncovered, stirring once.

Remove sauce from microwave, cover and set aside.

Place mussels, lemon quarters and wine in another 12-cup (*3-L*) casserole; cover and microwave 6 minutes.

Shell mussels and add to sauce; mix and serve over your choice of hot pasta.

1 serving	*290 calories*	*23 g carbohydrate*
18 g protein	*14 g fat*	*2.1 g fiber*

1. Place butter, onions, mushrooms, parsley and paprika in casserole. Cover and microwave 3 minutes.

2. Mix in flour until well incorporated. Season.

3. Pour in milk, stirring well; then sprinkle with nutmeg. Microwave 8 minutes, uncovered, stirring once.

4. After mussels have been cooked and shelled, incorporate them into hot sauce.

Vegetable Shrimp Dish

serves 4

Microwave setting: HIGH
Cooking time: 12 minutes

1 tsp	(*5 ml*) vegetable oil
½	eggplant, peeled and diced
½	seedless cucumber, peeled and diced
½ tsp	(*2 ml*) fennel seeds
½	large green pepper, diced
1	tomato, diced
2	green onions, thinly sliced
½ cup	(*125 ml*) grated Swiss cheese
1 lb	(*500 g*) cooked shrimp, shelled and deveined
dash	paprika
	salt and pepper

Place oil, eggplant, cucumber, fennel seeds and paprika in 12-cup (*3-L*) casserole; season well. Cover and microwave 8 minutes.

Add green pepper, tomato and green onions; season again. Sprinkle in cheese and mix; cover and microwave 3 minutes.

Stir in cooked shrimp and finish microwaving 1 minute. Serve in coquille dishes.

1 serving	*184 calories*	*6 g carbohydrate*
22 g protein	*8 g fat*	*1.6 g fiber*

Shrimp Mix in White Sauce

serves 4

Microwave settings: HIGH, MEDIUM
Cooking time: 5 minutes

1 tbsp	(*15 ml*) butter	
2	large green onions, diced	
1	green pepper, diced	
6 oz	(*170 g*) package cooked frozen shrimp, thawed	
1½ cups	(*375 ml*) white sauce, * heated	
½ cup	(*125 ml*) grated Gruyère cheese	
	salt and pepper	
dash	paprika	

Place butter, green onions and green pepper in 12-cup (*3-L*) casserole. Cover and microwave 3 minutes at HIGH.

Mix in shrimp and season. Pour in white sauce and sprinkle with paprika. Microwave 1 minute, uncovered, at MEDIUM.

Incorporate cheese and microwave 1 more minute, uncovered, at MEDIUM.

Serve with toasted bread and vegetables in season.

* *See Poached Salmon with Egg Sauce, page 338.*

1 serving	*326 calories*	*11 g carbohydrate*
20 g protein	*22 g fat*	*0.6 g fiber*

Fresh Shrimp Fresco

serves 4

Microwave setting: HIGH
Cooking time: 4 minutes

1 lb	(*500 g*) fresh medium shrimp
½ cup	(*125 ml*) water
2	lemon slices

Rinse shrimp under cold running water to clean. Place in 12-cup (*3-L*) casserole; add ½ cup (*125 ml*) water and slices of lemon. Cover and microwave 3 minutes.

Using tongs, remove shrimp that are pink in color—they are cooked. Mix remaining shrimp well, cover and microwave 1 more minute.

Place all cooked shrimp in cold water to stop cooking process. Peel and devein; serve or use in other recipes.

1 serving	*73 calories*	*0 g carbohydrate*
16 g protein	*1 g fat*	*0 g fiber*

Ginger Teriyaki Shrimp

serves 4

Microwave setting: HIGH
Cooking time: 7 minutes (preheating required)

1 tbsp	(*15 ml*) vegetable oil
2	carrots, pared and thinly sliced
2 tbsp	(*30 ml*) finely chopped fresh ginger
6–8	large fresh mushrooms, cleaned and sliced
1 lb	(*500 g*) medium shrimp, shelled and deveined
1 tbsp	(*15 ml*) olive oil
1 tbsp	(*15 ml*) teriyaki sauce
	juice ½ lemon
	salt and pepper
	few sprigs fresh watercress

Place vegetable oil, carrots and ginger in 12-cup (*3-L*) casserole. Cover and microwave 4 minutes.

Add mushrooms and sprinkle them with lemon juice. Season, cover and microwave 2 minutes. Set casserole aside.

Place browning plate in microwave and preheat 10 minutes at HIGH.

Meanwhile, place shrimp in bowl. Toss with olive oil and teriyaki sauce; marinate until browning plate is ready.

When ready, quickly drain shrimp, pouring liquid into casserole containing vegetables.

Place shrimp on hot browning plate, season and microwave 30 seconds.

Turn shrimp over; microwave another 30 seconds.

Transfer shrimp to vegetables in casserole, mix well and serve with fresh watercress as decoration.

1 serving	*164 calories*	*6 g carbohydrate*
17 g protein	*8 g fat*	*2.1 g fiber*

Rolled Sole Filets in Wine Sauce

serves 2

Microwave setting: MEDIUM-HIGH
Cooking time: 7 minutes

1 tbsp	(*15 ml*) butter
2	large sole filets, rolled
6	fresh mushrooms, cleaned and sliced
1 tbsp	(*15 ml*) chopped fresh parsley
2 tbsp	(*30 ml*) dry white wine
4	cherry tomatoes, halved
	juice 1 lemon
	salt and pepper

Place butter, fish, lemon juice, mushrooms and parsley in 12-cup (*3-L*) casserole; season.

Pour in wine and add tomatoes; cover and microwave 4 minutes.

Turn rolls over, adjust seasoning and cover; finish microwaving 3 minutes.

Serve at once with additional vegetables, if desired.

1 serving	*199 calories*	*6 g carbohydrate*
19 g protein	*11 g fat*	*2.2 g fiber*

Fresh Mussels

serves 2

Microwave setting: HIGH
Cooking time: 6 minutes

2 lb	(*900 g*) fresh mussels
1	lemon, quartered
¼ cup	(*50 ml*) dry white wine

Rinse mussels under plenty of cold running water. Scrub shells and remove beards with small knife. If you find any open shells, discard them—do not cook!

Place cleaned mussels in 12-cup (*3-L*) casserole. Add lemon and wine; cover and microwave 6 minutes.

Serve "au naturel" with juices.

1 serving	*143 calories*	*7 g carbohydrate*
22 g protein	*3 g fat*	*0 g fiber*

Chicken Livers Sauté-Style

serves 2

Microwave settings: HIGH, MEDIUM-HIGH
Cooking time: 8 minutes (preheating required)

½ lb	*(250 g)* chicken livers, cleaned, fat removed
1 tbsp	*(15 ml)* chopped fresh parsley
2	shallots, chopped
1 tsp	*(5 ml)* vegetable oil
1 tbsp	*(15 ml)* teriyaki sauce
1	garlic clove, smashed and chopped
1 tbsp	*(15 ml)* butter
½	zucchini, sliced
½	red pepper, sliced
1	celery stalk, sliced
4	fresh mushrooms, cleaned and sliced
dash	paprika
	few drops lemon juice
	salt and pepper

Place livers, parsley and shallots in bowl; season with paprika. Add vegetable oil, teriyaki sauce and garlic; mix well and set aside.

Place butter, vegetables and few drops lemon juice in 12-cup *(3-L)* casserole. Cover and microwave 5 minutes at HIGH.

Remove casserole and set aside, covered, on counter.

Place browning plate in microwave and preheat 10 minutes at HIGH.

When browning plate is ready, add chicken livers and seasonings; microwave 1 minute at MEDIUM-HIGH.

Turn livers over, season and continue microwaving 1 minute at MEDIUM-HIGH.

Set cooked livers aside and quickly reheat vegetables in casserole 1 minute at HIGH

Mix livers into vegetables, correct seasoning and serve at once.

1 serving	*270 calories*	*9 g carbohydrate*
27 g protein	*14 g fat*	*3.2 g fiber*

Calf Liver with Green Grapes

serves 2

Microwave settings: MEDIUM-HIGH, HIGH
Cooking time: 2 minutes (preheating required)

2	slices calf liver
1 tbsp	(*15 ml*) vegetable oil
1 tbsp	(*15 ml*) lemon juice
1 tbsp	(*15 ml*) teriyaki sauce
20	green seedless grapes
¼ cup	(*50 ml*) chicken stock, heated
	salt and pepper

Place browning plate in microwave and preheat 10 minutes at HIGH.

Trim all fat from liver and place slices on large plate. Add oil, lemon juice and teriyaki sauce; pepper well but do not salt. Let marinate, turning slices over once, until browning plate is ready.

Reserving marinade for later use, place slices of liver on hot browning plate. Microwave 1 minute at MEDIUM-HIGH.

Turn slices over, remove from browning plate and set aside.

Quickly pour reserved marinade into browning plate with juices from liver. Add grapes and chicken stock; microwave 1 minute, uncovered, at HIGH.

Serve at once with liver and accompany with assorted vegetables.

1 serving	*227 calories*	*11 g carbohydrate*
21 g protein	*11 g fat*	*0.3 g fiber*

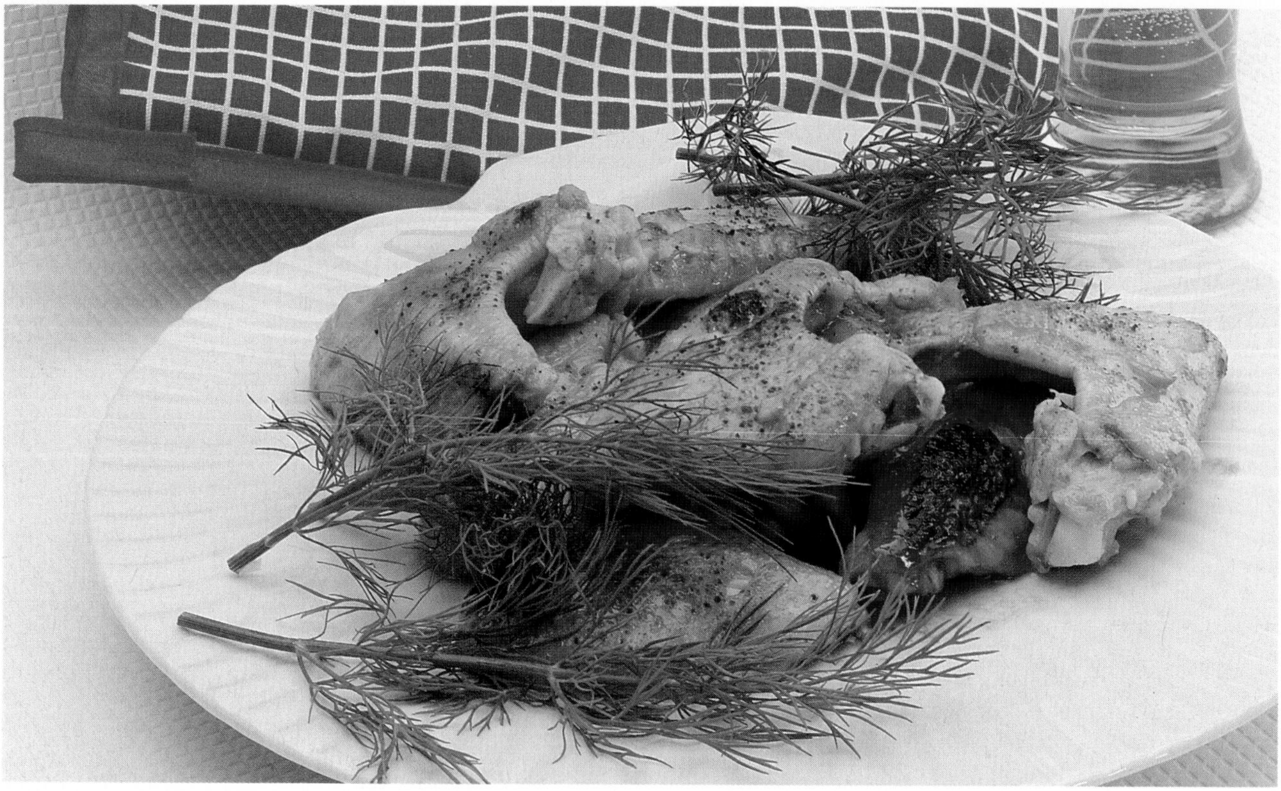

Tasty Grilled Chicken Wings

serves 2

Microwave setting: HIGH
Cooking time: 6 minutes (preheating required)

8	chicken wings, tips removed
2 tbsp	(*30 ml*) chopped fresh ginger
1 tbsp	(*15 ml*) liquid honey
1 tbsp	(*15 ml*) vegetable oil
	juice 1 lemon
	salt and pepper
	paprika to taste
	few drops Tabasco sauce

Place wings, ginger, honey, oil and lemon juice in bowl; season with salt, pepper and paprika to taste. Sprinkle in Tabasco sauce and mix well.

Meanwhile, place browning plate in microwave and preheat 10 minutes at HIGH.

When browning plate is ready, add wings and microwave 3 minutes.

Turn wings over, quickly season with more salt, pepper and paprika, and continue microwaving 3 minutes, depending on size of wings.

Serve.

1 serving *274 calories* *11 g carbohydrate*
26 g protein *14 g fat* *0 g fiber*

Chicken with Bananas and Coconut

serves 2

Microwave setting: MEDIUM-HIGH
Cooking time: 9 minutes

2 tbsp	(*30 ml*) butter
1	whole chicken breast, skinned, split into 2 and boned
6	fresh mushrooms, cleaned and sliced
1 tsp	(*5 ml*) curry powder
½ cup	(*125 ml*) sultana raisins
1	large banana, sliced thick
¼	papaya, peeled and sliced
1 tbsp	(*15 ml*) grated coconut
	juice ½ lemon
	juice 1 orange
	salt and pepper

Place butter, chicken, mushrooms, lemon juice, orange juice and curry powder in 12-cup (*3-L*) casserole; season well. Cover and microwave 6 minutes.

Turn chicken over and add raisins; cover and cook 2 minutes.

Stir in banana, papaya and coconut; correct seasoning. Cover and microwave 1 more minute.

1 serving	*513 calories*	*59 g carbohydrate*
31 g protein	*17 g fat*	*6.5 g fiber*

Teriyaki Strip Loin Steaks

serves 2

Microwave setting: HIGH
Cooking time: 1 minute 30 seconds (preheating required)

1 tbsp	(*15 ml*) oil
1 tbsp	(*15 ml*) teriyaki sauce
1 tsp	(*5 ml*) herbes de Provence
2	7 oz (*200 g*) strip loin steaks, ½ in. (*1.2 cm*) thick
	salt and pepper

Preheat browning oil in microwave for 10 minutes at HIGH.

Meanwhile, brush oil and teriyaki sauce over both sides of meat. Sprinkle sides with herbs and set aside.

As soon as grill is ready, add steaks and place in microwave for 1 minute.

Turn steaks over, season and continue microwaving 30 seconds for rare meat.

Serve with baked potatoes.

1 serving	*340 calories*	*1 g carbohydrate*
48 g protein	*16 g fat*	*0 g fiber*

Mixed Meat Patties with Vegetables

serves 4

Microwave setting: HIGH
Cooking time: 14 minutes (preheating required)

1 lb	(*500 g*) lean ground beef
½ lb	(*250 g*) sausage meat
1 tsp	(*5 ml*) vegetable oil
4	eggplants, peeled and thinly sliced
1	garlic clove, smashed and chopped
1	green pepper, thinly sliced
1	celery stalk, thinly sliced
½ cup	(*125 ml*) grated Gruyère cheese
	salt and pepper
dash	paprika
	few drops Tabasco sauce
	olive oil
	teriyaki sauce

Mix both meats together in food processor. Season well with salt, pepper, paprika and Tabasco sauce; mix again.

Shape meat into thin, flat patties; arrange on plate. Sprinkle with some olive oil and teriyaki sauce; marinate at least 15 minutes.

Meanwhile, pour vegetable oil into 12-cup (*3-L*) casserole. Add eggplant slices and season; cover and microwave 7 minutes.

Add garlic, green pepper and celery; cover and cook 2 minutes.

Add cheese, season and mix. Microwave 2 minutes, uncovered. Set vegetables aside.

Place browning plate in microwave and preheat 10 minutes at HIGH.

When browning plate is ready, add patties and microwave 1 minute. Turn patties over; continue microwaving 1 minute.

Remove from microwave and set aside. Reheat vegetables in casserole 1 minute, uncovered. Serve at once.

1 serving	*626 calories*	*8 g carbohydrate*
45 g protein	*46 g fat*	*3.2 g fiber*

Mock Beef Stroganoff with Kidney Beans

serves 4

Microwave setting: HIGH
Cooking time: 12 minutes

1	onion, chopped
1 tsp	(*5 ml*) oil
1 tbsp	(*15 ml*) chopped fresh parsley
½ lb	(*250 g*) fresh mushrooms, cleaned and sliced
1 lb	(*500 g*) lean ground beef
1 tsp	(*5 ml*) Pickapeppa sauce
2	garlic cloves, smashed and chopped
1 cup	(*250 ml*) canned red kidney beans, drained
1 cup	(*250 ml*) tomato sauce
3 tbsp	(*45 ml*) sour cream
	salt and pepper
	few drops Worcestershire sauce

Place onion, oil and parsley in 12-cup (*3-L*) casserole; cover and microwave 3 minutes.

Add mushrooms and ground beef; season well. Add Pickapeppa sauce, garlic and Worcestershire sauce; mix well.

Mix in kidney beans and microwave 8 minutes, uncovered, stirring once.

Stir in tomato sauce and microwave 1 minute, uncovered.

Mix in sour cream and serve. Accompany with fresh vegetables.

1 serving *364 calories* *22 g carbohydrate*
33 g protein *16 g fat* *6.9 g fiber*

Quick Sautéed Beef Tenderloin Slices

serves 4

Microwave setting: HIGH
Cooking time: 1 minute (preheating required)

1 tsp	(*5 ml*) vegetable oil
2 tbsp	(*30 ml*) teriyaki sauce
1 tbsp	(*15 ml*) chopped fresh ginger
4	slices beef tenderloin, ½ in. (*1.2 cm*) thick
	juice ½ lime
	freshly ground pepper

Place browning plate in microwave and preheat 10 minutes at HIGH. Pour oil and teriyaki sauce onto large plate. Add ginger and lime juice; pepper generously—do not salt.

Place slices of tenderloin in marinade and let stand until browning plate is ready. Be sure to turn meat over to marinate other side.

Place meat on browning plate and microwave 1 minute for rare meat.

Remove browning plate from oven, turn slices over and let stand 1 minute.

Serve with fresh vegetables.

1 serving *195 calories* *1 g carbohydrate*
32 g protein *7 g fat* *0 g fiber*

Lunch-Box Chocolate Cake

serves 4

Microwave settings: HIGH, MEDIUM
Cooking time: 14 minutes

4 oz	(*125 g*)	semisweet chocolate
2 tbsp	(*30 ml*)	water
2 tbsp	(*30 ml*)	butter
¼ cup	(*50 ml*)	heavy cream
3		egg yolks
3 tbsp	(*45 ml*)	sugar
3 tbsp	(*45 ml*)	flour
3		egg whites, beaten stiff with pinch of salt
		extra whipped cream for topping and chocolate sprinkles for decoration

Place chocolate and water in large glass bowl. Microwave 2 minutes, uncovered, at HIGH.

Mix in butter. Add cream and mix well. Mix in egg yolks; then add sugar and mix well.

Mix in flour until well incorporated. Using spatula, fold in beaten egg whites until thoroughly incorporated.

Pour batter into 8-cup (*2-L*) glass pie plate and microwave 12 minutes, uncovered, at MEDIUM. Cool thoroughly before serving and garnish cake as desired.

1 serving	*504 calories*	*26 g carbohydrate*
10 g protein	*40 g fat*	*1.2 g fiber*

Sour Cream Bundt Cake

serves 6–8

Microwave setting: HIGH
Cooking time: 14 minutes

1 cup	(*250 ml*) sour cream
1 cup	(*250 ml*) plain yogurt
1 cup	(*250 ml*) brown sugar
2 cups	(*500 ml*) sifted all-purpose flour
1 tbsp	(*15 ml*) baking powder
¼ tsp	(*1 ml*) baking soda
1	egg
1	apple, cored, peeled and diced
2 tbsp	(*30 ml*) Lamb's light rum
1 tsp	(*5 ml*) cinnamon
	grated rind 1 lemon

Place sour cream and yogurt in bowl and mix together. Add brown sugar and mix until lump-free, using spatula; set aside.

In second bowl, combine flour, baking powder and soda. Sift together; incorporate into sour cream mixture.

Stir in lemon rind. Add egg and mix well.

Mix in apple, then rum, then cinnamon.

Butter 8-cup (*2-L*) bundt mold. Pour in batter and microwave 14 minutes, uncovered. At halfway mark, rotate mold ¼ turn.

Cool on wire rack before serving. Glaze if desired or serve plain.

1 serving	*326 calories*	*61 g carbohydrate*
7 g protein	*6 g fat*	*1.5 g fiber*

Kiwi Dessert Sauce

serves 4

Microwave setting: HIGH
Cooking time: 8 minutes

3	kiwis, peeled and diced
½ cup	(*125 ml*) granulated sugar
½ cup	(*125 ml*) water
1 tsp	(*5 ml*) cornstarch
1 tbsp	(*15 ml*) cold water
2	ripe mangoes, peeled, flesh cut into wedges
4	scoops vanilla ice cream
	fresh sweet cherries, pitted

Purée kiwis in food processor; set aside.

Place sugar and ½ cup (*125 ml*) water in 12-cup (*3-L*) casserole. Microwave 5 minutes, uncovered.

Mix cornstarch with 1 tbsp (*15 ml*) water; stir into liquid sugar until well incorporated.

Add kiwis, mix and microwave 3 minutes, uncovered. Transfer sauce to bowl and freeze 10 minutes.

To serve, ladle sauce over dessert plate to cover bottom; arrange wedges of mango and scoop of ice cream. Decorate with cherries.

1 serving — 376 calories — 72 g carbohydrate
4 g protein — 8 g fat — 2.5 g fiber

RUSH HOUR COOKING II

Fast, fun cooking
for those on the run

Gourmet Pita Pizza

serves 4

1 tbsp	(*15 ml*) olive oil
1	garlic clove, smashed and chopped
1 tbsp	(*15 ml*) chopped fresh parsley
1	onion, chopped
2	shallots, chopped
28 oz	(*796 ml*) can tomatoes, drained and chopped
2 tbsp	(*30 ml*) tomato paste
½	jalapeño pepper, chopped
4	large whole-wheat or plain pita bread
½	green pepper, thinly sliced
½ lb	(*250 g*) fresh mushrooms, cleaned and sliced
2 cups	(*500 ml*) grated mozzarella cheese
	salt and pepper
pinch	sugar
	sliced pepperoni sausage
dash	paprika

Heat oil in large skillet. Add garlic, parsley, onion and shallots; cook 5 to 6 minutes over low heat.

Stir in tomatoes and season well; cook 20 minutes over low heat.

Mix in tomato paste and chopped jalapeño pepper. Sprinkle in sugar, stir and finish cooking 7 to 8 minutes over low heat.

At this point, the sauce is ready and may be stored for later use. Let cool and then cover with plastic wrap touching surface. Refrigerate up to 4 days.

To prepare pizza, preheat oven to 400°F (*200°C*).

Arrange pita bread on cookie sheets. Spread tomato sauce over bread and garnish with green pepper, mushrooms and pepperoni slices.

Top with grated cheese and season with salt, pepper and paprika. Cook 12 minutes in oven.

1 serving *854 calories* *70 g carbohydrate*
40 g protein *46 g fat* *4.0 g fiber*

1. Begin gourmet tomato sauce by sautéing garlic, parsley, onion and shallots 5 to 6 minutes in hot olive oil.

2. Stir in tomatoes and season well; cook 20 minutes over low heat.

3. Mix in tomato paste and jalapeño pepper. (Decrease amount of hot pepper for a milder sauce.) Sprinkle in sugar to offset bitterness that may be caused by tomato paste; stir well. Finish cooking sauce 7 to 8 minutes over low heat. Prepare to make pizza or cool sauce for refrigeration.

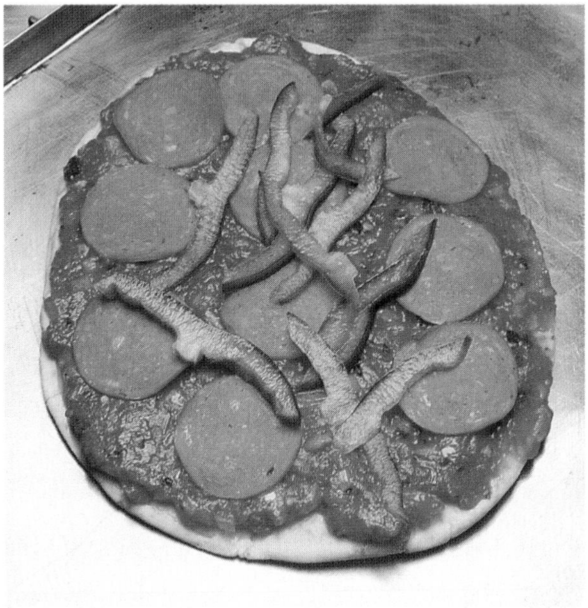

4. Garnish pita bread with vegetables and pepperoni slices. You can substitute our suggestions with zucchini slices, julienned carrot and anything else that might intrigue you.

Quick Shrimp Salad on French Baguette

serves 2

12	medium shrimp
2	slices lemon
½	celery stalk, chopped
¼	green pepper, chopped
2	tomato slices, chopped
1 tsp	(*5 ml*) chopped fresh parsley
1 tsp	(*5 ml*) Dijon mustard
2 tbsp	(*30 ml*) mayonnaise
	few drops lemon juice
	salt and pepper
	few drops Tabasco sauce
	fresh French baguette

Place shrimp in saucepan and pour in enough cold water to cover. Add lemon slices and bring to boil.

Immediately remove pan from heat and let stand 5 to 6 minutes on cutting board. Drain shrimp, peel and devein.

Dice shrimp and place in bowl with vegetables; toss together. Add parsley, mustard and mayonnaise; mix well.

Season salad with lemon juice, salt, pepper and Tabasco sauce.

Serve on opened slices of baguette.

1 serving *747 calories* *95 g carbohydrate*
49 g protein *19 g fat* *6.4 g fiber*

Salad in a Bun

serves 4

1 cup	(*250 ml*) frozen mixed vegetables
4	slices cooked ham, cut into strips
3	hard-boiled eggs, chopped
1 tbsp	(*15 ml*) chopped fresh chives
3 tbsp	(*45 ml*) mayonnaise
	salt and pepper
	juice 1 lemon
	whole-wheat or kaiser buns

Cook frozen vegetables according to directions on package. Cool in cold water, drain well and place in bowl.

Add ham and eggs; season with salt and pepper.

Sprinkle in chives and mix in mayonnaise. Add lemon juice and mix well again.

Slice tops off buns and scoop out most of insides. Spoon vegetable salad into hollow buns and serve with tops as decoration. If desired, accompany with sliced fresh fruit.

1 serving *360 calories* *37 g carbohydrate*
17 g protein *16 g fat* *2.5 g fiber*

Ten-Minute Western Sandwiches for Two

serves 2

1 tbsp	(*15 ml*) butter
½	onion, chopped
1 cup	(*250 ml*) chopped cooked ham
½	green pepper, chopped
1 tsp	(*5 ml*) chopped fresh parsley
4	large eggs
4	slices toasted bread
	salt and pepper

Melt butter in nonstick frying pan over high heat. Add onion, ham, green pepper and parsley and cook 3 to 4 minutes.

Meanwhile, break eggs into bowl and beat well with fork; season lightly.

Pour eggs over ham mixture in pan. Mix slightly, reduce heat to medium and continue cooking 2 minutes.

Using metal spatula, turn flat omelet over; continue cooking 1 minute.

Slice omelet into 4 pieces and assemble sandwiches. If desired, serve with chips.

1 serving *454 calories* *33 g carbohydrate*
31 g protein *22 g fat* *1.1 g fiber*

Double Fish Salad

serves 4

2	cooked sole filets
1 lb	(*500 g*) cooked shrimp
2	blanched carrots, sliced
1 cup	(*250 ml*) blanched snow pea pods
2	large apples, cored and sliced with skin
1	green onion, chopped
1 tbsp	(*15 ml*) chopped fresh parsley
4 tbsp	(*60 ml*) olive oil
2 tbsp	(*30 ml*) red wine vinegar
	salt and pepper
	lemon juice to taste
	romaine lettuce leaves

Break sole filets into small pieces and place in bowl with shrimp.

Add vegetables and apples; toss ingredients together.

Sprinkle in parsley, oil and vinegar; season well and toss thoroughly.

Season salad with lemon juice to taste and serve on bed of fresh crisp lettuce leaves.

1 serving	*376 calories*	*18 g carbohydrate*
40 g protein	*16 g fat*	*5.0 g fiber*

Hot Chicken and Asparagus Salad

serves 4

1	apple, cored, peeled and sliced
1 tsp	(*5 ml*) lemon juice
2	green onions, sliced
1	celery stalk, chopped
2	boneless half chicken breasts, cooked and still hot
2	tomatoes, cored, halved and sliced
1	endive, separated into leaves
2	bunches fresh asparagus, pared if needed, cooked and still hot
2 tbsp	(*30 ml*) mayonnaise
2 tbsp	(*30 ml*) heavy cream
2	fresh mint leaves, chopped
4 tbsp	(*60 ml*) chopped nuts
	salt and pepper

Place apple in large bowl and toss with lemon juice. Add green onions and celery; season well.

Slice chicken into large strips and add to bowl. Mix in tomatoes and endive leaves.

Cut asparagus stalks into 3 and add to bowl.

Mix in mayonnaise and cream. Season and add chopped mint; mix well. Toss in nuts and serve decorated with slices of fresh fruit.

1 serving *263 calories* *14 g carbohydrate*
18 g protein *15 g fat* *3.9 g fiber*

Baby Shrimp Salad

serves 4

2	6-oz (*170-g*) packages cooked baby shrimp
1	celery stalk, chopped
½	red pepper, chopped
1 tbsp	(*15 ml*) chopped fresh parsley
1	red apple, cored, peeled and coarsely chopped
1 tbsp	(*15 ml*) lemon juice
¼ lb	(*125 g*) green beans, cooked and diced
1 cup	(*250 ml*) blanched broccoli flowerets
1	green onion, blanched and sliced
4 tbsp	(*60 ml*) mayonnaise
	salt and white pepper
dash	paprika

Rinse shrimp in cold water, drain well and pat dry with paper towels.

Place shrimp in large bowl with celery, red pepper, parsley and apple. Sprinkle in lemon juice and season well.

Add cooked vegetables and mix well.

Spoon in mayonnaise and season with paprika; mix until thoroughly incorporated.

Correct seasoning and serve.

1 serving *248 calories* *12 g carbohydrate*
23 g protein *12 g fat* *4.8 g fiber*

Tomatoes with Sausage-Rice Stuffing

serves 4

4	large tomatoes, well cleaned
1 tbsp	(*15 ml*) vegetable oil
2	garlic cloves, smashed and chopped
1	onion, finely chopped
1 cup	(*250 ml*) chopped pork sausage meat
1 tsp	(*5 ml*) chopped fresh thyme
1 tsp	(*5 ml*) chopped fresh chives
1 tbsp	(*15 ml*) chopped fresh parsley
4	thin slices cooked ham, diced small
1¼ cups	(*300 ml*) cooked long-grain rice
1 cup	(*250 ml*) grated well-aged white Cheddar cheese
	salt and pepper
pinch	cayenne pepper

Preheat oven to 375°F (*190°C*).

Cut off slice from bottom of each tomato so that it stands flat. Using paring knife, cut out top and reserve for decoration. Scoop out about ¾ of pulp and either discard or keep for other uses.

Season tomato cavities, sprinkle with a few drops oil and set aside in baking dish.

Heat oil in skillet over medium heat. Cook garlic and onion 3 minutes.

Stir in sausage meat and fresh herbs; season with salt and pepper. Cook 3 minutes over medium heat.

Add ham, mix well and continue cooking 3 minutes.

Stir in rice, correct seasoning and cook another 3 to 4 minutes.

Incorporate cheese and correct seasoning; sprinkle with cayenne pepper to taste. Cook 2 minutes.

Spoon stuffing into tomatoes and bake 30 minutes in oven or according to size of tomatoes.

Serve with tomato hats as decoration.

1 serving	*339 calories*	*22 g carbohydrate*
20 g protein	*19 g fat*	*2.9 g fiber*

1. Cut off slice from bottom of each tomato. Remove top and reserve for decoration. Scoop out about ¾ of pulp to make room for stuffing. Be sure to leave sturdy shell.

2. Add sausage meat and fresh herbs to garlic and onion.

3. Mix in ham and continue cooking 3 minutes.

4. Stir in rice, correct seasoning and cook another 3 to 4 minutes.

Welsh Rarebit

serves 2

2	¾-in. (*2-cm*) thick slices Italian bread, toasted
3 cups	(*750 ml*) grated well-aged Cheddar cheese
¼ tsp	(*1 ml*) paprika
1 tsp	(*5 ml*) dry mustard
½ cup	(*125 ml*) beer
	freshly ground pepper

Set toasted bread aside on serving platter.

Place cheese and paprika in bowl. Pepper to taste. Add mustard and mix well.

Pour beer into nonstick frying pan and bring to boil. Continue cooking to reduce liquid by half.

Add cheese and cook 7 to 8 minutes over medium heat, stirring once or twice.

Spoon over bread and serve.

1 serving *816 calories* *22 g carbohydrate*
47 g protein *60 g fat* *0.8 g fiber*

Superstar Hot Dogs

serves 2

1 tbsp	(*15 ml*) vegetable oil
1	onion, thinly sliced
2	hot dog buns, toasted or steamed
2	beef, pork or veal sausage-type hot dogs, cooked
½	pickled hot banana pepper, thinly sliced
2	slices tomato, halved
	mustard, relish and catsup

Time the cooking of the onions with the preparation of the buns and hot dogs so everything is ready and hot at the same time.

Heat vegetable oil in small frying pan. Add onion, cover and cook 15 minutes over medium heat. Stir several times during cooking.

To assemble hot dogs, spoon some of onion mixture into buns and add hot dog.

Top with condiments to taste followed by remaining onion, sliced banana pepper and tomato.

Serve with pickles and nacho chips.

1 serving	*533 calories*	*38 g carbohydrate*
21 g protein	*33 g fat*	*2.8 g fiber*

Onion Quiche with Mint Seasoning

serves 4–6

2 tbsp	(*30 ml*) butter
1	large Spanish onion, thinly sliced
1 tbsp	(*15 ml*) chopped fresh parsley
2	eggs
1	egg yolk
2	fresh mint leaves, chopped
1 tsp	(*5 ml*) chopped fresh chives
1 cup	(*250 ml*) heavy cream
1 cup	(*250 ml*) grated Cheddar cheese
	pie dough
	beaten egg
	salt and pepper

Preheat oven to 375°F (*190°C*). Roll out dough on floured surface and line 9-in. (*23-cm*) quiche mold. Prick bottom with fork and brush with beaten egg. Set aside.

Melt butter in skillet over medium heat. Add onion and parsley; cover and cook 15 minutes.

Remove cover and continue cooking 4 to 5 minutes.

Meanwhile, mix eggs and additional yolk together in small bowl. Add mint, chives and cream; whisk everything together and season generously.

When onions are nicely browned, transfer to bottom of quiche crust. Top with cheese.

Pour egg mixture over cheese and place quiche on cookie sheet; bake in oven for 35 minutes.

1 serving	*437 calories*	*15 g carbohydrate*
11 g protein	*37 g fat*	*0.8 g fiber*

1. There are many good-quality prepared pie doughs available on the market, but if time permits by all means make your own. Be sure to prick the bottom with a fork and brush with beaten egg.

2. Cook Spanish onion with parsley in hot butter for 15 minutes over low heat. Cover pan.

3. Just before onion is done, mix together ingredients for creamy filling that will bind quiche. The chopped mint will lend an interesting flavor.

4. Make quiche by filling bottom of crust with onion and topping with Cheddar cheese.

Ham and Apple Stuffed Crepes

serves 4

2	apples, cored, peeled and diced
3 tbsp	(*45 ml*) butter
1	red pepper, chopped
3	green onions, sliced
½ lb	(*250 g*) fresh mushrooms, cleaned and diced
2 cups	(*500 ml*) cubed leftover cooked ham
1 tbsp	(*15 ml*) chopped fresh parsley
¼ tsp	(*1 ml*) marjoram
4 tbsp	(*60 ml*) flour
2 cups	(*500 ml*) chicken stock, heated
1½ cups	(*375 ml*) grated Gruyère cheese
8	crepes *
	lemon juice
	salt and pepper
dash	paprika
pinch	nutmeg
	few crushed chillies
pinch	powdered cloves

Place apples in bowl filled with lemony cold water. Set aside.

Reserve 1 tsp (*5 ml*) butter; melt remainder in large skillet over medium heat. Add red pepper, green onions and mushrooms; cook 3 to 4 minutes.

Drain apples, add to pan and correct seasoning. Mix in ham, cover and cook 6 minutes over low heat.

Add parsley and all seasonings; mix well. Stir in flour until well incorporated; cover and cook 3 minutes over low heat.

Pour in chicken stock, adjust seasoning and bring to boil. Cook 5 to 6 minutes, uncovered, over medium heat.

Mix in half of cheese and cook 2 minutes.

Preheat oven to 400°F (*200°C*).

Lay crepes flat on cutting board. Using slotted spoon, divide filling onto crepes; fold each in half and then in half again to form triangle. Place in large baking dish, pour in remaining sauce and top with rest of cheese.

Dot with 1 tsp (*5 ml*) butter, season with pepper and bake 5 minutes.

* *See Crepes Stuffed with Veal, page 240.*

1 serving	*825 calories*	*71 g carbohydrate*
43 g protein	*41 g fat*	*4.9 g fiber*

1. Cook red pepper, green onions and mushrooms 3 to 4 minutes in hot butter.

2. Add apples and ham; cover and cook 6 minutes over low heat.

3. Add parsley and all seasonings; mix well. Stir in flour until well incorporated; cover and cook 3 minutes over low heat.

4. Pour in chicken stock, adjust seasoning and bring to boil. Resume cooking.

Baked Ham Slices with Double Mushroom Sauce

serves 4

3 tbsp	(*45 ml*) butter
1	small onion, finely chopped
1 cup	(*250 ml*) fresh mushrooms, cleaned and sliced
1 cup	(*250 ml*) fresh oyster mushrooms,* cleaned and sliced
¼ tsp	(*1 ml*) nutmeg
3 tbsp	(*45 ml*) flour
2 cups	(*500 ml*) milk, heated
8	¼-in. (*0.65-cm*) thick slices cooked ham
2	egg yolks
	salt and pepper

Preheat oven to 350°F (*180°C*).

Melt butter in skillet over medium heat. Add onion and cook, covered, 3 minutes.

Add both types of mushrooms and nutmeg; season well. Cover and continue cooking 3 minutes.

Mix in flour until well incorporated. Cook 2 minutes, uncovered, over low heat.

Pour in milk, mix well and season again; continue cooking 8 minutes.

Roll ham slices and place in baking dish.

Remove sauce from heat and add egg yolks; mix very well. Pour sauce over ham and bake 5 to 6 minutes in oven.

Serve with garden salad.

* *Oyster mushrooms are a wild variety available most often during the fall and winter months.*

1 serving	*314 calories*	*17 g carbohydrate*
21 g protein	*18 g fat*	*1.7 g fiber*

Scrumptious Potato Omelet

serves 4

3 tbsp	(*45 ml*) butter
4	potatoes, peeled, halved and thinly sliced
1	small onion, chopped
1 tbsp	(*15 ml*) chopped fresh chives
1 tbsp	(*15 ml*) chopped fresh basil
1 tsp	(*5 ml*) chopped fresh parsley
1 tbsp	(*15 ml*) milk
8	beaten eggs
	salt and pepper

The success of an omelet is often determined by the pan. Choose a medium-large nonstick frying pan that has a smooth surface. Add butter and melt over medium heat.

Place potatoes in pan and cover; cook 8 minutes, stirring 2 or 3 times.

Add onion and all fresh herbs; season with salt and pepper. Cook 3 to 4 minutes, uncovered. Check potatoes for doneness and cook a little longer if needed.

Beat milk into eggs. Increase heat to high and pour eggs over potatoes. Season lightly and let cook 1 minute without stirring.

Gently stir omelet to help eggs set and continue cooking 1 to 2 minutes or until eggs have taken shape but are still soft. Then, using spatula, flip omelet over and cook 1 more minute.

Fold omelet in half and serve at once.

1 serving	*356 calories*	*29 g carbohydrate*
15 g protein	*20 g fat*	*2.9 g fiber*

Ham and Potato Hash Browns

serves 4

2 tbsp	(*30 ml*) butter
1	small onion, finely chopped
1 lb	(*500 g*) leftover cooked ham, chopped
1 tbsp	(*15 ml*) chopped fresh parsley
3	large cooked potatoes, peeled and diced small
1 tbsp	(*15 ml*) chopped fresh chives
	salt and pepper
	vegetable oil, if needed

Melt butter in large frying pan. Add onion, ham and parsley; cook 3 minutes over high heat.

Add potatoes and season well. Continue cooking 8 to 10 minutes, stirring occasionally and adding oil if needed. Toward the end of cooking, start to flatten potatoes with large metal spatula.

Sprinkle chives over potatoes, mix well and finish cooking 2 minutes before serving.

1 serving	*407 calories*	*30 g carbohydrate*
29 g protein	*19 g fat*	*2.9 g fiber*

Poached Eggs with Chasseur Sauce

serves 4

1 tbsp	(*15 ml*) butter
3	slices bacon, diced
1	small onion, chopped
¼ lb	(*125 g*) fresh mushrooms, cleaned and quartered
2 tbsp	(*30 ml*) flour
¼ cup	(*50 ml*) dry white wine
1¼ cups	(*300 ml*) beef stock, heated
1 tsp	(*5 ml*) tomato paste
8	poached eggs
8	slices toasted French bread
	salt and pepper
	few drops Pickapeppa sauce

Melt butter in small saucepan over medium heat. Add bacon and cook 4 to 5 minutes. Mix in onion and cook another 3 minutes.

Add mushrooms, season and cook 3 to 4 minutes. Mix in flour until well incorporated; cook 2 minutes over low heat.

Pour in wine, stir well and add beef stock, tomato paste and Pickapeppa sauce. Cook 15 minutes over medium heat.

Set each poached egg on slice of toasted bread and top with sauce. Serve at once.

1 serving	*330 calories*	*24 g carbohydrate*
18 g protein	*18 g fat*	*2.3 g fiber*

Eggplant-Filled Crepes

serves 4

3 tbsp	(*45 ml*) butter
1	onion, chopped
1	green onion, sliced
1	garlic clove, smashed and chopped
1	eggplant, peeled and diced
1 tbsp	(*15 ml*) chopped fresh parsley
½ tsp	(*2 ml*) oregano
½ tsp	(*2 ml*) thyme
¼ tsp	(*1 ml*) tarragon
2	tomatoes, cored and cubed
1 cup	(*250 ml*) grated Gruyère cheese
8	crepes *
	salt and pepper
pinch	sugar

Melt 2 tbsp (*30 ml*) butter in large skillet over medium heat. Add onion, green onion and garlic; cook 3 to 4 minutes.

Add eggplant and all seasonings; cover and cook 20 minutes, stirring occasionally.

Stir in tomatoes, season and add sugar. Mix, cover and cook 15 minutes.

Add half of cheese, correct seasoning and cook another 2 minutes.

Preheat oven to 400°F (*200°C*).

Lay crepes flat on cutting board. Divide filling onto crepes; fold each in half and then in half again to form triangle. Place in large baking dish and top with remaining cheese. Dot with leftover butter.

Cook 4 minutes in oven and serve.

* *For crepe batter, see Crepes Stuffed with Veal, page 240. Having a stack of cooked crepes on hand in your refrigerator or freezer makes it easy to prepare a delicious dinner in very little time.*

1 serving *612 calories* *58 g carbohydrate*
23 g protein *32 g fat* *3.8 g fiber*

1. Cook onion, green onion and garlic in hot butter 3 to 4 minutes over medium heat.

2. Add eggplant and all seasonings; cover and cook 20 minutes, stirring occasionally.

3. Stir in tomatoes, season and add sugar to offset any bitterness. Mix, cover and cook another 15 minutes.

4. Add half of cheese, correct seasoning and cook 2 minutes. Prepare to stuff crepes.

Watercress Pesto Pasta

serves 4

2 cups	(*500 ml*) fresh watercress, washed and well dried
1 cup	(*250 ml*) fresh parsley, washed and well dried
2	garlic cloves, smashed and chopped
1 cup	(*250 ml*) grated Romano cheese
4	portions cooked penne noodles, hot
	olive oil
	freshly ground pepper

Place watercress and parsley in food processor; blend until well chopped.

Add garlic and continue blending several minutes. Add cheese and blend again until incorporated.

Incorporate just enough oil to make paste. Season with pepper to taste and blend once more.

Place hot noodles in bowl and add pesto sauce; toss to coat evenly.

Serve immediately.

1 serving	*447 calories*	*43 g carbohydrate*
17 g protein	*23 g fat*	*3.3 g fiber*

Veal and Vegetable Pasta Toss

serves 4

2 tbsp	(*30 ml*) butter
2	veal cutlets, trimmed of fat and cut into strips
4	large fresh oyster mushrooms, cleaned and sliced thick
½	red pepper, cut into strips
2	green onions, sliced thick
2	fresh mint leaves, finely chopped
¾ cup	(*175 ml*) chicken stock, heated
1 tsp	(*5 ml*) cornstarch
2 tbsp	(*30 ml*) cold water
4	portions cooked spinach fettuccine, hot
	salt and pepper

Melt butter in large frying pan over high heat. Add strips of veal and cook 2 minutes, browning all sides.

Season meat well, remove and keep hot in oven.

Add all vegetables and chopped mint to frying pan; season well. Cook 3 minutes over high heat, adding a bit of butter if needed.

Remove vegetables from pan and place in oven with meat.

Pour chicken stock into pan and bring to boil. Mix cornstarch with water; stir into sauce until well incorporated. Reduce heat and cook 1 minute.

Return meat and vegetables to frying pan with sauce. Simmer several minutes; then toss with hot pasta and serve.

1 serving *382 calories* *44 g carbohydrate*
20 g protein *14 g fat* *2.5 g fiber*

Seafood Spirals

serves 4

2 tbsp	(*30 ml*) butter
1	shallot, chopped
½ lb	(*250 g*) fresh mushrooms, cleaned and sliced
1 tbsp	(*15 ml*) chopped fresh parsley
2 tbsp	(*30 ml*) flour
1½ cups	(*375 ml*) hot milk
4 oz	(*125 g*) canned crabmeat, well drained
4	portions cooked spiral noodles,* hot
	salt and pepper

Melt butter in saucepan over medium heat. Add shallot, mushrooms and parsley; cook 3 to 4 minutes.

Mix in flour until well incorporated. Cook 2 minutes over low heat.

Season well and pour in milk; mix and continue cooking 8 to 10 minutes over low heat.

Add crabmeat, mix well and correct seasoning. Cook 2 minutes over very low heat.

Spoon over noodles and serve.

** You can use leftover pasta by rinsing it in hot water, draining well and sautéing it in a bit of butter before topping with sauce.*

1 serving	*362 calories*	*52 g carbohydrate*
16 g protein	*10 g fat*	*3.3 g fiber*

1. Cook shallot, mushrooms and parsley in hot butter for 3 to 4 minutes over medium heat.

2. Mix in flour until well incorporated. This will help thicken the sauce. Be sure to reduce heat to low and cook flour 2 minutes.

3. After seasoning, pour in milk; mix and continue cooking 8 to 10 minutes over low heat.

4. Add crabmeat, mix well and correct seasoning. Cook 2 minutes over very low heat.

Open-Faced Veal and Mushroom Sandwiches

serves 2

2	veal scallopini *
2 tbsp	(*30 ml*) butter
4	thick slices fresh Italian bread, toasted
1 tbsp	(*15 ml*) garlic butter
8	fresh mushrooms, cleaned and sliced
1 tsp	(*5 ml*) chopped fresh parsley
¼ cup	(*50 ml*) chicken stock, heated
	salt and pepper

Lightly season veal with pepper only. Melt butter in frying pan and cook veal 2 minutes over medium-high heat.

Turn pieces over, season well and continue cooking 2 minutes.

Place 2 slices of bread on each heated dinner plate. Rest veal over bread and keep warm in oven.

Melt garlic butter in frying pan. Add mushrooms and parsley; cook 2 minutes over high heat.

Pour in chicken stock and season; reduce liquid by half.

Pour sauce over open-faced sandwiches and serve.

* *Scallopini are pounded pieces of veal cutlet usually about ¼ in.* (0.65 cm) *thick.*

1 serving *576 calories* *38 g carbohydrate*
34 g protein *32 g fat* *4.2 g fiber*

Lemon Veal Scallopini

serves 4

4	veal scallopini
2 tbsp	(*30 ml*) butter
¼ cup	(*50 ml*) chicken stock, heated
1 tbsp	(*15 ml*) chopped fresh parsley
	salt and pepper
	juice 1 lemon
	lemon slices

Lightly season veal with pepper only.

Melt butter in large frying pan over medium-high heat. Add veal and cook 2 minutes.

Turn veal over, season with salt and pepper and continue cooking 2 minutes. Be careful not to overcook veal. Remove and keep warm on hot serving platter covered with foil.

Add chicken stock, parsley and lemon juice to frying pan. Increase heat to high and reduce liquid for 3 minutes.

Immediately pour sauce over veal and garnish with lemon slices. Serve at once and accompany with fresh asparagus, if desired.

1 serving	*283 calories*	*1 g carbohydrate*
27 g protein	*19 g fat*	*0.1 g fiber*

Veal Scallopini with Chinese Flair

serves 4

1 lb	(*500 g*) veal scallopini, trimmed of fat
1 cup	(*250 ml*) seasoned flour
2 tbsp	(*30 ml*) butter
1	celery stalk, sliced into pieces 2 in. (*5 cm*) long
1	zucchini, thinly sliced
1 tsp	(*5 ml*) sesame seeds
½ cup	(*125 ml*) chicken stock, heated
3 tbsp	(*45 ml*) plum sauce
1 tsp	(*5 ml*) cornstarch
2 tbsp	(*30 ml*) cold water
	salt and pepper

Lightly dredge veal in flour. Melt butter in frying pan and add meat; cook 2 minutes over medium heat.

Turn veal over, season well and continue cooking another 2 minutes. Remove veal from pan and set aside.

Add vegetables and sesame seeds to pan. Mix well, cover and cook 3 minutes.

Pour in chicken stock and bring to boil. Stir in plum sauce, reduce heat and cook 2 minutes.

Mix cornstarch with water; stir into sauce until well incorporated and cook 1 minute. Reheat veal in sauce 1 minute over low heat. Serve.

1 serving *453 calories* *35 g carbohydrate*
31 g protein *21 g fat* *2.6 g fiber*

Pan-Fried Veal Scallopini

serves 4

4	large veal scallopini, trimmed of fat
1 cup	(*250 ml*) seasoned flour
2	eggs
1 cup	(*250 ml*) milk
2 tbsp	(*30 ml*) peanut oil
	breadcrumbs *
	salt and pepper

Preheat oven to 350°F (*180°C*).

Lightly dredge veal in flour. Beat eggs with milk and dip pieces of veal in mixture. Thoroughly coat with breadcrumbs, pressing in with fingertips.

Heat oil in large frying pan. When hot, add veal and cook 2 minutes over medium heat. Turn meat over, season and cook another 3 minutes.

Transfer veal to ovenproof platter and cook 4 to 5 minutes in oven. Serve with lemon wedges.

* *Choose good quality, tasty breadcrumbs as they are a significant factor in the overall taste of the recipe.*

1 serving *529 calories* *39 g carbohydrate*
37 g protein *25 g fat* *3.3 g fiber*

Veal Chops Sesame

serves 4

4	1-in. (*2.5-cm*) thick veal chops, trimmed of fat
1 cup	(*250 ml*) seasoned flour
4 tbsp	(*60 ml*) butter
1 lb	(*500 g*) fresh mushrooms, cleaned and sliced
1 tbsp	(*15 ml*) chopped fresh parsley
	salt and pepper
	sesame oil *

Dredge veal in flour.

Heat half of butter in large frying pan over medium heat. Add veal and cook 5 minutes.

Turn chops over, season well and continue cooking 3 to 4 minutes, depending on size.

Meanwhile, heat remaining butter in separate frying pan and cook mushrooms with parsley about 3 minutes over high heat. Be sure to season well.

Sprinkle mushrooms with sesame oil and continue cooking 1 minute.

When chops are done, serve at once with mushrooms.

* *This product can be found in Chinese shops or gourmet specialty stores.*

1 serving 536 calories 32 g carbohydrate
30 g protein 32 g fat 4.4 g fiber

Veal Scallopini Marsala

serves 4

4	veal scallopini
2½ tbsp	(*40 ml*) butter
¼ cup	(*50 ml*) Marsala wine
1 tbsp	(*15 ml*) chopped fresh parsley
	salt and pepper

Lightly season veal with pepper only.

Melt 2 tbsp (*30 ml*) butter in large frying pan over medium-high heat. Add veal and cook 2 minutes.

Turn veal over, season with salt and pepper and continue cooking 2 minutes. Be careful not to overcook veal. Remove and keep warm on hot serving platter covered with foil.

Pour wine into frying pan and add remaining butter and parsley. Reduce liquid 3 minutes over high heat.

Pour sauce over veal immediately and serve at once. Accompany with tomatoes or sautéed mushrooms, which take only minutes to prepare.

1 serving	*293 calories*	*0 g carbohydrate*
26 g protein	*21 g fat*	*0.1 g fiber*

Italian Breaded Pork Cutlets

serves 4

4	pork cutlets, ¼ in. (*0.65 cm*) thick
1 cup	(*250 ml*) seasoned flour
1 cup	(*250 ml*) heavy cream
1 cup	(*250 ml*) spicy Italian breadcrumbs
2 tbsp	(*30 ml*) peanut oil
1¼ cups	(*300 ml*) your favorite tomato sauce, heated
	salt and pepper

Preheat oven to 350°F (*180°C*).

Dredge cutlets in flour; then dip in cream and thoroughly coat with breadcrumbs.

Heat oil in large frying pan over high heat. Add cutlets and cook 2 minutes on each side. Transfer to baking dish and finish cooking 7 minutes in oven.

When ready to serve, spoon tomato sauce over heated dinner plates. Set cutlets on sauce and decorate, if desired, by grating a little hard-boiled egg yolk over meat. Serve with sautéed vegetables.

1 serving *808 calories* *53 g carbohydrate*
41 g protein *48 g fat* *2.6 g fiber*

Barbecued Pork Platter

serves 4

4	fresh pork sausages, parboiled 4 minutes
4	small pork chops, trimmed of fat
2 tbsp	(*30 ml*) olive oil
1 tbsp	(*15 ml*) teriyaki sauce
1 tsp	(*5 ml*) lemon juice
1	garlic clove, smashed and chopped
	few drops sesame oil
	freshly ground pepper

Place all ingredients in large bowl and marinate 15 minutes. Meanwhile, preheat barbecue at HIGH and oil grill.

When ready to barbecue, simply place meat on grill. Reduce heat to MEDIUM and cook about 15 minutes or according to size and thickness of meat.

Turn often to avoid charring and baste frequently with any leftover marinade.

Serve with barbecued vegetables, if desired. Accompany with fresh country-style bread.

1 serving	*358 calories*	*1 g carbohydrate*
30 g protein	*26 g fat*	*0 g fiber*

Pork Stir-Fry

serves 4

⅓ cup	(*75 ml*) vegetable oil
3	pork chops, trimmed of fat and cut into strips
3 cups	(*750 ml*) boiled rice
2 tbsp	(*30 ml*) light soy sauce
2	beaten eggs
2 tbsp	(*30 ml*) chopped fresh chives
	salt and pepper

Heat 2 tbsp (*30 ml*) oil in wok or large, heavy frying pan. When oil starts to smoke, add pork and stir-fry 4 to 5 minutes over high heat.

Remove meat and set aside on plate.

Add remaining oil to wok and heat to smoking point. Quickly add rice and cook 7 to 8 minutes, mixing occasionally.

Return pork to wok with rice and season well. Cook another 3 minutes.

Sprinkle in soy sauce, mix well and pour in beaten eggs. Reduce heat to low and stir quickly until eggs are cooked.

Sprinkle with chopped chives and serve.

1 serving *496 calories* *40 g carbohydrate*
21 g protein *28 g fat* *1.3 g fiber*

Rice and Vegetable Pilaf Dinner

serves 4

1 tbsp	(*15 ml*)	butter
2		green onions, chopped
1		celery stalk, chopped
1 cup	(*250 ml*)	long-grain rice, rinsed and drained
1 tbsp	(*15 ml*)	basil
½ tsp	(*2 ml*)	oregano
¼ tsp	(*1 ml*)	crushed chillies
1½ cups	(*375 ml*)	chicken stock, heated
1 tbsp	(*15 ml*)	olive oil
6		cooked asparagus tips, cut into 3
1		carrot, pared and thinly sliced
1		green pepper, cut into strips
½		seedless cucumber, thinly sliced
1		large tomato, cored and cut into wedges
1		garlic clove, smashed and chopped
		salt and pepper
		sesame oil to taste (optional)

Preheat oven to 350°F (*180°C*).

Heat butter in ovenproof casserole over medium heat. Add green onions and celery; cook 2 to 3 minutes.

Add rice and mix well. Season with salt, pepper, basil, oregano and crushed chillies. Cook 2 to 3 minutes or until rice starts to stick to bottom of casserole. Mix well.

Pour in chicken stock; cover and bring to boil. Place in oven and bake 18 minutes, covered.

About 5 minutes before rice is done, begin preparing vegetables. Heat olive oil in frying pan over high heat.

Add vegetables and garlic; season well. Cook 2 to 3 minutes, stirring once. Season with sesame oil if desired.

Serve with rice.

1 serving	*159 calories*	*21 g carbohydrate*
3 g protein	*7 g fat*	*2.8 g fiber*

Calf Liver with Spanish Onion

serves 4

4 tbsp	*(60 ml)* butter
1	large tomato, cored, halved and sliced
1	Spanish onion, halved and sliced
1 tsp	*(5 ml)* chopped fresh basil
4	large slices calf liver
1 cup	*(250 ml)* seasoned flour
	salt and pepper

Melt half of butter in skillet over medium heat. Add tomato, onion and basil; season well and cook 20 to 25 minutes. Stir occasionally.

Dredge liver in flour. Melt remaining butter in frying pan over low heat. Cook liver 3 minutes on first side. Turn pieces over, season and continue cooking 2 minutes.

Serve with tomato and onion mixture.

1 serving *462 calories* *38 g carbohydrate*
37 g protein *18 g fat* *2.7 g fiber*

Calf Liver with Mushrooms and Herbs

serves 4

4	slices fresh calf liver
3 tbsp	(*45 ml*) butter
½ lb	(*250 g*) fresh mushrooms, cleaned and quartered
2 tbsp	(*30 ml*) chopped fresh parsley
1 tbsp	(*15 ml*) chopped fresh tarragon
	flour
	salt and pepper

Dredge liver in flour. Melt 2 tbsp (*30 ml*) butter in frying pan over medium heat. Add liver and season; cook 2 to 3 minutes each side.

Transfer liver to heated serving platter and keep hot in oven.

Add remaining butter to pan. Cook mushrooms, parsley and tarragon 2 to 3 minutes over high heat, seasoning generously with salt and pepper.

Serve with liver and, if desired, accompany with steamed asparagus.

1 serving *262 calories* *7 g carbohydrate*
27 g protein *14 g fat* *1.8 g fiber*

Poached Chicken in White Wine

serves 4

2 tbsp	(*30 ml*) butter
2	whole chicken breasts, skinned, boned and split into 2
½ cup	(*125 ml*) dry white wine
1 tbsp	(*15 ml*) chopped fresh parsley
6	large fresh oyster mushrooms, cleaned and cut in half
½	seedless cucumber, seeded and sliced thick
1 cup	(*250 ml*) chicken stock, heated
1 tbsp	(*15 ml*) cornstarch
2 tbsp	(*30 ml*) cold water
	salt and pepper

Melt butter in large skillet over low heat. Add chicken, wine and parsley; season well. Cover and cook 10 minutes.

Turn chicken over. Add mushrooms and cucumber; season again. Cover and continue cooking 6 to 7 minutes.

Remove chicken from pan and keep hot in oven.

Add chicken stock to pan and bring to boil, uncovered.

Mix cornstarch with water; stir into sauce until well incorporated. Cook 1 minute over low heat.

Ladle sauce over chicken and serve. Accompany with fresh bread.

1 serving *213 calories* *5 g carbohydrate*
28 g protein *9 g fat* *1.3 g fiber*

Creamed Chicken on Toast

serves 4

2	whole chicken breasts, skinned and cut into large cubes
2 tbsp	(*30 ml*) butter
¼ lb	(*125 g*) fresh mushrooms, cleaned and quartered
2	shallots, chopped
1 tsp	(*5 ml*) chopped fresh parsley
1½ cups	(*375 ml*) chicken stock, heated
¼ cup	(*50 ml*) heavy cream (optional)
	flour
	salt and pepper
	toasted bread

Dredge chicken in flour and season cubes generously. Melt butter in skillet over medium heat. Add chicken pieces, cover and cook 10 minutes, stirring occasionally.

Add mushrooms, shallots and parsley. Season, cover and continue cooking 5 minutes.

Pour in chicken stock and mix well. Add cream and stir; cook 3 to 4 minutes, uncovered.

Spoon over toast and serve. This dish is especially good when a light meal is what you want.

1 serving *282 calories* *10 g carbohydrate*
29 g protein *14 g fat* *1.2 g fiber*

Cheddar Chicken Surprise

serves 4

2	whole chicken breasts, skinned, boned and split into two
1 cup	(*250 ml*) grated well-aged white Cheddar cheese
4	large thin slices Black Forest ham
1 cup	(*250 ml*) seasoned flour
2	beaten eggs
1 cup	(*250 ml*) breadcrumbs
2 tbsp	(*30 ml*) peanut oil
	salt and pepper

Slice each piece of chicken breast open to form cavity. Stuff with cheese and reshape meat with hands. Wrap in slice of ham.

Carefully dredge chicken in flour and then dip in beaten egg. Thoroughly coat with breadcrumbs. Chicken must be well coated or cheese may leak during cooking.

Preheat oven to 375°F (*190°C*).

Heat oil in large ovenproof frying pan. When hot, add chicken and cook 2 to 3 minutes on each side over medium-high heat to brown breadcrumbs. Season well when turning over.

Transfer to oven and finish cooking 10 minutes or longer depending on size of breasts.

Serve with fresh rolls if desired.

1 serving	*622 calories*	*46 g carbohydrate*
51 g protein	*26 g fat*	*2.1 g fiber*

1. Slice each piece of chicken breast open to form cavity for cheese. Stuff and reshape meat with hands.

2. Wrap in slice of ham. The flavor of the ham will have a considerable effect on the taste of the recipe.

3. Dredge in flour, being careful to keep ham taut.

4. Dip in beaten eggs; then coat thoroughly with breadcrumbs.

Sesame-Flavored Chicken Fry

serves 4

2	whole chicken breasts, skinned and cut into 2-in. (*5 cm*) pieces
1 tbsp	(*15 ml*) vegetable oil
1	zucchini, thinly sliced
1	large carrot, pared and thinly sliced
1	red pepper, thinly sliced
3	green onions, cut into sticks
1 tbsp	(*15 ml*) soy sauce
	flour
	salt and pepper
	few drops sesame oil *

Dredge chicken pieces in flour. Heat vegetable oil in skillet over medium heat. Add chicken, cover and cook 3 to 4 minutes. Remove chicken from pan and set aside.

Stir in zucchini and carrot; season well. Cover and cook 6 minutes over medium heat, stirring occasionally.

Add red pepper, green onions, soy sauce and sesame oil. Return chicken to pan, cover and cook 3 minutes. Serve.

* *Look for this product in your local Chinese shop or in gourmet specialty stores. If not available, substitute with a hot pepper sauce such as Tabasco. Although the overall taste will be different, it will be just as nice.*

1 serving 231 calories 13 g carbohydrate
29 g protein 7 g fat 2.8 g fiber

Beef Tenderloin with Oyster Mushrooms

serves 4

1 tbsp	(*15 ml*) vegetable oil
8	slices beef tenderloin
8	large fresh oyster mushrooms, cleaned and cut into large pieces
1	garlic clove, smashed and chopped
1 tbsp	(*15 ml*) chopped fresh chives
2	tomatoes, cored, halved and sliced
	salt and pepper

Heat oil in frying pan over medium-high heat. Add slices of beef and sear 1 to 2 minutes, depending on thickness. Turn over, season and sear other side 1 minute.

Remove meat from pan and set aside.

Add mushrooms, garlic and chives to pan; cook 3 to 4 minutes.

Add tomatoes and season well; continue cooking 3 to 4 minutes.

Return meat to pan and cook 1 to 2 minutes until reheated. Serve at once.

1 serving *347 calories* *5 g carbohydrate*
48 g protein *15 g fat* *2.2 g fiber*

Greek Meatballs

serves 4

1 tbsp	(*15 ml*) butter
2	onions, chopped
4	slices white bread, crusts trimmed
½ cup	(*125 ml*) milk
1¼ lb	(*625 g*) lean ground beef
1	garlic clove, smashed and chopped
1 tsp	(*5 ml*) oregano
1	egg
2 tbsp	(*30 ml*) sour cream
1 tbsp	(*15 ml*) vegetable oil
dash	paprika
	salt and pepper

Melt butter in small saucepan. Add onions and cook 4 to 5 minutes over medium heat.

Meanwhile, place bread in bowl and pour in milk; set aside to soak.

When onions are done, place in food processor with meat. Add garlic, all seasonings and egg.

Squeeze out excess milk from bread and add bread to food processor. Mix several minutes to combine ingredients well.

Spoon in sour cream and mix again until thoroughly combined. Transfer mixture to bowl and cover with plastic wrap. Refrigerate 1 hour. *

When ready to cook meatballs, take mixture from refrigerator. With oiled hands, shape into small balls.

Heat oil in large frying pan over medium heat. Cook meatballs 3 to 4 minutes on each side or longer, depending on size. Do not crowd pan; cook in batches if necessary.

Serve meatballs with spicy dipping sauce, with pasta in tomato sauce or with a light salad.

* *To accommodate your schedule, you can prepare the first half of the recipe in the morning and have the meatballs chill while you are at work.*

1 serving	*402 calories*	*19 g carbohydrate*
41 g protein	*18 g fat*	*1.9 g fiber*

1. Onions should always be precooked before adding them to meatball or hamburger meat mixture. Sautéing them in butter will lend a very nice flavor to the meatballs.

2. When onions are done, place them with meat in food processor. Be sure to put meat on the bottom or onions will be difficult to incorporate. Add garlic, all seasonings and egg.

3. Add soaked bread and blend several minutes until well combined. Add sour cream, blend again and chill.

4. When cooking meatballs, use medium heat. Avoid excess stirring—let each side sear properly before turning.

Ginger-Basted Shrimp Kebabs

serves 4

20	large shrimp, shelled, deveined and cleaned
3	green onions, cut into 2-in. (*5-cm*) lengths
1 cup	(*250 ml*) blanched snow pea pods
2	onions, cut into wedges
2	large carrots, pared, sliced ½ in. (*1.2 cm*) thick and blanched
2 tbsp	(*30 ml*) vegetable oil
2 tbsp	(*30 ml*) teriyaki sauce
1 tbsp	(*15 ml*) lime juice
2 tbsp	(*30 ml*) chopped fresh ginger
	salt and pepper

Alternate shrimp and vegetables on skewers.

Mix remaining ingredients together in small bowl and brush over kebabs.

Place skewers in oven about 6 in. (*15 cm*) from top element. Broil 3 to 4 minutes on each side, depending on size. If desired, they can be cooked on grill in the same time.

Be sure to baste several times during cooking.

1 serving *265 calories* *15 g carbohydrate*
31 g protein *9 g fat* *4.7 g fiber*

Courvoisier Shrimp Sauté

serves 4

2 tbsp	(*30 ml*) butter
1¾ lb	(*800 g*) medium shrimp, shelled, deveined and cleaned
3 tbsp	(*45 ml*) Courvoisier cognac
1	carrot, pared and finely diced
1	celery stalk, finely diced
1 tbsp	(*15 ml*) finely chopped fresh parsley
1 tsp	(*5 ml*) finely chopped fresh tarragon
2	shallots, chopped
1 cup	(*250 ml*) dry white wine
1 cup	(*250 ml*) heavy cream
	salt and pepper
	few drops lime juice

Heat butter in large frying pan over high heat. Add shrimp and cook 3 minutes, without stirring.

Turn shrimp over, season and cook another 3 minutes. Pour in cognac and flambé.

As soon as alcohol has burned off, remove shrimp and set aside.

Add vegetables, parsley, tarragon and shallots to pan. Cook 3 to 4 minutes over high heat. Season well.

Pour in wine and continue cooking 3 to 4 minutes to reduce liquid by half.

Add cream and continue cooking, stirring occasionally, until sauce has thickened.

Reduce heat to low and place shrimp in sauce. Simmer several minutes until reheated.

Sprinkle with lime juice and serve.

1 serving	*393 calories*	*6 g carbohydrate*
27 g protein	*29 g fat*	*0.8 g fiber*

Tempura Shrimp

serves 4

2 lb	(*900 g*) medium shrimp
2 tbsp	(*30 ml*) teriyaki sauce
1 tbsp	(*15 ml*) lemon juice
1 tbsp	(*15 ml*) honey
1	garlic clove, smashed and chopped
	salt and pepper
	commercial tempura batter mix
	lemon slices

Peel and devein shrimp, leaving tails intact. Wash thoroughly in cold water, drain and pat dry with paper towels.

Place shrimp in bowl; add teriyaki sauce, lemon juice, honey and garlic. Season with pepper and let stand 30 minutes.

Meanwhile, prepare batter according to directions on package.

Preheat plenty of peanut oil in electric deep-fryer set at 375 °F (*190 °C*).

Coat shrimp in batter and deep-fry, in several batches, about 2 to 3 minutes or until golden brown. Drain well on paper towels before serving.

Accompany with lemon slices.

1 serving	*374 calories*	*21 g carbohydrate*
32 g protein	*18 g fat*	*0.4 g fiber*

ECONOMICAL FARE

Delicious, tempting recipes that will save you money but won't disappoint your palate

Cheryl's Hot Penne Salad

serves 4

1 tbsp	(*15 ml*) olive oil
1	onion, cubed small
1	green pepper, diced
2	celery stalks, sliced
2	carrots, pared and thinly sliced
1 tbsp	(*15 ml*) chopped fresh ginger
3 cups	(*750 ml*) cooked penne, still warm
1 tbsp	(*15 ml*) chopped fresh parsley
2 tbsp	(*30 ml*) olive oil
2 tbsp	(*30 ml*) wine vinegar
1 tbsp	(*15 ml*) Dijon mustard
1 cup	(*250 ml*) canned chickpeas, drained
	salt and pepper

Heat 1 tbsp (*15 ml*) oil in saucepan over high heat. Add vegetables and ginger; cook 4 to 5 minutes.

Place warm pasta in bowl. Add parsley, 2 tbsp (*30 ml*) oil, vinegar and mustard; toss until well mixed.

Add chickpeas and season well; toss again.

Stir in hot vegetables, toss once more and serve in attractive bowl, decorated with lettuce leaves if desired.

1 serving	*336 calories*	*48 g carbohydrate*
9 g protein	*12 g fat*	*6.6 g fiber*

Penne Abigail

serves 6

2 tbsp	(*30 ml*) olive oil
1	medium onion, chopped
2	shallots, chopped
½	hot green pepper, seeded and chopped
1	small zucchini, diced with skin
1 lb	(*500 g*) lean ground beef
28 oz	(*796 ml*) can tomatoes, drained and chopped
1 tbsp	(*15 ml*) chopped fresh parsley
1½ cups	(*375 ml*) canned red kidney beans, drained
1 tsp	(*5 ml*) basil
½ tsp	(*2 ml*) chili powder
5 cups	(*1.2 L*) cooked penne pasta
1 cup	(*250 ml*) grated mozzarella cheese
	salt and pepper
	few drops Pickapeppa sauce

Heat oil in large, deep skillet. Add onion, shallots, hot pepper and zucchini; cook 7 to 8 minutes over high heat.

Mix in beef and continue cooking 3 to 4 minutes, stirring several times during cooking.

Season meat well and add tomatoes, parsley and kidney beans. Mix well and sprinkle in basil, chili powder and Pickapeppa sauce.

Mix again, correct seasoning and cook 8 to 10 minutes over high heat.

Reduce heat to medium and continue cooking 15 minutes.

Stir in penne noodles and cook 3 to 4 minutes. Add cheese and continue cooking another 2 minutes or until cheese is melted.

1 serving	*448 calories*	*38 g carbohydrate*
29 g protein	*20 g fat*	*2.5 g fiber*

White Spaghetti and Peas

serves 4

3 tbsp	(*45 ml*) butter
3 tbsp	(*45 ml*) flour
2 cups	(*500 ml*) milk, heated
4	slices cooked back bacon, cut into thin strips
½	green pepper, cut into strips
1 tbsp	(*15 ml*) chopped lemon rind
1 cup	(*250 ml*) frozen green peas, cooked
4	portions cooked spaghetti, hot
1 cup	(*250 ml*) grated mozzarella cheese
pinch	nutmeg
	salt and pepper

Melt 2 tbsp (*30 ml*) butter in saucepan over medium heat. Add flour and mix well with wooden spoon; cook 3 minutes over low heat, stirring constantly.

Pour in hot milk and mix well; continue cooking 8 to 10 minutes over low heat. Stir frequently.

Sprinkle in nutmeg, season and set white sauce aside.

Melt remaining butter in skillet. Add bacon, green pepper and lemon rind; season well. Cook 3 minutes over medium heat.

Stir in peas, pasta and white sauce. Add cheese, mix well and cook 2 minutes over medium heat before serving.

1 serving	*559 calories*	*60 g carbohydrate*
28 g protein	*23 g fat*	*3.9 g fiber*

Stuffed Cannelloni

serves 4

1 tbsp	(*15 ml*) vegetable oil
1	medium onion, chopped
8	large fresh mushrooms, cleaned and chopped
1	green onion, chopped
1 tsp	(*5 ml*) chopped lime rind
½ tsp	(*2 ml*) cumin
3	jumbo green olives, chopped
6 oz	(*170 g*) lean ground beef
3 oz	(*30 g*) feta cheese, crumbled
12	cooked cannelloni
1 cup	(*250 ml*) tomato sauce
½ cup	(*125 ml*) chicken stock, heated
pinch	paprika
	salt and pepper
	freshly grated Parmesan cheese

Preheat oven to 325°F (*160°C*).

Heat oil in frying pan. Add chopped onion, mushrooms, green onion and lime rind; season well.

Sprinkle in all seasonings and cook 4 to 5 minutes over medium heat.

Stir in olives and ground beef; mix well, season again and continue cooking 4 minutes.

Mix in feta cheese and cook 3 more minutes.

Transfer mixture to bowl of food processor and blend. Spoon stuffing into pastry bag fitted with plain nozzle.

Stuff cannelloni and place in baking dish. Mix tomato sauce with chicken stock and pour over pasta.

Cover dish with foil and bake 1 hour. Serve with Parmesan cheese.

1 serving	*412 calories*	*45 g carbohydrate*
22 g protein	*16 g fat*	*2.7 g fiber*

Lamb Shoulder Stew with Carrots

serves 4

3 lb	(*1.4 kg*) boneless lamb shoulder, trimmed of fat
2	shallots, chopped
1 cup	(*250 ml*) dry white wine
1 tbsp	(*15 ml*) olive oil
2 tbsp	(*30 ml*) peanut oil
3 tbsp	(*45 ml*) flour
2½ cups	(*625 ml*) beef stock, heated
2 tbsp	(*30 ml*) tomato paste
1 tsp	(*5 ml*) olive oil
1	onion, cut into 6
1	garlic clove, smashed and chopped
3	carrots, pared and cut into thick sticks
½ tsp	(*2 ml*) oregano
1 tbsp	(*15 ml*) chopped fresh parsley
1 tsp	(*5 ml*) soy sauce
	salt and pepper
dash	paprika

Cut meat into cubes. Place in bowl and season with salt and pepper.

Add shallots, wine and 1 tbsp (*15 ml*) olive oil; marinate 1 hour.

Preheat oven to 350°F (*180°C*).

Heat peanut oil in large skillet. Drain lamb, reserving marinade, and place meat in hot oil. Cook 7 to 8 minutes over high heat.

Turn cubes over, season and continue cooking 2 to 3 minutes.

Sprinkle in flour and mix very well. Reduce heat to medium and continue cooking 5 minutes or until flour browns and starts to stick to bottom of pan. Stir occasionally to avoid burning.

Pour in beef stock and reserved marinade. Mix well and bring to boil.

Mix in tomato paste and set skillet aside.

Heat 1 tsp (*5 ml*) olive oil in small frying pan. Cook onion and garlic 3 to 4 minutes over high heat.

Transfer onion and garlic to skillet containing lamb. Add carrots, seasonings and soy sauce; mix well. Cover and bring to boil.

Place stew in oven, cover and cook 2 hours. Add beef stock during cooking if necessary.

Serve over egg noodles.

1 serving	*669 calories*	*15 g carbohydrate*
69 g protein	*37 g fat*	*2.5 g fiber*

Beef Sauté with Figs

serves 4

2 tbsp (*30 ml*) peanut oil
1 lb (*500 g*) fast-fry inside round beef, sliced on angle
12 figs, halved
1 apple, cored and sectioned with skin
12 water chestnuts, sliced
1 green pepper, thinly sliced
½ cup (*125 ml*) canned chick peas, drained
1½ tbsp (*25 ml*) cornstarch
3 tbsp (*45 ml*) cold water
1 cup (*250 ml*) beef stock, heated
salt and pepper
few drops Pickapeppa sauce

Heat 1 tbsp (*15 ml*) oil in frying pan over high heat. Add meat and sear 2 minutes on both sides. Season well, remove meat from pan and set aside.

Add remaining oil to pan and heat. Cook figs, apple, water chestnuts, green pepper and chick peas 3 to 4 minutes over high heat. Be sure to season well during cooking.

Mix cornstarch with water. Pour beef stock into frying pan, stir in diluted cornstarch and add Pickapeppa sauce. Mix well and simmer 2 to 3 minutes.

Place meat in sauce, cook 30 seconds and serve over buttered noodles.

1 serving *478 calories* *54 g carbohydrate*
34 g protein *14 g fat* *13.4 g fiber*

Curried Meatballs

serves 4

1 lb	(*500 g*) lean ground beef
¼ tsp	(*1 ml*) chili powder
2 tbsp	(*30 ml*) chopped fresh parsley
1	beaten egg
2 tbsp	(*30 ml*) vegetable oil
1½	large onions, finely chopped
1	celery stalk, finely diced
1	red apple, cored, peeled and chopped
2 tbsp	(*30 ml*) curry powder
1 tbsp	(*15 ml*) butter
2 tbsp	(*30 ml*) flour
1½ cups	(*375 ml*) chicken stock, heated
	salt and pepper
	few drops hot pepper sauce

Place meat, chili powder, half of parsley, egg, some salt and hot pepper sauce in food processor. Blend until meat forms ball. Shape mixture into small meatballs and set aside.

Heat oil in large skillet. Cook onions, celery, apple and remaining parsley 6 to 7 minutes over medium heat.

Sprinkle in curry powder and mix well. Cook 5 to 6 minutes over low heat.

Add butter to pan and continue cooking 1 minute.

Place meatballs in pan and cook 5 to 6 minutes over medium heat, turning meatballs over often.

Sprinkle in flour, mix and continue cooking 2 to 3 minutes.

Pour in chicken stock and season very well. Bring to boil and cook 15 minutes over low heat.

Serve on rice.

1 serving 377 calories 18 g carbohydrate
29 g protein 21 g fat 2.8 g fiber

1. Cook onions, celery, apple and remaining parsley in hot oil for 6 to 7 minutes over medium heat.

2. Sprinkle in curry powder and mix well. Cook 5 to 6 minutes over low heat. Add butter and continue cooking 1 minute.

3. Place meatballs in pan and cook 5 to 6 minutes over medium heat, turning meatballs over often.

4. Sprinkle in flour, mix and continue cooking 2 to 3 minutes.

Leftover Meatballs à la Lyonnaise

serves 4

1 tbsp	(*15 ml*) peanut oil
3	onions, thinly sliced
1	garlic clove, smashed and chopped
1 tbsp	(*15 ml*) chopped fresh parsley
½ tsp	(*2 ml*) celery seeds
1 tsp	(*5 ml*) cumin
1 tbsp	(*15 ml*) butter
2 tbsp	(*30 ml*) flour
2 cups	(*500 ml*) chicken stock, heated
12	leftover cooked meatballs
¼ cup	(*50 ml*) grated mozzarella cheese
	salt and pepper

Heat oil in skillet over high heat. Add onions, garlic and parsley; cover and cook 15 minutes over medium heat.

Add seasonings and butter; mix well. Stir in flour and cook 2 minutes.

Pour in chicken stock, mix well and bring to boil. Correct seasoning.

Place meatballs in sauce. Add cheese and simmer until reheated. Garnish servings with leftover cooked vegetables.

1 serving	*336 calories*	*13 g carbohydrate*
26 g protein	*20 g fat*	*1.9 g fiber*

Rice with Tarragon Mushrooms

serves 4

1 tbsp (*15 ml*) butter
2 shallots, chopped
1 garlic clove, smashed and chopped
½ celery stalk, finely diced
1 tbsp (*15 ml*) chopped lemon rind
1 cup (*250 ml*) long-grain rice, rinsed and drained
1½ cups (*375 ml*) chicken stock, heated
1 tbsp (*15 ml*) peanut oil
½ lb (*250 g*) fresh mushrooms, cleaned and halved
1 tsp (*5 ml*) tarragon
salt and pepper

Preheat oven to 350°F (*180°C*).

Melt butter in ovenproof casserole over medium heat. Add shallots, garlic, celery and lemon rind; cook 3 minutes.

Stir in rice and season well. Continue cooking 2 to 3 minutes or until rice starts to stick to bottom of casserole.

Pour in chicken stock, mix and bring to boil. Correct seasoning, cover and cook 15 minutes in oven.

About 5 minutes before rice is cooked, heat oil in frying pan over high heat.

Add mushrooms and tarragon; season well. Sauté 2 to 3 minutes. Stir into rice in casserole and finish cooking 3 minutes in oven.

1 serving 255 calories 43 g carbohydrate
5 g protein 7 g fat 1.7 g fiber

Quick Curried Rice

serves 4

2 tbsp	(*30 ml*) butter
½	celery stalk, diced
1	medium onion, diced
1½ tbsp	(*25 ml*) curry powder (or to taste)
1 cup	(*250 ml*) long-grain rice, rinsed and drained
1½ cups	(*375 ml*) chicken stock, heated
	salt and pepper

Prejeat oven to 350°F (*180°C*).

Place butter, celery and onion in ovenproof casserole. Season with pepper and cook 3 minutes over medium heat.

Sprinkle in curry powder and mix well; continue cooking 4 to 5 minutes over low heat.

Add rice and mix well; season to taste. Cook 2 to 3 minutes to evaporate any water from rice and allow it to brown.

When rice starts to stick to bottom of casserole, pour in chicken stock. Stir and bring to boil over high heat.

Cover casserole and cook 18 minutes in oven.

1 serving *242 calories* *43 g carbohydrate*
4 g protein *6 g fat* *0.7 g fiber*

1. Cook celery and onion with butter in ovenproof casserole for 3 minutes over medium heat. Be sure to season well with pepper.

2. Add curry to taste and mix well; continue cooking 4 to 5 minutes over low heat.

3. Mix in rice and season to taste. Cook 2 to 3 minutes to allow any water to evaporate and to brown rice.

4. When rice starts to stick to bottom of casserole, add the hot chicken stock.

Leftover Beef Chinese Style

serves 4

2 tbsp	(*30 ml*) peanut oil
1 lb	(*500 g*) fast-fry inside round beef, sliced on angle
½	yellow pepper, sliced
1	zucchini, sliced
2	leaves Chinese cabbage, sliced
2	Italian-type plum tomatoes, quartered
1	apple, cored and sectioned with skin
2 tbsp	(*30 ml*) chopped fresh ginger
1 tbsp	(*15 ml*) chopped fresh parsley
	salt and pepper

Heat oil in frying pan over high heat. Add meat and sear slices 2 minutes on each side. Season well, remove meat from pan and set aside.

Add all vegetables, apple, ginger and parsley to pan. Season and continue cooking 3 minutes over high heat.

Return meat to pan, mix and cook another 30 seconds. Serve immediately.

1 serving *289 calories* *12 g carbohydrate*
31 g protein *13 g fat* *3.5 g fiber*

Hamburger Steaks in Sherry Sauce

serves 4

1½ lb	(*750 g*) lean ground beef
1	beaten egg
1 tbsp	(*15 ml*) chopped fresh parsley
1	onion, chopped and cooked
¼ tsp	(*1 ml*) chili powder
1½ tbsp	(*25 ml*) olive oil
1 lb	(*500 g*) fresh mushrooms, cleaned and sliced
¼ tsp	(*1 ml*) tarragon
4 tbsp	(*60 ml*) sherry wine
1½ cups	(*375 ml*) beef gravy, heated (commercial or homemade)
	salt and pepper

Blend meat, egg, parsley, onion, chili powder, salt and pepper in food processor until mixture forms ball. Shape into hamburger steaks.

Brush both sides of meat with 1 tsp (*5 ml*) oil. Place frying pan over high heat; when hot, add steaks and cook 3 to 4 minutes.

Turn steaks over, reduce heat to medium and continue cooking another 3 to 4 minutes or longer, depending on size and your preference. Be sure to season well during cooking. When done, remove from pan, set aside and keep hot.

Heat remaining oil in frying pan. Add mushrooms and tarragon; cook 2 minutes over high heat.

Season, pour in sherry and cook 3 minutes over high heat.

Add beef gravy, mix well and finish cooking 2 to 3 minutes. Pour over steaks and serve.

1 serving *501 calories* *13 g carbohydrate*
47 g protein *29 g fat* *3.7 g fiber*

Ground Beef Rice Casserole

serves 4

1 tbsp	(*15 ml*) vegetable oil
½	medium onion, coarsely chopped
2	garlic cloves, smashed and chopped
½	green pepper, diced
½	celery stalk, thinly sliced
1	leaf Chinese cabbage, thinly sliced
¼ tsp	(*1 ml*) basil
¼ tsp	(*1 ml*) chili powder
½ lb	(*250 g*) lean ground beef
2 tbsp	(*30 ml*) chopped orange rind
1 cup	(*250 ml*) tomato sauce, heated
2 cups	(*500 ml*) cooked rice
½ cup	(*125 ml*) grated mozzarella cheese
pinch	thyme
pinch	ground ginger
	salt and pepper

Preheat oven to 400°F (*200°C*).

Heat oil in frying pan over high heat.

Reduce heat to medium and cook onion and garlic 3 minutes.

Add green pepper, celery and cabbage; sprinkle in all seasonings. Mix well and continue cooking 5 minutes.

Correct seasoning and mix in ground beef; continue cooking 5 to 6 minutes.

Stir in orange rind and tomato sauce; season to taste. Bring to boil over high heat.

Mix in rice, correct seasoning and add cheese; mix again. Wrap frying pan handle in foil (or transfer to another utensil) and finish cooking 8 to 10 minutes in oven.

Decorate with orange slices and tomato wedges, if desired.

1 serving	*351 calories*	*34 g carbohydrate*
20 g protein	*15 g fat*	*2.0 g fiber*

Stuffed Beef Flank

serves 4

1¼ lb	(*625 g*) beef flank
2 tbsp	(*30 ml*) vegetable oil
½ lb	(*250 g*) fresh mushrooms, cleaned and finely chopped
2 tbsp	(*30 ml*) chopped lemon rind
2	green onions, chopped
½ tsp	(*2 ml*) oregano
1 cup	(*250 ml*) cooked rice
3 tbsp	(*45 ml*) steak sauce
1	onion, quartered and sectioned
1 cup	(*250 ml*) beer
1 cup	(*250 ml*) beef gravy
2 tbsp	(*30 ml*) tomato paste
	salt and pepper
	paprika to taste

Preheat oven to 350°F (*180°C*).

Using sharp knife, split flank into two lengthwise. Cut only ¾ of the way through thickness of meat so that flank can be opened into one large piece.

Season opened flank with pepper and paprika; then pound with wooden mallet to tenderize and flatten thin. Set aside.

Heat 1 tbsp (*15 ml*) oil in large skillet. Add mushrooms, lemon rind and green onions; season well.

Add oregano and mix well; cook 4 to 5 minutes over medium heat.

Stir in rice and continue cooking 4 to 5 minutes.

Pour mixture into food processor and blend well. Incorporate steak sauce by mixing for 2 to 3 minutes.

Spread stuffing over beef flank. Roll and tie with kitchen string.

Heat remaining oil in skillet over high heat. Add flank and sear well on all sides until brown. Season well.

Add onion and continue cooking 3 to 4 minutes. Remove meat from pan and set aside.

Pour beer into skillet containing onion. Stir in beef gravy and tomato paste; correct seasoning.

Place meat in sauce. Cover and bring to boil. Place pan in oven and cook 1½ hours.

1 serving	*384 calories*	*28 g carbohydrate*
41 g protein	*12 g fat*	*3.0 g fiber*

Beef and Vegetable Stew

serves 4

4 lb	(*1.8 kg*) blade steak with bone
2½ tbsp	(*40 ml*) peanut oil
2	garlic cloves, smashed and chopped
½ tsp	(*2 ml*) basil
¼ tsp	(*1 ml*) oregano
¼ tsp	(*1 ml*) chili powder
1	bay leaf
4 tbsp	(*60 ml*) flour
3 cups	(*750 ml*) beef stock, heated
2 tbsp	(*30 ml*) tomato paste
2	large onions, cubed
¼ tsp	(*1 ml*) Worcestershire sauce
2	celery stalks, cubed
2	parsnips, pared and cubed
2	large carrots, pared and cubed
	salt and pepper
pinch	thyme

Preheat oven to 350°F (*180°C*).

Bone meat and cut into cubes. Reserve bone for making your own homemade stock, if desired. Trim excess fat.

Heat 2 tbsp (*30 ml*) oil in large, deep skillet over high heat. Add meat and sear on all sides.

Season meat well and add garlic and all seasonings; mix. Continue cooking 3 to 4 minutes over high heat.

Stir in flour and mix until well incorporated. Cook 5 to 6 minutes over low heat.

Pour in beef stock, stir and bring to boil. Mix in tomato paste and bring to boil again. Simmer 3 to 4 minutes over low heat.

Heat remaining oil in frying pan. Cook onions with Worcestershire sauce 2 to 3 minutes over high heat.

Add onions to meat mixture, cover and cook 1 hour in oven.

Add remaining vegetables to stew, mix, cover and cook 1 more hour in oven.

1 serving	*892 calories*	*41 g carbohydrate*
110 g protein	*32 g fat*	*6.4 g fiber*

1. When the oil is hot, add cubes of meat and begin searing.

2. All sides of the cubes must be browned before the meat is seasoned.

3. Add garlic and seasonings; continue cooking 3 to 4 minutes.

4. Sprinkle flour over meat; stir well to incorporate.

Delicious Blade Roast

serves 4

3 lb	(*1.4 kg*) blade roast, boned
2	garlic cloves, peeled and halved
1 tbsp	(*15 ml*) bacon fat
3	onions, quartered
1	bay leaf
½ tsp	(*2 ml*) basil
1½ cups	(*375 ml*) beer
	salt and pepper
pinch	thyme

Preheat oven to 350°F (*180°C*).

Using small paring knife, cut incisions in meat and insert garlic pieces.

Place bacon fat in ovenproof casserole and place over high heat. When hot, add roast and sear until brown on both sides. Season well with salt and pepper after second side starts to brown.

Add onions and continue cooking 4 to 5 minutes.

Sprinkle in seasonings, season and pour in beer. Cover and cook 1 hour in oven.

Turn roast over and season again. Cover and continue cooking 1 hour.

Serve with vegetables.

1 serving	*569 calories*	*13 g carbohydrate*
82 g protein	*21 g fat*	*1.7 g fiber*

Corned Beef Brisket and Cabbage

serves 4–6

2 lb	(*900 g*) corned beef brisket
1	large cabbage, quartered
2	large carrots, pared and halved
1 tsp	(*5 ml*) sweet basil
¼ tsp	(*1 ml*) thyme
2	bay leaves
2	parsley sprigs
	few black peppercorns
	salt and freshly ground pepper

Place brisket in large saucepan and pour in enough water to cover meat by 2 in. (*5 cm*). Cover with lid and bring to boil for 2 to 3 minutes.

Skim surface, cover again and cook 1 hour over medium heat.

Add vegetables, basil, thyme, bay leaves and peppercorns; season well. Cover and continue cooking 1 hour over medium heat.

Remove vegetables and transfer to bowl.

Cover saucepan and finish cooking 30 minutes or longer, depending on size.

Remove brisket from liquid, slice and serve with cooked vegetables and mustard.

1 serving	*614 calories*	*13 g carbohydrate*
37 g protein	*46 g fat*	*6.8 g fiber*

Beef and Kidney Pie

serves 2

2 tbsp	(*30 ml*) clarified butter
1 tsp	(*5 ml*) olive oil
1 lb	(*500 g*) top sirloin, trimmed of fat and cut into medium cubes
1 lb	(*500 g*) beef kidney, trimmed of fat and cut into medium cubes
2	small onions, cut into 6
½ tsp	(*2 ml*) basil
½ tsp	(*2 ml*) chili powder
1	large carrot, pared and cubed
2	small potatoes, peeled and cubed
3 tbsp	(*45 ml*) flour
3 cups	(*750 ml*) beef stock, heated
	salt and pepper
pinch	thyme
dash	paprika
	few crushed chilies
	pie dough (commercial or leftover)
	milk

Preheat oven to 350°F (*180°C*).

Heat clarified butter and oil in skillet. Add sirloin and cook 4 to 5 minutes over medium heat. Season well and turn beef to brown all sides. Remove cubes from pan and set aside.

Place beef kidney in hot skillet. Sear 4 to 5 minutes over medium heat, turning pieces to brown all sides. Season well.

Return sirloin to skillet with kidney. Add onions and all seasonings; mix well.

Add remaining vegetables and sprinkle in flour. Mix and cook 3 to 4 minutes over low heat.

Stir in beef stock and season well. Cook 2 to 3 minutes over medium heat.

Divide mixture between two individual baking dishes. Cover with rolled pie dough and crimp edges against lip of dish.

Score 4 small holes along top of each pie crust to allow steam to escape and finish by brushing dough with a bit of milk.

Cook 1 hour in oven.

1 serving	*1312 calories*	*65 g carbohydrate*
128 g protein	*60 g fat*	*5.9 g fiber*

1. Trim and cut meat and vegetables before beginning the recipe.

2. Both the sirloin and kidney should be seared in hot oil over medium heat. Be sure to turn pieces to brown on all sides.

3. Add onions and all seasonings to meat in pan; mix well.

4. Add remaining vegetables, sprinkle with flour and season well.

Chicken Pot Pie

serves 4

2	whole chicken breasts, skinned and boned
2	potatoes, peeled and cubed small
2	carrots, pared and sliced ¼ in. (*0.65 cm*) thick
1	onion, cut into 8
¼ tsp	(*1 ml*) tarragon
1 tbsp	(*15 ml*) chopped fresh parsley
4 tbsp	(*60 ml*) butter
3 cups	(*750 ml*) cold water
3 tbsp	(*45 ml*) flour
dash	paprika
	salt and pepper
	few drops Worcestershire sauce
	ready-to-use pie dough

Split chicken breasts into halves and cut each half into four pieces, for a total of 16 pieces.

Place chicken, potatoes, carrots, onion, tarragon, parsley, paprika and 1 tbsp (*15 ml*) butter in deep skillet. Season well and pour in cold water. Sprinkle in Worcestershire sauce, cover and bring to boil.

Reduce heat to medium and cook chicken and vegetables until both are completely cooked. The meat should no longer be pink in the center and the vegetables should be tender.

Using slotted spoon, remove vegetables and chicken and divide them into four individual-size baking dishes; set aside. Reserve cooking liquid in skillet.

Heat remaining butter in saucepan. When bubbly, add flour and mix very well; cook 2 minutes, stirring frequently.

Stir in reserved cooking liquid and mix thoroughly with whisk. Cook 4 to 5 minutes over medium heat to thicken sauce.

Preheat oven to 350°F (*180°C*).

Pour sauce into each baking dish and cover with ready-to-use pie dough. Crimp edges with fingers and score dough 3 times to allow steam to escape.

Place pies in oven and cook 30 minutes.

1 serving *441 calories* *33 g carbohydrate*
30 g protein *21 g fat* *3.3 g fiber*

Shepherd's Pie

serves 4

4	potatoes, cooked in skins and still hot
2 tbsp	(*30 ml*) butter
¾ cup	(*175 ml*) milk, heated
1 tbsp	(*15 ml*) peanut oil
3	onions, finely chopped
2	green onions, finely chopped
2	celery stalks, finely chopped
¼ tsp	(*1 ml*) chili powder
½ tsp	(*2 ml*) basil
1 lb	(*500 g*) lean ground beef
12 oz	(*341 ml*) can whole kernel corn, drained
2 tbsp	(*30 ml*) melted butter
	salt and pepper
pinch	nutmeg
pinch	thyme

Preheat oven to 350°F (*180°C*).

Grease baking dish with butter and set aside.

Peel cooked potatoes, cut up and mash until smooth. Add 2 tbsp (*30 ml*) butter and season with salt, pepper and nutmeg; mix well.

Incorporate hot milk to potatoes and set aside.

Heat oil in large, deep skillet. Cook onions, green onions and celery with all seasonings 3 to 4 minutes over high heat.

Mix well and add meat. Cook 4 to 5 minutes and season well.

Stir in corn and continue cooking 2 to 3 minutes.

Spread half of mashed potatoes in bottom of greased baking dish. Cover with meat mixture.

Spoon remaining potatoes in pastry bag fitted with large star nozzle and cover meat mixture. Season well and sprinkle with melted butter.

Cook 20 minutes in oven.

1 serving	*713 calories*	*77 g carbohydrate*
36 g protein	*29 g fat*	*6.3 g fiber*

Chicken Livers with Mixed Vegetables

serves 4

1 tbsp	(*15 ml*) vegetable oil
1¼ lb	(*625 g*) chicken livers, well cleaned
1 tbsp	(*15 ml*) melted butter
3	green onions, sliced
1	large zucchini, sliced thick
1	red pepper, thinly sliced
6	water chestnuts, sliced
½ tsp	(*2 ml*) tarragon
1 tsp	(*5 ml*) chopped fresh parsley
1½ cups	(*375 ml*) beef stock, heated
1 tbsp	(*15 ml*) cornstarch
2 tbsp	(*30 ml*) cold water
	salt and pepper
pinch	thyme
pinch	paprika

Heat oil in frying pan over high heat. Add chicken livers when oil is very hot and cook 2 minutes.

Turn livers over, season and continue cooking 3 minutes over high heat.

Turn a second time, season again and continue cooking 3 minutes.

Remove livers and set aside.

Add melted butter to pan; then add all vegetables and water chestnuts. Season with salt and pepper and add all seasonings. Cook 4 to 5 minutes over high heat.

Pour in beef stock, stir and bring to boil.

Mix cornstarch with water; stir into sauce and cook 1 minute over medium heat.

Place livers in sauce, correct seasoning, reheat 1 minute and serve.

1 serving	*290 calories*	*9 g carbohydrate*
32 g protein	*14 g fat*	*2.1 g fiber*

Chicken Wings Brière

serves 4

24	chicken wings
2 tbsp	(*30 ml*) chopped fresh ginger
1	garlic clove, smashed and chopped
1 tsp	(*5 ml*) Worcestershire sauce
1 tsp	(*5 ml*) Pickapeppa sauce
2 tbsp	(*30 ml*) olive oil
¼ cup	(*50 ml*) catsup
	juice 1 lemon
	salt and pepper

Snip off tips from wings and discard. Blanch wings 8 to 10 minutes.

Mix together in bowl ginger, garlic, Worcestershire sauce and Pickapeppa sauce. Add lemon juice, oil and catsup; mix again and season with pepper.

Drain blanched wings and place in bowl containing marinade; let stand 15 minutes.

Place wings in roasting pan and broil in preheated oven 3 to 4 minutes on each side, basting during cooking.

Season and serve.

1 serving	*329 calories*	*5 g carbohydrate*
39 g protein	*17 g fat*	*0 g fiber*

Chicken Vol-au-Vent

serves 4

2	whole chicken breasts, split into 2, skinned and diced large
2½ tbsp	(*40 ml*) butter
1 tsp	(*5 ml*) chopped fresh parsley
2 cups	(*500 ml*) chicken stock, heated
¼ tsp	(*1 ml*) tarragon
2	onions, cut into 6
½ lb	(*250 g*) fresh mushroom caps, cleaned and halved
1 cup	(*250 ml*) frozen green peas
2 tbsp	(*30 ml*) flour
4	large cooked vol-au-vent shells
	juice ¼ lemon
	salt and pepper
pinch	thyme
pinch	nutmeg

Place chicken in deep skillet. Add 1 tbsp (*15 ml*) butter, parsley and lemon juice. Poach 2 minutes over very low heat.

Turn pieces over and season. Pour in chicken stock, add all seasonings and onions. Mix well and bring to boil.

Cover and cook 10 minutes over low heat.

Add mushrooms and peas. Season, cover and cook 8 minutes over medium heat.

Remove skillet from heat. Using slotted spoon, remove chicken and vegetables; set aside. Reserve cooking liquid.

Melt remaining butter in saucepan. Add flour and mix well. Cook 2 minutes over medium heat.

Incorporate reserved cooking liquid from chicken into saucepan by mixing well with whisk. Season to taste and cook sauce 6 to 7 minutes over medium heat, stirring only once during cooking.

Place chicken and vegetables in sauce without adding the juice that may have collected. Cook 3 to 4 minutes.

Fill pastry shells with chicken mixture and serve.

1 serving	*627 calories*	*42 g carbohydrate*
36 g protein	*35 g fat*	*7.9 g fiber*

1. Place chicken in deep skillet. Add 1 tbsp (15 ml) butter, parsley and lemon juice. Poach 2 minutes over very low heat.

2. Turn pieces over and season. Pour in chicken stock and add all seasonings and onions. Mix well and bring to boil. Cover and cook 10 minutes over low heat.

3. Add mushrooms and peas. Season, cover and cook 8 minutes over medium heat.

4. Remove chicken and vegetables and set aside.

Breaded Chicken Breasts

serves 4

2	whole chicken breasts, split into 2, skinned and boned
1 cup	(*250 ml*) flour
2	beaten eggs
1 cup	(*250 ml*) breadcrumbs
2 tbsp	(*30 ml*) peanut or vegetable oil
1 tbsp	(*15 ml*) butter
	salt and pepper

Place each chicken breast between 2 sheets of waxed paper; pound with mallet until quite thin.

Season chicken with salt and pepper; dredge in flour. Dip in beaten eggs, and then coat with breadcrumbs.

Heat oil and butter in large frying pan. Add chicken and cook 3 to 4 minutes on each side over medium heat or until done.

Serve with your favorite sauce.

1 serving	*465 calories*	*32 g carbohydrate*
37 g protein	*21 g fat*	*2.1 g fiber*

Veal Croquettes

serves 4

2 tbsp	(*30 ml*) butter
1	onion, finely chopped
1 lb	(*500 g*) lean ground veal
1 tbsp	(*15 ml*) curry powder
1½ cups	(*375 ml*) thick white sauce,* heated
2	egg yolks
1 cup	(*250 ml*) all-purpose flour
2	beaten eggs
1½ cups	(*375 ml*) seasoned breadcrumbs
	salt and pepper
	peanut oil for frying

Place butter and onion in skillet. Cook 4 to 5 minutes over low heat.

Add meat and season well. Sprinkle in curry powder and mix well with wooden spoon. Cook 7 to 8 minutes over high heat, stirring to break up lumps.

When meat is cooked, stir in white sauce and cook 2 minutes over medium-high heat.

Remove pan from heat and incorporate egg yolks. Return to burner and cook 2 minutes over medium heat, stirring constantly.

Transfer mixture to large dinner plate and smooth with spatula until flat. Let cool 30 minutes; then cover with plastic wrap and refrigerate a minimum of 4 hours before using.

Preheat plenty of peanut oil in deep-fryer at 375°F (*190°C*).

Shape cold croquette mixture into cylindrical-type rolls. Roll each in flour, coat lightly with beaten egg and finish by rolling in breadcrumbs.

Deep-fry croquettes until golden brown.

Serve with your favorite sauce.

* *See Poached Salmon with Egg Sauce, page 338.*

1 serving	*717 calories*	*54 g carbohydrate*
42 g protein	*37 g fat*	*1.8 g fiber*

Veal Burgers

serves 4

1½ lb	(*750 g*) lean ground veal
1	beaten egg
2 tbsp	(*30 ml*) vegetable oil
1	large green pepper, thinly sliced
2	apples, cored and thinly sliced, with skin
1 tbsp	(*15 ml*) butter
1	large onion, halved and thinly sliced
4	cooked potatoes, peeled and cut into ¼-in. (*0.65-cm*) slices
pinch	paprika
	few drops Worcestershire sauce
	salt and pepper

Place meat, egg, paprika and Worcestershire sauce in food processor. Season and blend until meat forms ball. Shape into 4 burgers.

Heat oil in large frying pan over medium heat. Add burgers and cook 3 to 4 minutes. Turn over, season and continue cooking 3 to 4 minutes depending on size and preference.

Remove meat from pan, set aside and keep hot.

Add green pepper and apples to pan; season well. Cook 3 minutes over medium heat.

Meanwhile, melt butter in another frying pan. Add onion and potatoes; season well. Cook 3 to 4 minutes over medium heat.

Serve green pepper and apples over burgers. Accompany with potatoes on the side or in separate plates.

1 serving *626 calories* *45 g carbohydrate*
44 g protein *30 g fat* *5.4 g fiber*

Veal Stew

serves 2

2 lb	(*900 g*) veal shoulder, cubed and trimmed of fat
1	celery stalk, cubed
1	onion, quartered
1	large potato, peeled and cubed
3	parsley sprigs
½ tsp	(*2 ml*) tarragon
1	bay leaf
2 tbsp	(*30 ml*) butter
2 tbsp	(*30 ml*) flour
2 tbsp	(*30 ml*) heavy cream
	salt and pepper
dash	paprika

Place veal in saucepan and cover with cold water. Bring to boil and continue cooking 3 minutes.

Drain meat, rinse under cold water and place in clean saucepan.

Add celery, onion, potato, salt and pepper. Add seasonings and bay leaf; pour in enough cold water to cover.

Cover saucepan and bring to boil. Cook 1 hour 15 minutes over medium-low heat.

Remove vegetables from saucepan and set aside. Continue cooking veal until tender. Remove with slotted spoon and reserve liquid.

Melt butter in separate saucepan. Add flour and mix well. Cook 2 minutes over low heat, stirring constantly.

Pour in cooking liquid from veal; mix well with whisk. Stir in cream and season to taste.

Place vegetables and veal in sauce, stir and simmer 1 minute or until reheated.

1 serving	*1049 calories*	*27 g carbohydrate*
98 g protein	*61 g fat*	*2.8 g fiber*

Crepes Stuffed with Veal

serves 4

1 cup	*(250 ml)* all-purpose flour
3	large eggs
1 cup	*(250 ml)* milk
¼ cup	*(50 ml)* tepid water
3 tbsp	*(45 ml)* tepid melted butter
1 tbsp	*(15 ml)* chopped fresh parsley
2 tbsp	*(30 ml)* butter
1	onion, chopped
1	celery stalk, diced small
½ lb	*(250 g)* fresh mushrooms, cleaned and sliced
½ tsp	*(2 ml)* tarragon
¼ tsp	*(1 ml)* celery seeds
¾ lb	*(375 g)* lean ground veal
2 cups	*(500 ml)* cheesy white sauce *
¾ cup	*(175 ml)* grated mozzarella cheese
	salt and white pepper
pinch	paprika

Place flour and pinch of salt in large bowl. Whisk in eggs until smooth. Whisk in milk and water; then strain batter through sieve into clean bowl.

Mix in melted butter, parsley and paprika; season. Cover with sheet of plastic wrap touching surface and chill 1 hour. Prepare crepes using crepe batter.

Preheat oven to 400°F *(200°C)*.

Melt 2 tbsp *(30 ml)* butter in frying pan over medium heat. Cook onion and celery 4 minutes. Add mushrooms and seasonings; mix well. Cook 3 to 4 minutes.

Mix in meat and correct seasoning; brown meat 3 minutes. Cover and cook another 3 minutes.

Pour in cheesy white sauce, cook another 2 minutes and remove pan from heat. Stuff crepes with mixture and place in baking dish. Top with leftover stuffing and cheese. Melt in oven 7 to 8 minutes.

* *See Broccoli with Old-Fashioned Cheddar Sauce, page 386.*

1 serving *845 calories* *48 g carbohydrate*
44 g protein *53 g fat* *3.5 g fiber*

1. *It is necessary to use all-purpose flour for the crepe batter.*

2. *After flour and pinch of salt have been placed in a bowl, add eggs. Blend together with whisk until smooth and lump-free.*

3. *After liquids have been incorporated, pour batter through wire sieve into clean bowl.*

4. *Making crepes is easiest with a special pan. If not available, use a short-rimmed frying pan.*

Zesty Sliced Pork

serves 4

2 tbsp	(*30 ml*) peanut oil
3	pork cutlets, fat trimmed and cut into strips ½ in. (*1.2 cm*) wide
1	carrot, pared and sliced
6	large fresh mushrooms, cleaned and sliced
1 tbsp	(*15 ml*) chopped fresh ginger
2	stalks short bok choy, sliced thick
1 tbsp	(*15 ml*) soy sauce
	salt and pepper

Heat oil in frying pan over high heat. Add meat and carrot; cook 3 minutes.

Turn meat strips over, season and continue cooking 3 minutes.

Add mushrooms and ginger; continue cooking 2 minutes.

Correct seasoning and add bok choy; sprinkle in soy sauce, mix and cook 2 minutes.

Serve immediately.

1 serving *282 calories* *4 g carbohydrate*
26 g protein *18 g fat* *1.9 g fiber*

Braised Pork Shoulder with Vegetables

serves 4

1 tbsp	*(15 ml)* peanut oil
3 lb	*(1.4 kg)* pork shoulder butt, boned
2	garlic cloves, peeled and halved
2	onions, halved
1 cup	*(250 ml)* dry white wine
28 oz	*(800 ml)* canned tomatoes
1 tsp	*(5 ml)* basil
¼ tsp	*(1 ml)* thyme
½ tsp	*(2 ml)* oregano
1	bay leaf
½	turnip, cut into large cubes
2 tbsp	*(30 ml)* cornstarch
4 tbsp	*(60 ml)* cold water
	salt and pepper
	few drops Worcestershire sauce
	few drops Pickapeppa sauce

Heat oil in large saucepan. Meanwhile, make several incisions in pork with small knife and insert garlic pieces.

Sear meat 8 minutes over medium-high heat. Be sure to turn meat to brown all sides and season at the end of cooking.

Add onions and continue cooking 7 to 8 minutes over medium heat.

Pour in wine and cook 3 more minutes.

Add tomatoes with juice, add all seasonings including bay leaf and cover. Cook 1¼ hours over low heat, stirring occasionally.

Add turnip, season and continue cooking, covered, 1¼ hours or longer depending on size of shoulder butt.

Remove meat from saucepan and set aside.

Mix cornstarch with water; stir into sauce. Add Worcestershire sauce and Pickapeppa sauce and bring to boil. Cook 2 to 3 minutes.

Slice meat and serve with vegetables and sauce. Garnish with green peas.

1 serving	*709 calories*	*22 g carbohydrate*
72 g protein	*37 g fat*	*3.4 g fiber*

Feta-Stuffed Eggplant Shells

serves 2

1	large eggplant
1 tbsp	(*15 ml*) olive oil
1 tbsp	(*15 ml*) peanut oil
½	onion, chopped
½ lb	(*250 g*) lean ground beef
½	red pepper, chopped
½ tsp	(*2 ml*) sweet basil
½ tsp	(*2 ml*) chili powder
3 oz	(*90 g*) feta cheese, crumbled
4	slices mozzarella cheese, about 1 in. (*2.5 cm*) wide
	salt and pepper

Preheat oven to 400°F (*200°C*).

Slice eggplant into two equal halves lengthwise. Score flesh in a crisscross pattern and brush with olive oil. Place in baking dish and cook 30 minutes in oven.

Using spoon, scoop out most of the cooked flesh while still leaving sturdy shell; set aside.

Heat peanut oil in large frying pan. Add onion, beef and red pepper; season well.

Add basil and chili powder to pan and mix well. Cook 5 to 6 minutes over medium heat.

Chop eggplant flesh and add to pan. Continue cooking 3 to 4 minutes.

Add feta cheese and cook 2 minutes or until melted.

Spoon filling into eggplant shells and top with slices of mozzarella. Broil until melted and serve at once.

1 serving *703 calories* *14 g carbohydrate*
47 g protein *51 g fat* *3.5 g fiber*

Pork Cutlets in Mustard Sauce

serves 4

2 tbsp	(*30 ml*) vegetable oil
4	pork cutlets, fat trimmed
1 lb	(*500 g*) fresh mushrooms, cleaned and sliced
1	apple, cored, peeled and sliced thick
1½ cups	(*375 ml*) chicken stock, heated
1 tbsp	(*15 ml*) cornstarch
2 tbsp	(*30 ml*) cold water
1 tbsp	(*15 ml*) Dijon mustard
	salt and pepper

Heat half of oil in frying pan. When hot, add pork cutlets and cook 3 to 4 minutes over medium-high heat.

Turn cutlets over, season well and continue cooking 3 to 4 minutes, depending on size.

Remove cutlets from frying pan and keep hot.

Add remaining oil, mushrooms and apple to pan. Season and cook 3 minutes over high heat.

Stir in chicken stock and bring to boil. Mix cornstarch with water; stir into sauce and cook 3 to 4 minutes over low heat.

Remove pan from heat and stir in mustard. Place pork in sauce and serve.

1 serving	*394 calories*	*13 g carbohydrate*
36 g protein	*22 g fat*	*3.8 g fiber*

Hot Italian Sausages with Eggplant

serves 4

3 tbsp	(*45 ml*) peanut oil
1	eggplant, peeled and diced
1	onion, diced
2	garlic cloves, smashed and chopped
3	green onions, chopped
1¼ lb	(*625 g*) hot Italian sausages
	salt and pepper
	chopped fresh parsley

Heat 2 tbsp (*30 ml*) oil in large frying pan. When hot, add eggplant, onion, garlic and green onions; season well. Cover and cook 20 minutes over medium heat, stirring frequently.

Mix in sausages and add remaining oil. Partly cover and continue cooking 15 minutes.

Reduce heat to low and finish cooking 7 to 8 minutes. Sprinkle with parsley and serve.

1 serving *501 calories* *8 g carbohydrate*
25 g protein *41 g fat* *1.9 g fiber*

Garlicky Sweet Sausages

serves 4

2 tbsp	(*30 ml*) peanut oil
3	potatoes, peeled, halved and thinly sliced
1¼ lb	(*625 g*) sweet Italian sausages
2	garlic cloves, smashed and chopped
1	onion, thinly sliced
¾ cup	(*175 ml*) chicken stock, heated
	salt and pepper

Heat half of oil in large frying pan over high heat. Add potatoes and season; cook, partly covered, 15 minutes. Be sure to stir frequently.

Add sausages and remaining oil; season well. Partly cover and continue cooking 10 to 12 minutes over medium heat. Turn sausages over twice during cooking.

Stir in garlic and onion. Cook, partly covered, 10 minutes, stirring several times.

Pour in chicken stock and bring to boil. Correct seasoning and cook 5 minutes, uncovered, over low heat. Serve.

1 serving	*537 calories*	*25 g carbohydrate*
26 g protein	*37 g fat*	*2.6 g fiber*

Hot Sausages in Tomato Sauce

serves 4

1 tbsp	(*15 ml*) olive oil
1	onion, chopped
1	celery stalk, diced
½	small hot pepper, chopped
2	garlic cloves, smashed and chopped
28 oz	(*796 ml*) can tomatoes, drained and chopped
½ tsp	(*2 ml*) oregano
1 tbsp	(*15 ml*) chopped fresh parsley
5 oz	(*150 ml*) canned tomato paste
½ cup	(*125 ml*) beef stock, heated
1 tbsp	(*15 ml*) peanut oil
1¼ lb	(*625 g*) hot Italian sausages, blanched 7 minutes
	salt and pepper
pinch	sugar

Heat olive oil in large, deep skillet. When hot, add onion, celery, hot pepper and garlic; cook 5 to 6 minutes over medium heat.

Stir in tomatoes and season. Add sugar, oregano, parsley, tomato paste and beef stock. Stir well and bring to boil. Cook 20 minutes over medium heat.

Heat peanut oil in frying pan. When hot, add sausages and cook 15 minutes over medium heat, turning pieces over frequently.

Serve with tomato sauce.

1 serving — 538 calories — 22 g carbohydrate
27 g protein — 38 g fat — 3.1 g fiber

Sweet Italian Sausages with Tomatoes

serves 4

2 tbsp	(*30 ml*)	peanut oil
1¼ lb	(*625 g*)	sweet Italian sausages
½ tsp	(*2 ml*)	sweet basil
1		onion, halved and sliced
6		Italian-type plum tomatoes, quartered
1		small hot yellow pepper, chopped
1		large apple, cored, peeled and thinly sliced
1½ cups	(*375 ml*)	beef stock, heated
1 tbsp	(*15 ml*)	cornstarch
3 tbsp	(*45 ml*)	cold water
		salt and pepper
		few drops soy sauce

Heat oil in large, deep skillet over high heat. When hot, add sausages and reduce heat to medium. Cook, partly covered, 10 minutes, turning pieces over 2 or 3 times during cooking.

Sprinkle in basil and season well. Add vegetables and apple; continue cooking, partly covered, another 10 minutes.

Remove sausages from pan and set aside.

Increase heat to high and cook vegetables another 2 minutes.

Stir in beef stock, season and bring to boil.

Mix cornstarch with water; stir into sauce. Sprinkle in soy sauce and finish cooking 2 minutes.

Serve immediately with sausages.

1 serving	*526 calories*	*20 g carbohydrate*
26 g protein	*38 g fat*	*4.0 g fiber*

Chili Con Carne

serves 4

2 tbsp	(*30 ml*) vegetable oil
2	onions, chopped
2	garlic cloves, smashed and chopped
1	yellow pepper, chopped
1½ lb	(*750 g*) lean ground beef
½ tsp	(*2 ml*) caraway seeds
½ tsp	(*2 ml*) celery seeds
19 oz	(*540 ml*) can red kidney beans, drained
1½ cups	(*375 ml*) stewed tomatoes
1¼ cups	(*300 ml*) beef stock, heated
4 tbsp	(*60 ml*) tomato paste
pinch	cayenne
pinch	paprika
	few crushed red peppers
	salt and pepper
pinch	sugar

Preheat oven to 350°F (*180°C*).

Heat oil in large, deep skillet. Add onions, garlic and yellow pepper; cook 7 to 8 minutes over medium heat.

Stir in meat and season. Add all seasonings and mix very well. Cook 5 to 6 minutes over medium heat.

Stir in kidney beans and continue cooking 4 to 5 minutes.

Add tomatoes and sugar; cook 2 to 3 minutes. Stir in beef stock and tomato paste; correct seasoning. Bring to boil.

Cover pan and cook 45 minutes in oven. Serve chili with fresh bread, if desired.

1 serving *547 calories* *36 g carbohydrate*
49 g protein *23 g fat* *10.8 g fiber*

1. Heat oil in large, deep skillet. Cook onions, garlic and yellow pepper 7 to 8 minutes over medium heat.

2. Stir in meat and season. Add all seasonings and mix very well. Cook 5 to 6 minutes over medium heat.

3. Stir in kidney beans and continue cooking 4 to 5 minutes.

4. Add tomatoes and sugar; cook 2 to 3 minutes.

Stuffed Green Peppers

serves 4

1 tbsp	(*15 ml*) vegetable oil
3	figs, finely chopped
1	onion, finely chopped
1	celery stalk, finely chopped
1 cup	(*250 ml*) cooked rice
1 cup	(*250 ml*) whole kernel corn
½ tsp	(*2 ml*) tarragon
2	green peppers, halved across width, seeded and blanched 6 minutes
1 tbsp	(*15 ml*) olive oil
2	shallots, chopped
½ lb	(*250 g*) fresh mushrooms, cleaned and sliced
28 oz	(*796 ml*) can tomatoes, drained and chopped
1 tsp	(*5 ml*) tomato paste
½ cup	(*125 ml*) chicken stock, heated
	salt and pepper
pinch	sugar

Preheat oven to 350°F (*180°C*).

Heat vegetable oil in frying pan. Add figs, onion and celery; season well. Cook 4 to 5 minutes over medium heat.

Stir in rice and corn. Correct seasoning, add tarragon and mix well. Cook 4 to 5 minutes.

Pour mixture into food processor and blend for 2 minutes; set aside.

Place blanched peppers in large, deep skillet and fill with stuffing; set aside.

Heat olive oil in frying pan. Add shallots and mushrooms; cook 3 to 4 minutes over high heat.

Add tomatoes, sugar, tomato paste and chicken stock; mix well. Bring to boil. Season and continue cooking 2 to 3 minutes over medium heat.

Pour sauce over stuffed peppers and cook, uncovered, 45 minutes in oven.

Serve with your favorite grated cheese.

1 serving	*318 calories*	*48 g carbohydrate*
9 g protein	*10 g fat*	*8.6 g fiber*

Stuffed Cabbage Leaves in Sauce

serves 4

8	large curly cabbage leaves, well washed and dried
2 tbsp	(*30 ml*) peanut oil
1	green pepper, finely chopped
2	green onions, finely chopped
½ lb	(*250 g*) fresh mushrooms, cleaned and finely chopped
½	onion, finely chopped
2	garlic cloves, smashed and chopped
¼ tsp	(*1 ml*) chili powder
½ tsp	(*2 ml*) sweet basil
¼ tsp	(*1 ml*) thyme
1 tbsp	(*15 ml*) chopped fresh parsley
1 lb	(*500 g*) lean ground beef
2 tbsp	(*30 ml*) tomato paste
¼ cup	(*50 ml*) chicken stock, heated
3 oz	(*90 g*) feta cheese, chopped
2 tbsp	(*30 ml*) butter
14 oz	(*400 ml*) canned tomato sauce, heated
	salt and pepper

Preheat oven to 350° F (*180°C*).

Remove tough stems from bottom of cabbage leaves. Place leaves in salted boiling water. Cover and cook 4 to 5 minutes.

Drain leaves and place each on separate piece of paper towel. Pat dry with another piece of towel. Transfer to serving platter and set aside.

Heat oil in large, deep skillet over high heat. Add green pepper, green onions, mushrooms, onion and garlic; season well. Sprinkle in seasonings and parsley; mix well. Cook 8 minutes, covered, over medium heat.

Stir in beef and season; continue cooking, covered, 7 to 8 minutes.

Add tomato paste and chicken stock; mix well. Cook 4 to 5 minutes, uncovered.

Stir in cheese and continue cooking 2 minutes.

Spoon stuffing on each cabbage leaf. Fold sides over to meet and roll.

Melt butter in frying pan. Place stuffed rolls in pan and cook 6 to 7 minutes on each side over high heat.

Transfer to baking dish and pour in tomato sauce. Cover with foil and prick wrap with knife for steam vents.

Bake 1 hour in oven. If desired, garnish portions with vegetables.

1 serving	*499 calories*	*21 g carbohydrate*
34 g protein	*31 g fat*	*6.4 g fiber*

Pol's Favorite Meatloaf

serves 4–6

1 tbsp	(*15 ml*) butter
1	onion, chopped
2	garlic cloves, smashed and chopped
1 tbsp	(*15 ml*) chopped fresh parsley
2	green onions, sliced
1½ lb	(*750 g*) lean ground beef
½ lb	(*250 g*) lean ground veal
¼ cup	(*50 ml*) heavy cream
1	egg yolk
3	slices white bread, crusts trimmed
½ cup	(*125 ml*) milk
½ tsp	(*2 ml*) caraway seeds
¼ tsp	(*1 ml*) nutmeg
¼ tsp	(*1 ml*) thyme
½ tsp	(*2 ml*) savory
1	egg white, lightly beaten
3	long stalks celery, pared
3	bay leaves
	salt and pepper
	paprika to taste
	few crushed red peppers

Preheat oven to 350°F (*180°C*).

Melt butter in large skillet. Add onion, garlic, parsley and green onions; cook 3 to 4 minutes over low heat.

Place meat in mixing bowl and season well. Add cooked onion mixture and mix well.

Pour in cream and mix until incorporated. Add egg yolk and mix again.

Place bread in small bowl and pour in milk. Let stand several minutes; then squeeze out excess milk from bread and place pieces in bowl containing meat.

Incorporate well, add all seasonings and mix until well combined.

Add egg white and incorporate thoroughly. Press half of meat mixture into 5½ × 9½ in. (*14 × 24 cm*) loaf pan. Arrange celery stalks on meat (trim to size if necessary) and press in slightly.

Cover with remaining meat and press firmly to take shape of mold. Lay bay leaves on top.

Cover with sheet of perforated foil and place mold in roasting pan containing about 1 in. (*2.5 cm*) hot water. Cook 1 hour 15 minutes in oven. Remove foil at halfway point.

Serve meatloaf with condiments or a sauce such as onion sauce.

1 serving	*403 calories*	*11 g carbohydrate*
38 g protein	*23 g fat*	*1.4 g fiber*

1. Place meat in mixing bowl and season well. Add cooked onion mixture and mix well.

2. After cream has been incorporated, add egg yolk and mix again.

3. Place pieces of soaked bread in bowl containing meat and incorporate well.

4. To make meatloaf, fill mold with half of meat mixture. Arrange pared celery stalks on meat and press in slightly.

Baked Red Cabbage

serves 4

1	head red cabbage, cut into 6 pieces
2 tbsp	(*30 ml*) bacon fat
1	garlic clove, smashed and chopped
1 tbsp	(*15 ml*) wine vinegar
4	thick slices back bacon, rolled in cornmeal and broiled
	salt and pepper

Preheat oven to 400°F (*200°C*).

Parboil cabbage in salted boiling water for 45 minutes, covered.

Drain well and set aside.

Heat bacon fat in large, deep skillet over high heat. Add garlic and cabbage; season generously. Cook 6 to 7 minutes.

Cover pan and finish cooking in oven for 45 minutes.

Sprinkle cabbage with wine vinegar and let stand several minutes. Serve with broiled back bacon.

1 serving	*190 calories*	*14 g carbohydrate*
11 g protein	*10 g fat*	*8.5 g fiber*

WINING AND DINING ON LAND

Main course recipes for every-day dining, unexpected company and formal entertaining

Cognac-Braised Quails

serves 4

2 tbsp	(*30 ml*) butter
8	quails, cleaned and trussed
2	onions, cut into small wedges
1	garlic clove, smashed and chopped
3 tbsp	(*45 ml*) Courvoisier cognac
1 cup	(*250 ml*) dry red wine
½ tsp	(*2 ml*) basil
¼ tsp	(*1 ml*) thyme
1	bay leaf
1½ cups	(*375 ml*) light beef gravy, heated
	salt and pepper

Preheat oven to 350°F (*180°C*).

Heat butter in large ovenproof casserole or skillet over medium heat. Add quails and sear birds about 6 to 8 minutes, browning on all sides.

Add onions and garlic; cook another 2 minutes.

Pour in cognac and flambé or, if preferred, cook 2 minutes over high heat to evaporate alcohol.

Add wine, bring to boil and add all seasonings. Stir in gravy, cover and cook 30 minutes in oven.

1 serving	*373 calories*	*11 g carbohydrate*
44 g protein	*17 g fat*	*1.1 g fiber*

Grilled Half Chicken

serves 2

2 tbsp (*30 ml*) sunflower oil
1 tbsp (*15 ml*) teriyaki sauce
1 tbsp (*15 ml*) lemon juice
2 garlic cloves, smashed and chopped
3 lb (*1.4 kg*) chicken, cleaned and halved
few drops Tabasco sauce
salt and pepper

Preheat barbecue to medium.

Mix oil, teriyaki sauce, lemon juice, garlic and Tabasco sauce together; brush over chicken and season well.

Grill chicken about 1 hour 15 minutes, turning every 10 minutes to avoid charring. Baste frequently and season at least twice during cooking.

When chicken halves are done, serve with fresh rolls and a small salad.

1 serving	*685 calories*	*2 g carbohydrate*
86 g protein	*37 g fat*	*0 g fiber*

Coq au Vin

serves 4

3 tbsp	(*45 ml*) melted butter
5 lb	(*2.3 kg*) capon, cleaned, divided into 8 pieces and skinned
2	medium onions, in small wedges
3	garlic cloves, smashed and chopped
1 tbsp	(*15 ml*) chopped fresh chives
1 tbsp	(*15 ml*) chopped fresh parsley
2 cups	(*500 ml*) dry red wine
2 cups	(*500 ml*) light beef gravy, heated
1	bay leaf
½ lb	(*250 g*) fresh mushrooms, cleaned and halved
	salt and pepper

Preheat oven to 350°F (*180°C*).

Heat 1 tbsp (*15 ml*) butter in large ovenproof casserole. Add half of chicken and brown on all sides for 5 to 6 minutes over medium-high heat. Remove chicken and set aside.

Add another 1 tbsp (*15 ml*) butter and repeat for remaining chicken. Add onions, garlic, chives and parsley to casserole; cook 2 minutes.

Return first half of chicken to casserole and pour in wine; bring to boil.

Mix in gravy and season well. Drop in bay leaf, cover casserole and cook 45 minutes in oven.

About 10 minutes before chicken is done, quickly sauté mushrooms in remaining 1 tbsp (*15 ml*) of butter. Add to casserole and resume cooking.

Serve with rice, potatoes or other vegetable.

1 serving	*978 calories*	*15 g carbohydrate*
90 g protein	*62 g fat*	*2.7 g fiber*

Quick Baked Chicken with Vegetables

serves 4

2 tbsp	(*30 ml*) butter
2	whole chicken breasts, skinned, split into 2 and boned
½	celery stalk, diced
2	large tomatoes, diced large
½	cucumber, peeled, seeded and diced
1	shallot, chopped
½ tsp	(*2 ml*) herbes de Provence
	salt and pepper

Preheat oven to 350°F (*180°C*).

Heat butter in large ovenproof skillet over medium heat. Add chicken and brown 3 minutes on each side, seasoning well when turning over.

Add remaining ingredients, being sure to season well. Continue cooking 2 minutes.

Cover pan and finish cooking 10 to 12 minutes in oven.

Serve with fresh asparagus, if desired.

1 serving *213 calories* *5 g carbohydrate*
28 g protein *9 g fat* *1.6 g fiber*

Chicken Kiev

serves 4

2	whole chicken breasts, skinned, split into 2 and boned
4 tbsp	(*60 ml*) frozen garlic butter *
½ cup	(*125 ml*) seasoned flour
2	beaten eggs
1 cup	(*250 ml*) breadcrumbs
2 tbsp	(*30 ml*) peanut oil

Preheat oven to 350°F (*180°C*).

Using small knife, cut small pockets into flesh of breasts. Be careful that knife does not run through to other side. Insert slivers of frozen garlic butter and pat meat back into shape.

Dredge chicken in flour, dip in beaten eggs and coat thoroughly with breadcrumbs. Use your fingertips to press crumbs into meat.

Heat oil in large frying pan over medium-high heat. When hot, add chicken and brown 3 minutes on each side.

Transfer to ovenproof platter and finish cooking 10 to 12 minutes in oven.

Serve with slices of cantaloupe for a pretty presentation.

* *See Escargots with Garlic Butter, page 52.*

1 serving	*478 calories*	*27 g carbohydrate*
34 g protein	*26 g fat*	*0.8 g fiber*

Breaded Chicken Papaya

serves 4

1	ripe papaya, peeled and sliced
2	small whole chicken breasts, skinned, split into 2 and boned
½ cup	(*125 ml*) seasoned flour
2	beaten eggs
¼ cup	(*50 ml*) seasoned milk
1 cup	(*250 ml*) seasoned breadcrumbs
2 tbsp	(*30 ml*) sunflower oil
	juice ¼ lemon

Preheat oven to 375°F (*190°C*).

Place slices of fruit in small bowl and marinate in lemon juice while preparing chicken.

Place chicken breasts between sheets of waxed paper and pound each to an even ½ in. (*1.2 cm*) thickness.

Dredge in flour and shake off excess. Mix eggs with milk and dip chicken; coat thoroughly with breadcrumbs.

Heat oil in large ovenproof frying pan over high heat. When hot, add chicken and cook 3 minutes on each side.

Transfer to oven and finish cooking another 4 minutes or adjust time depending on original size of breasts.

Serve with lemony papaya slices.

1 serving *410 calories* *36 g carbohydrate*
35 g protein *14 g fat* *1.2 g fiber*

Vermouth Chicken with Green Grapes

serves 4

2 tbsp	(*30 ml*) butter
2 tbsp	(*30 ml*) chopped onion
2	whole chicken breasts, skinned and split into 2 pieces
½ tsp	(*2 ml*) tarragon
1 cup	(*250 ml*) green seedless grapes
1	green pepper, thinly sliced
2 tbsp	(*30 ml*) dry vermouth
1¼ cups	(*300 ml*) chicken stock, heated
1 tbsp	(*15 ml*) cornstarch
3 tbsp	(*45 ml*) cold water
	few drops Tabasco sauce
	salt and pepper

Heat butter in large skillet. Add onion and Tabasco sauce; cover and cook 3 minutes over low heat.

Set chicken breasts in pan and season well. Sprinkle in tarragon, cover and cook 16 to 18 minutes over medium-low heat. Turn chicken over once halfway through cooking time.

Add grapes and green pepper to pan; cook another 4 minutes.

When chicken is cooked, remove from pan and set aside.

Increase heat to high and add vermouth to pan; cook 2 minutes.

Mix in chicken stock and continue cooking 2 minutes; correct seasoning. Mix cornstarch with water; stir into sauce.

Return chicken to pan and simmer 2 to 3 minutes to reheat.

Serve with rice, potatoes or other vegetable.

1 serving	*229 calories*	*10 g carbohydrate*
27 g protein	*9 g fat*	*0.7 g fiber*

Boneless Chicken with Deglazed Lemon Sauce

serves 4

2 tbsp	(*30 ml*) butter
2	whole chicken breasts, skinned, split into 2 and boned
¼ cup	(*50 ml*) chicken stock, heated
1 tbsp	(*15 ml*) chopped fresh parsley
	salt and pepper
	juice 1 lemon

Preheat oven to 350°F (*180°C*).

Heat butter in large ovenproof frying pan over medium heat. Add chicken breasts and brown 3 minutes. Turn chicken over, season and brown another 3 minutes.

Transfer pan to oven and cook 10 to 12 minutes.

When chicken is cooked, remove from pan and set aside.

Place frying pan over high heat; add lemon juice and cook 1 minute.

Pour in chicken stock and add parsley; mix and cook another 2 minutes. Season.

Pour sauce over chicken and serve with a vegetable such as asparagus.

1 serving	*166 calories*	*1 g carbohydrate*
27 g protein	*6 g fat*	*0.1 g fiber*

Chicken Legs Supreme

serves 4

2 tbsp	(*30 ml*) melted butter
4	medium-size chicken legs, skinned and cut into 2 pieces
2	shallots, chopped
½	eggplant, peeled and diced
3 tbsp	(*45 ml*) flour
1 cup	(*250 ml*) dry red wine
1¼ cups	(*300 ml*) beef stock, heated
¼ tsp	(*1 ml*) thyme
½ tsp	(*2 ml*) marjoram
1 tbsp	(*15 ml*) grated orange rind
	salt and pepper
	few drops Tabasco sauce

Preheat oven to 350°F (*180°C*).

Place melted butter in large skillet over medium heat. When hot, add chicken pieces and shallots; season well. Cook 6 minutes, turning chicken over at 3-minute mark.

Add eggplant and mix well. Cover and cook 10 minutes.

Mix in flour and cook 2 minutes, uncovered, over medium heat.

Pour in wine, mix well, and add beef stock. Mix again. Sprinkle in seasonings, orange rind and Tabasco sauce. Bring to boil.

Cover pan and cook in oven 30 minutes. To keep skillet handle cool, wrap in foil.

Correct seasoning and serve.

1 serving	*258 calories*	*6 g carbohydrate*
27 g protein	*14 g fat*	*0.6 g fiber*

Chicken Breasts Florence on Rice

serves 4

2 tbsp	(*30 ml*) butter
2	whole chicken breasts, skinned, split into 2 and boned
1	green pepper, sliced
½ lb	(*250 g*) fresh mushrooms, cleaned and sliced
1	celery stalk, sliced thick
1½ cups	(*375 ml*) chicken stock, heated
2 tbsp	(*30 ml*) teriyaki sauce
1 tbsp	(*15 ml*) cornstarch
3 tbsp	(*45 ml*) cold water
	salt and pepper
	lemon wedges

Heat butter in large skillet over medium heat. Add chicken and cook 4 minutes. Turn over and season well; cook another 4 minutes.

Continue cooking 7 minutes or according to size of breasts, turning chicken over once. Be sure to season several more times.

When chicken is cooked, transfer to plate and keep hot in oven.

Add green pepper, mushrooms and celery to hot skillet. Cook 3 to 4 minutes over medium heat.

Season, pour in chicken stock and teriyaki sauce; bring to boil. Cook 4 to 5 minutes over medium heat.

Mix cornstarch with water; stir into sauce and cook 1 more minute.

Place chicken in sauce and let simmer 2 minutes to reheat.

Serve on a bed of white rice and garnish with lemon wedges.

1 serving *229 calories* *8 g carbohydrate*
29 g protein *9 g fat* *1.9 g fiber*

Sautéed Veal Cutlets with Wild Mushroom Sauce

serves 4

4	¼-in. (*0.65-cm*) thick veal cutlets, trimmed of fat
1 cup	(*250 ml*) lightly seasoned flour
1½ tbsp	(*25 ml*) butter
1½ cups	(*375 ml*) fresh oyster mushrooms, cleaned and halved
3	green onions, chopped
1 tbsp	(*15 ml*) chopped fresh parsley
½ cup	(*125 ml*) light beef consommé, heated
	juice ½ lemon
	salt and pepper

Dredge cutlets in flour and shake off excess. Heat butter in frying pan over medium-high heat. Add meat and sauté 3 minutes.

Turn cutlets over, season and sauté about 2 minutes, depending on size. Remove meat and keep hot in oven.

Add mushrooms, green onions and parsley to pan; cook 3 to 4 minutes over high heat.

Pour in consommé and bring to boil. Sprinkle in lemon juice, correct seasoning and serve at once with veal. Accompany with grilled tomato slices.

1 serving	*325 calories*	*16 g carbohydrate*
27 g protein	*17 g fat*	*1.9 g fiber*

Springtime Veal Scallopini

serves 4

2 lb	(*900 g*) veal scallopini,* cut into 2-in. (*5-cm*) squares
2 tbsp	(*30 ml*) butter
2	red peppers, cut into thick wedges
¼ lb	(*125 g*) fresh mushrooms, cleaned and sliced
2	shallots, chopped
	salt and pepper
	few drops lemon juice

Sauté veal** in hot butter over high heat for 1 minute. Turn pieces over, season lightly and cook 1 more minute. Remove from pan and set aside.

With veal set aside, add red peppers, mushrooms and shallots to hot pan. Cook 3 to 4 minutes over medium-high heat.

Season well, sprinkle in lemon juice and serve immediately with veal. Add more lemon juice if desired. Accompany with noodles.

* *Scallopini are pounded pieces of veal cutlet usually about ¼ in.* (0.65 cm) *thick.*

** *Cook veal in several batches (dividing butter) to avoid overcrowding and allow for proper searing.*

1 serving	*470 calories*	*3 g carbohydrate*
47 g protein	*30 g fat*	*1.1 g fiber*

Sausage-Stuffed Veal Scallopini

serves 4

2 tbsp	(*30 ml*) butter
12	fresh mushrooms, cleaned and chopped
2	shallots, chopped
1 tbsp	(*15 ml*) chopped fresh parsley
1 cup	(*250 ml*) ground sausage meat
¼ cup	(*50 ml*) heavy cream
4	large veal scallopini
	salt and pepper

Preheat oven to 350°F (*180°C*).

Heat half of butter in skillet over medium heat. Add mushrooms, shallots and parsley; cook 3 minutes.

Mix in sausage meat and reduce heat to low; cook another 4 to 5 minutes.

Pour in cream, increase heat to high and season well. Cook 3 to 4 minutes to reduce cream.

Transfer contents of pan to food processor and purée. Set stuffing aside to cool.

Spread cooled stuffing over opened, flat scallopini. Roll lengthwise, tuck in ends and tie with kitchen string.

Heat remaining butter in frying pan. Add veal and sear 2 to 3 minutes over medium-high heat, browning all sides. Season well.

Transfer to ovenproof casserole, cover and cook 10 to 12 minutes in oven.

Serve with potatoes and your choice of sauce.

1 serving	*454 calories*	*3 g carbohydrate*
34 g protein	*34 g fat*	*1.6 g fiber*

1. Cook mushrooms, shallots and parsley 3 minutes in hot butter.

2. Mix in sausage meat and cook 4 to 5 minutes over low heat.

3. Pour in cream, increase heat to high and season well. Reduce cream for 3 to 4 minutes.

4. After stuffing has been puréed and cooled, spread over entire surface of scallopini.

Veal Tenderloin Royale

serves 4

1 tbsp	(*15 ml*) vegetable oil
2	veal tenderloins,* 1 lb (*500 g*) each, fat trimmed
½	celery stalk, diced
1	medium onion, diced small
1	carrot, pared and diced
1	shallot, chopped
1 tbsp	(*15 ml*) chopped fresh chives
½ tsp	(*2 ml*) oregano
½ tsp	(*2 ml*) basil
½ cup	(*125 ml*) dry white wine
1¼ cup	(*300 ml*) light beef consommé, heated
1 tbsp	(*15 ml*) cornstarch
3 tbsp	(*45 ml*) cold water
	salt and pepper

Preheat oven to 375°F (*190°C*).

Heat oil in large ovenproof skillet over medium-high heat. When hot, add veal and sear on all sides until nicely browned.

Reduce heat to medium. Add all vegetables, shallot, chives and seasonings; cook another 2 minutes.

Season well and pour in wine; cook 2 minutes.

Mix in consommé and place skillet in oven; cook 16 minutes, uncovered.

Remove meat from pan and set aside.

Place skillet over low heat. Mix cornstarch with water and stir into sauce; cook 30 seconds or until thickened slightly.

Slice veal and serve with sauce. Accompany with fresh carrots and peas.

* *Veal tenderloin may be difficult to find in your local supermarket. Try your butcher, who should be able to provide you with this special and exceptionally tender cut.*

1 serving	*423 calories*	*7 g carbohydrate*
47 g protein	*23 g fat*	*1.2 g fiber*

Veal Chops with Sautéed Mango

serves 4

2 tbsp	(*30 ml*) butter
4	¾-in. (*2-cm*) thick veal chops
1	ripe mango
	salt and pepper
	juice ½ lemon

Heat butter in large frying pan over medium-high heat. Add veal and cook 3 minutes.

Turn chops over, season well and cook another 3 minutes over medium heat. Adjust cooking time depending on size of chops.

Meanwhile, peel half of mango; holding unpeeled half, slice flesh into thin wedges, running knife in towards pit. Peel second half and slice remaining flesh.

When veal is done, transfer to serving platter.

Quickly sauté mango wedges in frying pan for 1 minute. Sprinkle with lemon juice and serve at once with veal.

1 serving *298 calories* *10 g carbohydrate*
24 g protein *18 g fat* *0.8 g fiber*

Braised Veal Round-Roast Sunday Dinner

serves 4

3 lb	(*1.4 kg*) veal round roast, tied
1 cup	(*250 ml*) seasoned flour
2 tbsp	(*30 ml*) oil
2	onions, cut into 4 or 6
2	carrots, pared and diced large
2	small celery stalks, diced large
1 tbsp	(*15 ml*) chopped fresh parsley
½ tsp	(*2 ml*) oregano
¼ tsp	(*1 ml*) celery salt
1 cup	(*250 ml*) dry white wine
1 cup	(*250 ml*) chicken stock, heated
1 tbsp	(*15 ml*) cornstarch
3 tbsp	(*45 ml*) cold water
	salt and pepper
pinch	thyme
dash	crushed chilies

Preheat oven to 350°F (*180°C*). Dredge meat in flour.

Heat oil in large ovenproof casserole. When hot, add meat and sear on all sides over medium-high heat until nicely browned.

Add vegetables and season well. Continue cooking 2 minutes.

Sprinkle in parsley, oregano, celery salt, thyme and crushed chilies; mix well.

Pour in wine and cook 3 to 4 minutes over high heat. Add chicken stock and bring to boil. Cover casserole and cook 1 hour in oven.

Remove veal and transfer to serving platter; set aside.

Mix cornstarch with cold water; stir into sauce remaining in casserole and cook 1 to 2 minutes to thicken.

Slice meat and serve with sauce and vegetables. Accompany with slices of fresh baguette.

1 serving	*743 calories*	*25 g carbohydrate*
73 g protein	*39 g fat*	*3.2 g fiber*

Vegetable-Stuffed Veal Shoulder

serves 4

3 lb	(*1.4 kg*) boned veal shoulder roast*
2 tbsp	(*30 ml*) butter
1	onion, finely chopped
2	garlic cloves, smashed and chopped
½ tsp	(*2 ml*) tarragon
½ tsp	(*2 ml*) thyme
¼ tsp	(*1 ml*) sage
3½ tsp	(*17 ml*) chopped fresh parsley
3	slices white bread, crusts trimmed
¼ cup	(*50 ml*) light cream
12	large fresh mushrooms, cleaned and chopped
2 tbsp	(*30 ml*) olive oil
2	onions, cut into 6
½ tsp	(*2 ml*) rosemary
1	red pepper, diced large
2	zucchini, thickly sliced on angle
1 cup	(*250 ml*) dry white wine
1 cup	(*250 ml*) chicken stock, heated
	salt and pepper

* *Have your butcher prepare roast for stuffing by cutting it open and flattening it in one large piece.*

Heat butter in small saucepan. Add chopped onion, garlic, tarragon, ¼ tsp (*1 ml*) each of thyme and sage, and ½ tsp (*2 ml*) parsley; cook 2 minutes over medium heat. Meanwhile, soak bread in cream in small bowl.

Add mushrooms to saucepan and season well. Reduce heat to low, cover and cook 6 minutes. Remove cover and continue cooking 4 to 6 minutes.

Mash bread and squeeze out excess cream. Incorporate bread to stuffing in saucepan and set aside to cool slightly.

Preheat oven to 350°F (*180°C*).

Spread vegetable stuffing over opened meat. Close and secure with kitchen string; do not tie too tight.

Heat oil in large ovenproof casserole over high heat. When oil is very hot (smoking), add meat and sear on all sides until nicely browned. Add onions, rosemary and remaining parsley and thyme. Continue cooking 2 to 3 minutes over medium heat.

Mix in red pepper and zucchini; season well. Cook 2 more minutes. Pour in wine and cook 4 to 5 minutes over high heat. Pour in chicken stock, mix and bring to boil. Cover casserole and cook 1 hour in oven.

To serve, slice meat and serve with red pepper and zucchini. If preferred, you can purée the vegetables to make more of a sauce instead. Accompany with corn.

1 serving	*865 calories*	*29 g carbohydrate*
77 g protein	*49 g fat*	*6.8 g fiber*

Roast Veal Sirloin

serves 4

2½ lb	(*1.2 kg*) veal sirloin roast, tied
1 tbsp	(*15 ml*) butter
2	onions, cut into 4
	salt and pepper
	chopped fresh parlsey

Preheat oven to 425 °F (*220 °C*). Season meat generously with pepper.

Heat butter in roasting pan over medium-high heat. When hot, add meat and sear 8 to 10 minutes on all sides. Season lightly as meat is seared.

Add onions to pan and mix; cook another 2 minutes.

Transfer pan to oven and roast meat 40 minutes.

Serve with onions and pan juices. Accompany with Brussels sprouts and sprinkle with parsley.

1 serving	*561 calories*	*6 g carbohydrate*
60 g protein	*33 g fat*	*1.3 g fiber*

Stuffed Pork Tenderloin in Vegetable Gravy

serves 4

1 tbsp	(*15 ml*) butter
½	stalk celery, chopped
2	green onions, chopped
¼ lb	(*125 g*) fresh mushrooms, cleaned and chopped
½ tsp	(*2 ml*) oregano
½ tsp	(*2 ml*) basil
½ cup	(*125 ml*) cooked rice
2	pork tenderloins, trimmed of fat
1 tbsp	(*15 ml*) oil
2	leeks, cleaned * and sliced
2	green onions, sliced
1	garlic clove, smashed and chopped
½ tsp	(*2 ml*) herbes de Provence
½ cup	(*125 ml*) dry red wine
1½ cups	(*375 ml*) light beef gravy, heated
1 tsp	(*5 ml*) chopped fresh parsley
	salt and pepper

Preheat oven to 350°F (*180°C*).

Begin by preparing stuffing. Heat butter in skillet; cook celery, chopped green onions, mushrooms, oregano and basil 5 to 6 minutes over medium heat.

Mix in rice and continue cooking 2 minutes; correct seasoning. Transfer to food processor and blend stuffing; set aside to cool.

Without cutting all the way through, split tenderloins into 2 lengthwise to make one large piece. Open each tenderloin, place between 2 sheets of waxed paper and pound to double width.

Spread stuffing over flattened tenderloins and roll. Secure with kitchen string.

Heat oil in large ovenproof skillet. Sear tenderloins 6 to 8 minutes over medium-high heat, browning all sides.

Add leeks, sliced green onions, garlic and herbes de Provence; season well and cook another 2 to 3 minutes.

Pour in wine and gravy; mix, cover and cook in oven 35 minutes or according to size of tenderloins.

To serve, remove string, slice meat and accompany with sauce.

Sprinkle with parsley.

* *To clean leeks properly, slit each into 4 lengthwise, leaving about 1 in.* (2.5 cm) *uncut at base. This technique will free leaves, allowing you to run plenty of cold water between them to remove all traces of sand and dirt.*

1 serving	*616 calories*	*18 g carbohydrate*
64 g protein	*32 g fat*	*2.3 g fiber*

Pork Tenderloin Braised in Vegetable Broth

serves 4

1 tbsp	(*15 ml*) vegetable oil
2	1 lb (*500 g*) pork tenderloins, trimmed of fat
1	celery stalk, diced
2	carrots, pared and diced
1	zucchini, sliced ½ in. (*1.2 cm*) thick
1	garlic clove, smashed and chopped
1 tbsp	(*15 ml*) oregano
¼ cup	(*50 ml*) dry white wine
1½ cups	(*375 ml*) light chicken stock, heated
1 tbsp	(*15 ml*) cornstarch
3 tbsp	(*45 ml*) cold water
	salt and pepper

Preheat oven to 350°F (*180°C*).

Heat oil in large ovenproof skillet over medium-high heat. When very hot, add tenderloins and sear on all sides.

Add vegetables, garlic and oregano; increase heat to high and mix well. Cook 2 minutes.

Pour in wine and cook another 2 minutes.

Pour in chicken stock and season well. Cover skillet and cook 30 to 35 minutes in oven.

When cooked, remove meat from broth and set aside. Mix cornstarch with water; stir into broth and cook 1 minute to thicken.

Slice meat and serve with vegetable broth.

1 serving	*510 calories*	*9 g carbohydrate*
60 g protein	*26 g fat*	*2.5 g fiber*

Boneless Pork Chops with Pickle Sauce

serves 4

1 tbsp	(*15 ml*) butter
1	shallot, finely chopped
2	green onions, cut in 1-in. (*2.5-cm*) lengths
1	red pepper, cut into julienne
2	large dill pickles, cut into julienne
3 tbsp	(*45 ml*) red wine vinegar
¼ cup	(*50 ml*) dry white wine
1½ cups	(*375 ml*) light beef gravy, heated
1 tbsp	(*15 ml*) vegetable oil
4	¾-in. (*2-cm*) thick boneless pork chops
	salt and pepper

Begin by preparing pickle sauce. Heat butter in saucepan over medium heat. Add shallot, vegetables and pickles; sauté 2 minutes.

Stir in vinegar and wine; cook 2 minutes over high heat.

Mix in gravy and season well. Reduce heat to low and simmer sauce 4 to 6 minutes.

Meanwhile, prepare pork by heating oil in large frying pan.* When hot, add meat and sear 3 minutes over high heat.

Turn chops over, season well and reduce heat to medium. Cook another 3 minutes. Turn over a third time and finish cooking 2 minutes or longer, depending on thickness.

Arrange pork chops on dinner plates and spoon sauce over. Baked potatoes go nicely with this recipe.

** If pan is not large enough to hold 4 chops without crowding, then use two pans or cook meat in batches.*

1 serving	*383 calories*	*7 g carbohydrate*
37 g protein	*23 g fat*	*1.4 g fiber*

Old-Fashioned Pork Stew with Vegetables

serves 4

2 tbsp	(*30 ml*) bacon fat
3 lb	(*1.4 kg*) pork shoulder, trimmed of fat and cut into 1-in. (*2.5-cm*) cubes
1	garlic clove, smashed and chopped
1	onion, chopped
1 tbsp	(*15 ml*) soy sauce
3 tbsp	(*45 ml*) flour
2½ cups	(*625 ml*) beef stock, heated
1 tbsp	(*15 ml*) tomato paste
1	bay leaf
½ tsp	(*2 ml*) rosemary
1 tbsp	(*15 ml*) butter
2	carrots, pared and diced large
2	onions, quartered
2	potatoes, peeled and diced large
1 tsp	(*5 ml*) brown sugar
	salt and pepper

Preheat oven to 350°F (*180°C*).

Heat half of bacon fat in large ovenproof casserole over medium-high heat. When hot, add half of pork and sear 8 to 10 minutes on all sides over high heat. Remove pork and set aside.

Heat remaining bacon fat in casserole and sear rest of pork.

With both batches of pork in casserole, add garlic and chopped onion. Mix well and season; cook 3 minutes over medium-high heat.

Sprinkle in soy sauce and mix well. Add flour and stir with wooden spoon until incorporated; cook 3 more minutes over medium heat.

Pour in beef stock, mixing well; then add tomato paste, bay leaf and rosemay; bring to boil.

Cover casserole and cook stew 1 hour in oven.

Before end of cooking, melt butter in frying pan over medium heat. Add vegetables and brown sugar; sauté about 5 minutes.

Add vegetables to stew, mix well, and resume cooking for 1 hour or until meat is tender.

1 serving	*845 calories*	*34 g carbohydrate*
85 g protein	*41 g fat*	*4.3 g fiber*

Roast Loin of Pork Rosemary

serves 4

4 lb	(*1.8 kg*) loin of pork, boned*
1	shallot, peeled and cut into 4 pieces
3 tbsp	(*45 ml*) melted butter
1 tbsp	(*15 ml*) rosemary
2	onions, quartered
1	celery stalk, diced
2	carrots, pared and halved
3 tbsp	(*45 ml*) flour
1¾ cups	(*425 ml*) light beef stock, heated
2	small Chinese eggplants, sliced
2	zucchini, sliced
½	red pepper, cut into strips
	salt and pepper
	few drops Tabasco sauce

Preheat oven to 350°F (*180°C*). Allow 30 minutes per lb (*500 g*). Trim most of fat from pork and tie bone against meat with kitchen string. Place in roasting pan and stud with pieces of shallot. Brush 1 tbsp (*15 ml*) melted butter over meat. Sprinkle rosemary on meat and press with fingers to help herb adhere.

Place roasting pan in oven and cook about 2 hours, depending on weight. As soon as meat is seared, season generously. About halfway into cooking time, surround meat with onions, celery and carrots.

When pork is done, remove from pan but keep warm in oven. Discard bone.

Place roasting pan over medium heat and cook juices and vegetables 3 minutes.

Mix in flour with wooden spoon; continue cooking over low heat 5 minutes or until flour has browned.

Pour in beef stock, mixing well with whisk, and bring to boil. Continue cooking 5 minutes over medium heat; then correct seasoning and sprinkle in Tabasco sauce. Strain sauce and pour into gravy boat.

To prepare garnish, heat remaining butter in frying pan. Sauté eggplant, zucchini and red pepper 4 to 5 minutes over medium heat. Season well.

Serve garnish with pork and sauce. If desired, accompany with green peas.

* *Have butcher give you bone from the loin.*

1 serving	*862 calories*	*25 g carbohydrate*
87 g protein	*46 g fat*	*6.5 g fiber*

Kidney Sauté in Red Wine Sauce

serves 4

2	calf kidneys, well cleaned
3 tbsp	(*45 ml*) butter
½ lb	(*250 g*) fresh mushrooms, cleaned and quartered
2	shallots, chopped
¼ cup	(*50 ml*) dry red wine
1 cup	(*250 ml*) beef stock, heated
1 tbsp	(*15 ml*) cornstarch
2 tbsp	(*30 ml*) cold water
3 tbsp	(*45 ml*) heavy cream
	salt and pepper

Trim fat from kidneys and discard. Slice kidneys ¼ in. (*0.65 cm*) thick.

Heat 1 tbsp (*15 ml*) butter in large frying pan. When melted, increase heat to high and add half of kidneys; cook 2 minutes.

Turn kidneys over, season and cook another 2 minutes. Remove from pan and set aside. Add another 1 tbsp (*15 ml*) butter to hot pan and cook rest of kidneys following same procedure.

With all kidneys set aside, place remaining 1 tbsp (*15 ml*) butter in pan. Add mushrooms and shallots; cook 4 minutes over high heat.

Add red wine; cook another 3 minutes.

Pour in beef stock and season well. Mix cornstarch with water; stir into sauce and cook 3 to 4 minutes over medium heat.

Mix in cream and cook 2 more minutes.

Place kidneys in sauce and simmer 2 minutes to reheat. Serve with croutons, if desired.

1 serving *212 calories* *5 g carbohydrate*
12 g protein *16 g fat* *1.6 g fiber*

1. Choose very fresh calf kidneys for this recipe and be sure to clean them thoroughly.

2. Trim fat from kidneys and discard. Slice ¼ in. (0.65 cm) *thick.*

3. It is best to cook kidneys in two batches. Overcrowding the pan will cause the fat to boil instead of sauté.

4. After all kidneys have been sautéed and set aside, add rest of butter to pan and cook mushrooms and shallots 4 minutes over high heat.

Leg of Lamb Lorence

serves 4

3½ lb	(*1.6 kg*) leg of lamb, boned by butcher
2	garlic cloves, peeled and cut into 3
2 tbsp	(*30 ml*) melted butter
1 tsp	(*5 ml*) basil
½ tsp	(*2 ml*) oregano
3	small onions, quartered
2	celery stalks, diced
3 tbsp	(*45 ml*) flour
2 cups	(*500 ml*) light beef stock, heated
1 tbsp	(*15 ml*) tomato paste
pinch	thyme
	pepper

Preheat oven to 425 °F (*220 °C*). Allow 16 minutes per lb (*500 g*).

Remove the fell (thin covering) from lamb if not already done by butcher. Stud meat with slivers of garlic and brush with melted butter.

Place lamb in roasting pan, mix seasonings together and rub over meat. Place in oven and cook about 1 hour for "pink" meat. Adjust time if desired.

About halfway through cooking time, surround lamb with onions and celery; resume cooking.

When lamb is cooked, remove from roasting pan and transfer to serving platter; keep hot in oven.

Place roasting pan on stove over medium heat and cook juices 4 minutes.

Mix in flour with wooden spoon. Reduce heat to low and cook 5 to 6 minutes or until flour is lightly browned.

Pour in beef stock and stir in tomato paste; whisk well. Season with pepper only and bring to boil. Continue cooking 5 to 6 minutes over medium heat.

Pour sauce through sieve into bowl and prepare to serve with lamb.

Accompany with a variety of vegetables.

1 serving	*794 calories*	*12 g carbohydrate*
65 g protein	*54 g fat*	*1.7 g fiber*

Double Loin of Lamb 5th Avenue

serves 4

3 lb	(*1.4 kg*) double loin of lamb*
½ tsp	(*2 ml*) oregano
¼ tsp	(*1 ml*) thyme
¼ tsp	(*1 ml*) savory
2 tbsp	(*30 ml*) melted butter
½ cup	(*125 ml*) dry white wine
½	onion, finely chopped
1 tbsp	(*15 ml*) chopped fresh parsley
1 cup	(*250 ml*) beef stock, heated
	salt and pepper

Preheat oven to 450°F (*240°C*).

Lay lamb on cutting board and sprinkle with oregano, thyme and savory; pepper well. Roll and tie loins.

Place meat with bones in roasting pan and baste with melted butter. Pour wine over meat. Sear 12 minutes in oven.

Reduce heat to 350°F (*180°C*) and continue cooking about 25 minutes for "pink" lamb. Adjust time if you prefer medium.

When meat is done, remove from pan and set aside. Cover with foil to keep hot.

With bones still in pan, add onion and parsley; cook 3 minutes over high heat.

Pour in beef stock and bring to boil. Continue cooking 3 to 4 minutes over medium-high heat.

Slice lamb and serve with onion sauce. Accompany with fresh asparagus.

* *Have your butcher bone the loins and remove most of the fat. Bring the bones home too!*

1 serving	*741 calories*	*2 g carbohydrate*
64 g protein	*53 g fat*	*0.4 g fiber*

Lamb Chops with Broiled Eggplant Rounds

serves 4

3 tbsp	(*45 ml*) olive oil
3 tbsp	(*45 ml*) teriyaki sauce
1	garlic clove, smashed and chopped
½ tsp	(*2 ml*) rosemary
1	eggplant, cut into rounds ½ in. (*1.2 cm*) thick
8	lamb chops, trimmed of fat
	juice ½ lemon
	salt and freshly ground pepper

Preheat oven to 400°F (*200°C*).

Mix oil with teriyaki sauce, garlic, rosemary, lemon juice and pepper. Brush over eggplant rounds and lamb chops.

Place eggplant in roasting pan and change oven setting to broil. Place pan in oven 6 in. (*15 cm*) from top element. With oven door ajar, cook eggplant 5 to 6 minutes each side.

Meanwhile, cook basted lamb chops in hot frying pan over high heat for 3 to 4 minutes on each side, depending on thickness. Remember to season when turning meat over.

1 serving	*317 calories*	*4 g carbohydrate*
28 g protein	*21 g fat*	*0.7 g fiber*

Lamb Shoulder Stew

serves 4

2 tbsp	(*30 ml*) oil
3½ lb	(*1.6 kg*) lamb shoulder, trimmed of fat and cubed
2	onions, chopped
1	garlic clove, smashed and chopped
1 tbsp	(*15 ml*) chopped fresh ginger
3 tbsp	(*45 ml*) flour
3 cups	(*750 ml*) light chicken stock, heated
1	bay leaf
1	small head cauliflower, in flowerets
1	small zucchini, diced
	salt and pepper

Heat oil in large casserole. When hot, add meat and sear 5 to 6 minutes, turning to brown all sides.

Add onions, garlic and ginger; mix well and continue cooking 5 minutes.

Mix in flour and cook 1 minute over medium-low heat.

Pour in chicken stock, add bay leaf and season well. Bring to boil.

Partly cover casserole and cook 1 hour over low heat.

Add vegetables and continue cooking for 30 minutes.

1 serving *831 calories* *17 g carbohydrate*
67 g protein *55 g fat* *3.9 g fiber*

Country-Style Beef Bourguignon

serves 4

2 tbsp	(*30 ml*) light oil	
4 lb	(*1.8 kg*) boneless blade roast, trimmed of fat	
4	blanched garlic cloves	
1	bay leaf	
¼ tsp	(*1 ml*) thyme	
½ tsp	(*2 ml*) basil	
1 tbsp	(*15 ml*) chopped fresh parsley	
3	onions, cut into wedges	
⅓ cup	(*75 ml*) flour	
2 cups	(*500 ml*) dry red wine	
1 cup	(*250 ml*) beef stock, heated	
1 tbsp	(*15 ml*) cornstarch	
3 tbsp	(*45 ml*) cold water	
	salt and pepper	

Preheat oven to 350°F (*180°C*).

Heat oil in large ovenproof casserole over high heat. Add roast and sear 8 to 10 minutes, browning all sides.

Add garlic, bay leaf, thyme, basil and parsley; season well. Add onions and continue cooking 4 to 5 minutes over high heat.

Add flour, incorporating a little at a time, while turning meat over. Continue cooking another 4 to 5 minutes over medium heat.

Season meat well and pour in wine and beef stock; bring to boil. Cover and cook 3 hours in oven. Turn roast over several times during cooking.

Transfer cooked meat to serving platter and prepare to slice. If sauce is too thin, thicken with cornstarch diluted in cold water. Be sure to mix in well.

Accompany this dish with potatoes or broiled tomato halves.

1 serving	*720 calories*	*19 g carbohydrate*
98 g protein	*28 g fat*	*2.1 g fiber*

1. Sear meat in hot oil for 8 to 10 minutes, browning all sides. Avoid turning roast too often or meat will not be properly seared.

2. Add garlic, bay leaf, thyme, basil and parsley; season well. Add onions and continue cooking 4 to 5 minutes over high heat.

3. Add flour, incorporating it a little at a time, turning meat over. The flour will thicken the sauce during cooking. Continue cooking another 4 to 5 minutes over medium heat to remove raw taste of flour.

4. Season meat well and pour in wine and beef stock; bring to boil and prepare to finish cooking in oven.

Curried Blade Steak Stew

serves 4

2 tbsp	(*30 ml*) bacon fat
3½ lb	(*1.6 kg*) blade steak, trimmed of fat and cut into 1-in. (*2.5-cm*) cubes
2	onions, finely chopped
3 tbsp	(*45 ml*) curry powder
1 tbsp	(*15 ml*) cumin powder
3 tbsp	(*45 ml*) flour
3 cups	(*750 ml*) beef stock, heated
2 tbsp	(*30 ml*) tomato paste
1	bay leaf
1 tsp	(*5 ml*) rosemary powder
	salt and pepper

Preheat oven to 350°F (*180°C*).

Heat half of bacon fat in large frying pan. When hot, add half of meat and sear on all sides over high heat.

Remove meat when nicely browned and set aside. Add remaining fat and repeat procedure for rest of meat.

Transfer all seared meat to ovenproof casserole and season well.

Add onions to frying pan in which meat was seared. Sauté 3 to 4 minutes over high heat and transfer to casserole.

Sprinkle curry powder and cumin over meat; mix well and add flour. Mix with wooden spoon until completely incorporated.

Place casserole over medium heat and cook until flour begins sticking to bottom of casserole. Stir once or twice.

Pour in beef stock, mix well, and add tomato paste and remaining seasonings. Mix and cover casserole. Cook stew 2½ hours in oven.

Serve on bed of egg noodles.

1 serving	*621 calories*	*12 g carbohydrate*
87 g protein	*25 g fat*	*1.4 g fiber*

Braised Cross-Rib Roast Americana

serves 4

2 tbsp	(*30 ml*) bacon fat
5 lb	(*2.2 kg*) cross-rib roast, tied
2	celery stalks, cut into 4
2	carrots, pared and cut into 4
4	onions, quartered
1	garlic clove, peeled
3	parsley sprigs
2	bay leaves
½ tsp	(*2 ml*) thyme
1 tsp	(*5 ml*) chervil
½ tsp	(*2 ml*) basil
1 cup	(*250 ml*) dry white wine
3 cups	(*750 ml*) light beef gravy, heated
1 tbsp	(*15 ml*) chopped fresh parsley
	salt and pepper

Preheat oven to 325°F (*160°C*).

Heat bacon fat in large ovenproof casserole. When hot, add meat and sear on all sides over high heat.

Season meat and add all vegetables, garlic, parsley sprigs, bay leaves and seasonings. Cook 2 minutes over medium-high heat.

Pour in wine, increase heat to high and cook another 2 minutes.

Stir in gravy, season well and bring to boil.

Cover casserole and cook 3 hours in oven. Halfway through cooking time, turn meat over.

Remove meat from casserole and slice to serve. Accompany with sauce and, if desired, honey-glazed carrots. Sprinkle portions with chopped parsley.

1 serving	*962 calories*	*9 g carbohydrate*
119 g protein	*50 g fat*	*0 g fiber*

Tenderloin Steaks with Pepper Sauce

serves 4

1 tbsp	(*15 ml*) oil
1	green pepper, diced
½ lb	(*250 g*) fresh mushrooms, cleaned and diced
½ tsp	(*2 ml*) oregano
½ tsp	(*2 ml*) chopped fresh chives
1	garlic clove, smashed and chopped
1	tomato, diced
½ cup	(*125 ml*) chicken stock, heated
1 tbsp	(*15 ml*) tomato paste
4	6-oz (*170-g*) tenderloin steaks
	salt and pepper

Heat half of oil in skillet over high heat. Add diced green pepper and cook 1 minute.

Add mushrooms, oregano, chives and garlic; continue cooking 2 minutes.

Add tomato, chicken stock and tomato paste; season well. Mix and cook 6 to 8 minutes over medium-low heat.

Meanwhile, brush remaining oil over both sides of meat. Cook in hot frying pan over high heat for 3 minutes.

Turn steaks over, season well and continue cooking 2 minutes for rare meat. Serve with sauce. Accompany with potatoes, if desired.

1 serving	*305 calories*	*6 g carbohydrate*
41 g protein	*13 g fat*	*2.2 g fiber*

1. Heat half of oil in skillet over high heat and cook green pepper for 1 minute.

2. Add mushrooms, oregano, chives and garlic; continue cooking 2 minutes.

3. Add tomato, and then …

4. Add chicken stock and tomato paste; season well and mix. Cook 6 to 8 minutes over medium-low heat while you are preparing the steaks.

Tenderloin Steaks with Red Wine Onion Sauce

serves 4

1 tsp	(*5 ml*) butter
2	onions, sliced
¼ tsp	(*1 ml*) basil
1 tbsp	(*15 ml*) chopped fresh parsley
½ cup	(*125 ml*) dry red wine
1¼ cups	(*300 ml*) light beef consommé, heated
1 tsp	(*5 ml*) cornstarch
2 tbsp	(*30 ml*) cold water
4	6-oz (*170-g*) tenderloin steaks
1 tbsp	(*15 ml*) oil
	salt and pepper

Heat butter in saucepan over medium heat. Add onions, basil and parsley; cook 15 minutes over low heat, stirring frequently.

Pour in wine, increase heat to high and cook 2 to 3 minutes. Correct seasoning.

Add consommé and bring to boil. Mix cornstarch with water; stir into sauce and finish simmering 6 to 7 minutes over low heat.

Meanwhile, brush meat on both sides with oil and cook in hot frying pan over high heat for 3 minutes.

Turn steaks over, season well and continue cooking 2 minutes for rare meat.

Serve with sauce and garnish with croutons, if desired.

1 serving	*314 calories*	*7 g carbohydrate*
40 g protein	*14 g fat*	*1.1 g fiber*

1. Cook onions, basil and parsley in hot butter for 15 minutes over low heat, stirring frequently.

2. Pour in wine, increase heat to high and cook 2 to 3 minutes. Correct seasoning.

3. Add consommé and bring to boil.

4. Thicken sauce with diluted cornstarch and simmer 6 to 7 minutes while steaks are being cooked.

Strip Loin Steaks with Texas Garlic Sauce

serves 4

7	garlic cloves
1	egg yolk
½ cup	(*125 ml*) olive oil
1 tbsp	(*15 ml*) vegetable oil
4	8-oz (*250-g*) strip loin steaks, trimmed of fat
	salt and pepper

Peel garlic cloves and place them in small saucepan. Pour in 1 cup (*250 ml*) water and bring to boil. Continue cooking 4 to 5 minutes.

Drain cloves well, place in mortar and mash. Add egg yolk and incorporate using pestle.

Incorporate olive oil in thin stream, whisking constantly. Continue mixing until sauce is very thick. Pour through wire sieve and set aside.

Heat half of vegetable oil in large, heavy-bottomed frying pan over high heat. When oil starts to smoke, add 2 steaks and sear 3 minutes without touching.

Turn steaks over and season generously. Reduce heat to medium-high and sear second side 3 to 4 minutes for rare meat. For medium-rare, turn steaks a third time and cook another 3 to 4 minutes over medium heat.

Remove steaks from pan and keep hot in oven while cooking other 2 steaks.

To serve, ladle garlic sauce over one end of steaks and accompany with steamed snow pea pods.

1 serving	*653 calories*	*2 g carbohydrate*
51 g protein	*49 g fat*	*0 g fiber*

Strip Loin Steaks Louise

serves 4

2 tbsp	(*30 ml*) vegetable oil
4	8-oz (*250-g*) strip loin steaks, trimmed of fat
1 tbsp	(*15 ml*) butter
½ lb	(*250 g*) fresh oyster mushrooms, cleaned and sliced in half
2	green onions, sliced on angle
1	green pepper, halved and sliced on angle
¾ cup	(*175 ml*) prepared demi-glace roast gravy mix
dash	Worcestershire sauce
	salt and pepper

Mix 1 tbsp (*15 ml*) oil with Worcestershire sauce and baste over steaks; pepper well.

Cook steaks in 2 batches to avoid crowding the pan. If preferred, use 2 pans.

In a large, heavy-bottomed frying pan, heat half of remaining oil over high heat. When oil starts to smoke, add 2 steaks and sear them 3 minutes without touching.

Turn steaks over and season generously. Reduce heat to medium-high and sear second side 3 to 4 minutes for rare meat. For medium-rare, turn steaks over a third time and cook another 3 to 4 minutes over medium heat.

When steaks are done to taste, remove from pan and keep hot in oven. Add remaining oil and repeat procedure for other 2 steaks.

Meanwhile, heat butter in another frying pan over medium-high heat. Add vegetables and cook 4 to 5 minutes.

Season well and pour in demi-glace gravy; mix well and bring to quick boil.

Serve vegetables with steaks.

1 serving	*475 calories*	*6 g carbohydrate*
52 g protein	*27 g fat*	*2.1 g fiber*

Double Strip Loin Steak

serves 4

2 lb	(*900 g*) piece strip loin steak
2 tbsp	(*30 ml*) oil
1 tbsp	(*15 ml*) teriyaki sauce
½ tsp	(*2 ml*) herbes de Provence
2 tbsp	(*30 ml*) green peppercorns, mashed
	salt and pepper

Place meat on dinner plate. Mix oil with teriyaki sauce and pour over steak. Spread herbs and mashed peppercorns on top.

Using tongs, turn meat over to coat both sides with mixture; marinate 30 minutes.

Preheat oven to 425°F (*220°C*).

Place meat in hot heavy-bottomed frying pan and sear about 3 minutes on each side over high heat. Sear a little longer for medium-cooked meat. Be sure to season well when turning meat over.

Transfer to oven and finish cooking 10 to 12 minutes.

Slice as shown in technique and serve with vegetables such as fresh green beans and potatoes. Accompany with sauce, if desired.

1 serving	*411 calories*	*1 g carbohydrate*
50 g protein	*23 g fat*	*— g fiber*

1. Most likely your local supermarket will not carry this cut of meat. Just ask your butcher to cut a 2-lb (900-g) piece of strip loin steak for you.

2. Cover meat with marinade ingredients.

3. Turn steak over so that both sides are coated; let stand 30 minutes.

4. After searing and cooking meat, slice as shown here and serve.

Strip Steaks with Choron Sauce

serves 4

¾ lb	(*375 g*) unsalted butter
1 tbsp	(*15 ml*) chopped fresh parsley
1 tbsp	(*15 ml*) chopped shallot
1 tbsp	(*15 ml*) coarsely ground pepper
3 tbsp	(*45 ml*) red wine vinegar
2 tbsp	(*30 ml*) dry red wine
2	egg yolks
1 tbsp	(*15 ml*) tomato paste
1 tbsp	(*15 ml*) vegetable oil
4	8-oz (*250-g*) strip loin steaks, trimmed of fat
	salt and pepper

Place butter in stainless-steel bowl set over saucepan half-filled with hot water. Without touching bowl, melt over low heat.

Skim whitish foam from surface and discard. Set bowl aside.

Place parsley, shallot, ground pepper, vinegar and wine in clean saucepan. Cook over medium heat until liquid has evaporated. Transfer to clean stainless-steel bowl, add egg yolks and whisk well.

Set bowl over saucepan with hot water. Over very low heat, gradually add ¼ of clarified butter, whisking constantly.

Whisk in tomato paste. Add rest of butter using above technique; then strain sauce through wire sieve. Season and set aside.

Cook meat in 2 batches. Heat oil in large, heavy-bottomed frying pan over high heat. When smoking, add meat and sear 3 minutes. Turn over, season and sear 3 to 4 minutes over medium-high for rare meat. Repeat procedure. Serve with sauce.

1 serving *1058 calories* *1 g carbohydrate*
52 g protein *94 g fat* *0.1 g fiber*

1. When butter has melted in bowl, skim off whitish foam and discard.

2. Place parsley, shallot, coarsely ground pepper, wine vinegar and wine in saucepan. Cook over medium heat until all the liquid has evaporated.

3. With parsley mixture transferred to bowl, add egg yolks and mix well with whisk.

4. Butter must be incorporated very slowly in a thin stream while whisking constantly. Start by incorporating ¼ of the butter. Then mix in tomato paste. Continue adding rest of butter using the same technique.

Sirloin Tip Roast au Jus

serves 4

4 tbsp	(*60 ml*) dry mustard
3 lb	(*1.4 kg*) sirloin tip roast, tied
2	garlic cloves, peeled and halved
2 tbsp	(*30 ml*) melted butter
3	onions, cut into 6
1 cup	(*250 ml*) beef stock, heated
1 tsp	(*5 ml*) chopped fresh parsley
	salt and pepper

Preheat oven to 350°F (*180°C*). Allow 30 minutes per lb (*500 g*) for medium-done meat.

Mix mustard with just enough cold water to make paste; using back of small spoon, mix until smooth and lump-free.

Make several incisions in meat and stud with garlic slivers. Rub meat lightly with salt and cover with mustard paste.

Heat butter in roasting pan over medium heat. Place meat in pan and roast 1½ hours in oven or until meat is done to taste.

When cooked, remove meat from pan and set aside.

Add onions to pan and cook 4 minutes over medium-high heat. Pour in beef stock and mix in parsley; season and continue cooking 3 minutes.

Carve roast and serve with pan gravy. Accompany with fresh green beans.

1 serving	*554 calories*	*9 g carbohydrate*
80 g protein	*22 g fat*	*1.7 g fiber*

Inside Round Roast

serves 4

3 lb	(*1.4 kg*) inside round roast
2	garlic cloves, peeled and cut into 3
1 tsp	(*5 ml*) rosemary
1	onion, quartered
1 tbsp	(*15 ml*) chopped fresh parsley
	thin slices pork fat
	salt and freshly ground pepper

Preheat oven to 350°F (*180°C*). Allow 30 minutes per lb (*500 g*) for medium-done meat.

Make incisions in meat and stud with garlic slivers. Cover roast with slices of pork fat and secure with kitchen string.

Place roast in small roasting pan and cook 1 hour in oven.

Season well and sprinkle with rosemary; continue cooking another 30 minutes or until meat is done to taste.

When cooked, remove meat from pan and discard fat. Return meat to pan with drippings and let stand 15 minutes; then remove from pan and set aside on cutting board.

Place roasting pan over high heat and add onion; cook 2 minutes.

Season well with pepper and continue cooking 3 to 4 minutes. Strain sauce and serve with roast and onions. Sprinkle with parsley.

1 serving	*508 calories*	*3 g carbohydrate*
79 g protein	*20 g fat*	*0.6 g fiber*

Cross-Rib Roast with Tomatoes

serves 4

2 tbsp	(*30 ml*) bacon fat
3 lb	(*1.4 kg*) cross-rib roast, tied
3	onions, cut into 4
2	garlic cloves, smashed and chopped
28 oz	(*796 ml*) can tomatoes, drained
¼ tsp	(*1 ml*) thyme
½ tsp	(*2 ml*) marjoram
1	bay leaf
1 cup	(*250 ml*) V-8 juice
	salt and pepper
pinch	sugar

Preheat oven to 350°F (*180°C*).

Heat bacon fat in ovenproof casserole over high heat. When hot, add roast and sear on all sides for 8 to 10 minutes.

Add onions and garlic; continue cooking 6 to 7 minutes.

Season well, add tomatoes, all seasonings, V-8 juice and pinch of sugar. Cover and cook roast in oven 2 to 2½ hours.

Slice and serve with sauce and tomatoes. Accompany with homemade mashed potatoes, if desired.

1 serving	*693 calories*	*21 g carbohydrate*
78 g protein	*33 g fat*	*2.4 g fiber*

Outside Rump Roast Fire Island

serves 4

3 lb	(*1.4 kg*) outside rump roast, tied
1 cup	(*250 ml*) seasoned flour
2 tbsp	(*30 ml*) bacon fat
1	carrot, pared and diced
1	onion, diced
1	celery stalk, diced
1½ cups	(*375 ml*) chopped fresh tomatoes
1	bay leaf
¼ tsp	(*1 ml*) marjoram
2 cups	(*500 ml*) beef stock, heated
1 tbsp	(*15 ml*) tomato paste
	salt and pepper
pinch	sugar

Preheat oven to 350°F (*180°C*). Dredge meat in flour.

Heat bacon fat in large ovenproof casserole over medium heat. When hot, add roast and sear on all sides until nicely browned.

Add vegetables and all seasonings; continue cooking 5 minutes.

Add remaining ingredients and mix well. Correct seasoning and bring to boil.

Cover casserole and cook 2 hours in oven.

1 serving	*633 calories*	*24 g carbohydrate*
78 g protein	*25 g fat*	*3.3 g fiber*

Filet Mignon with Hunter Sauce

serves 4

1 tbsp	(*15 ml*) butter
3	green onions, diced
½ lb	(*250 g*) fresh mushrooms, cleaned and diced
1	garlic clove, smashed and chopped
1	shallot, chopped
2	tomatoes, diced large
½ tsp	(*2 ml*) oregano
½ cup	(*125 ml*) dry white wine
1 cup	(*250 ml*) light beef gravy, heated
4	7-oz (*200-g*) filet mignon steaks
1 tsp	(*5 ml*) oil
	salt and pepper

Heat butter in large skillet over medium-high heat. Add green onions, mushrooms, garlic and shallot; cook 3 to 4 minutes.

Add tomatoes and oregano; season well. Mix and cook 3 to 4 minutes over high heat.

Pour in wine and continue cooking 2 to 3 minutes.

Correct seasoning and incorporate beef gravy. Simmer over low heat until steaks are ready.

Brush steaks on both sides with oil. Cook in hot frying pan over high heat for 3 minutes. Turn steaks over, season and continue cooking 3 to 4 minutes for rare meat.

Serve with hunter sauce.

1 serving	*359 calories*	*7 g carbohydrate*
49 g protein	*15 g fat*	*1.5 g fiber*

1. Heat butter in large skillet over medium-high heat. Add green onions, mushrooms, garlic and shallot; cook 3 to 4 minutes.

2. Add tomatoes and oregano; season well. Mix and cook 3 to 4 minutes over high heat.

3. Pour in wine and continue cooking 2 to 3 minnutes.

4. Correct seasoning and incorporate beef gravy. Simmer sauce over low heat.

Flank Steak à la Provençale

serves 4

1	large flank steak, trimmed of fat
2 tbsp	(*30 ml*) vegetable oil
4 tbsp	(*60 ml*) teriyaki sauce
3	blanched garlic cloves, mashed
1 tbsp	(*15 ml*) olive oil
3	onions, cut into wedges
3	tomatoes, peeled and cut into wedges
2 tbsp	(*30 ml*) tomato paste
½ tsp	(*2 ml*) oregano
	salt and pepper
pinch	thyme

Score meat on both sides and place in shallow baking dish. Mix vegetable oil with teriyaki sauce and half of garlic; pour over meat and marinate 1½ hours in refrigerator. Turn meat occasionally to baste both sides.

When ready to cook meat, heat olive oil in skillet. Cook onions with remaining garlic 3 to 4 minutes over medium heat.

Mix well and cover; continue cooking 6 to 7 minutes over low heat.

Add tomatoes, tomato paste and seasonings to mixture; continue cooking 8 to 10 minutes over low heat. Do not cover.

Meanwhile, coat heavy frying pan, preferably cast-iron, with thin film of oil. Heat pan and add flank steak; sear 6 minutes over high heat.

Turn steak over, season generously and cook another 6 minutes, depending on thickness. Meat should be cooked rare to keep it tender.

Slice meat quite thinly on angle and serve with tomatoes.

1 serving *634 calories* *18 g carbohydrate*
82 g protein *26 g fat* *3.1 g fiber*

WINING AND DINING BY SEA

Tantalizing seafood entrées

Glorious Fish Salad

serves 4

½ cup	(*125 ml*) stuffed green olives
14 oz	(*400 ml*) canned miniature corn cobs, halved
2	hard-boiled eggs, sliced
1 cup	(*250 ml*) cooked green beans
1 cup	(*250 ml*) cooked snow pea pods
½	red pepper, thinly sliced
1	cooked potato, peeled and sliced
2 cups	(*500 ml*) leftover cooked fish, flaked into bite-size pieces
1 tbsp	(*15 ml*) Dijon mustard
2 tbsp	(*30 ml*) wine vinegar
1 tbsp	(*15 ml*) lemon juice
6 tbsp	(*90 ml*) olive oil
	salt and pepper

Place olives, corn, eggs, beans, pea pods, red pepper and potato in mixing bowl; season well.

Add fish, toss gently and season again. Set aside.

Place mustard in second bowl. Season and add vinegar, lemon juice and oil. Mix very well with whisk. Correct seasoning.

Pour dressing over salad ingredients, toss to coat evenly and serve on crisp lettuce leaves. Decorate platter with fruit.

1 serving	*469 calories*	*25 g carbohydrate*
27 g protein	*32 g fat*	*6.6 g fiber*

Elegant Curried Halibut Steaks

serves 2

1	halibut steak, cut into 2
2 tbsp	(*30 ml*) curry powder
1	carrot, pared and sliced
1	sprig dill
1 tsp	(*5 ml*) butter
½	onion, sliced
¼ lb	(*125 g*) fresh mushrooms, cleaned and sliced
2 tbsp	(*30 ml*) flour
2 tbsp	(*30 ml*) heavy cream
	salt and pepper

Place fish in buttered baking dish and sprinkle with half of curry powder. Add carrot and dill; pour in enough cold water to cover and season. Bring to boil over medium heat.

Turn fish over and let simmer about 5 to 6 minutes or until middle bone can be removed easily. Then remove fish and set aside, reserving 1½ cups (*375 ml*) of cooking liquid.

Melt butter in saucepan. Add onion, cover and cook 3 to 4 minutes over medium heat.

Add mushrooms; continue cooking 3 to 4 minutes.

Sprinkle in remaining curry powder and mix well. Cook 1 minute, uncovered.

Incorporate flour and cook 1 more minute.

Pour in reserved cooking liquid from fish and mix very well. Add cream and continue cooking sauce 7 to 8 minutes, stirring 2 or 3 times.

Arrange fish on plates and spoon sauce over. Surprise your guests by garnishing with purple grapes.

1 serving	*390 calories*	*16 g carbohydrate*
41 g protein	*18 g fat*	*3.4 g fiber*

Poached Halibut Pernod

serves 2

1	large halibut steak, cut into 2 across width
1 tbsp	(*15 ml*) chopped fresh parsley
1 tbsp	(*15 ml*) Pernod
1	shallot, chopped
	salt and pepper
	juice ½ lemon

Butter a frying pan and add fish; season with salt and pepper. Sprinkle in parsley, lemon juice, Pernod and shallot.

Cover with waxed paper touching surface and cook 4 to 5 minutes over medium heat.

Turn fish over; cover and continue cooking 4 to 5 minutes. When bone can be removed easily, fish is cooked.

Serve with vegetables.

1 serving — 262 calories — 5 g carbohydrate
38 g protein — 10 g fat — 0.1 g fiber

Halibut Steak with Garlic Butter

serves 2

½ lb	(*250 g*) unsalted butter, softened
1 tbsp	(*15 ml*) chopped fresh parsley
1	shallot, chopped
2	garlic cloves, smashed and chopped
1	large halibut steak, cut into 2
	pepper
	lemon juice
	Tabasco sauce

Mix butter with parsley; then add shallot and garlic. Using wooden spoon, mix until well blended. Season with pepper, lemon juice and Tabasco sauce. Mix again until thoroughly incorporated.

Butter baking dish with some of garlic butter. Add fish and spread more garlic butter on top. Pepper well.

Place in preheated oven and broil 7 minutes.

Turn fish over, spread with more garlic butter and continue broiling 7 to 8 minutes. Adjust time depending on size.

Serve with potatoes and onions.

1 serving	*413 calories*	*0 g carbohydrate*
38 g protein	*29 g fat*	*0 g fiber*

Golden Sautéed Halibut with Almonds

serves 4

2 tbsp	(*30 ml*) butter
1 tsp	(*5 ml*) oil
2	large halibut steaks, cut into 2 across width
2 tbsp	(*30 ml*) slivered almonds
	flour
	salt and pepper

Place 1 tbsp (*15 ml*) butter and oil in frying pan over medium heat.

Meanwhile, dredge fish in flour and season well. Add to hot pan and cook 3 minutes.

Turn fish over, season and increase heat to medium-high. Cook another 4 minutes or according to size. When bone can be removed easily, fish is done.

Transfer fish to hot serving platter and set aside.

Add remaining butter to still hot frying pan. Sauté almonds 2 minutes over medium-high heat.

Pour almonds and pan juices over fish and serve. Accompany with spinach, if desired.

1 serving *368 calories* *7 g carbohydrate*
40 g protein *20 g fat* *0.4 g fiber*

Pan-Fried Sole and Squash

serves 4

4	large sole filets
2 tbsp	(*30 ml*) butter
1 tbsp	(*15 ml*) oil
1	shallot, chopped
2	yellow summer squash, sliced
	flour
	salt and pepper
	juice 1 lemon

Dredge fish in flour and season with salt and pepper.

Place butter and oil in frying pan over medium-high heat. When hot, add fish and cook 3 minutes.

Turn filets over; continue cooking 3 minutes. Remove fish and set aside.

Quickly add shallot and squash to pan; sprinkle with lemon juice. Sauté 2 minutes and serve at once with fish.

1 serving	*231 calories*	*14 g carbohydrate*
19 g protein	*11 g fat*	*2.8 g fiber*

Breaded Sole Filets Sesame

serves 4

4	sole filets
2 tbsp	(*30 ml*) sesame seeds
1 cup	(*250 ml*) breadcrumbs
2	beaten eggs
1 tbsp	(*15 ml*) vegetable oil
1 tbsp	(*15 ml*) butter
	seasoned flour
	salt and pepper
	lemon slices

Dredge fish in flour. Mix sesame seeds with breadcrumbs and spread on plate.

Dip floured fish in beaten egg and coat with breadcrumbs, pressing lightly with fingertips.

Heat oil and butter in large frying pan. Add fish and cook filets 2 minutes over medium-high heat.

Turn filets over, season and continue cooking 2 to 3 minutes. Adjust time according to size of filets.

Accompany with lemon slices and, if desired, serve with squash.

1 serving	*317 calories*	*26 g carbohydrate*
24 g protein	*13 g fat*	*0.8 g fiber*

Rolled Sole Filets with Light Creamy Sauce

serves 4

4	large sole filets
1	carrot, pared and sliced on angle
12	large fresh mushrooms, cleaned and sliced
1	celery stalk, sliced
1	shallot, sliced
2	fresh lovage leaves
1 cup	*(250 ml)* dry white wine
½ cup	*(125 ml)* water
1 tbsp	*(15 ml)* chopped fresh parsley
2 tbsp	*(30 ml)* butter
2½ tbsp	*(40 ml)* flour
2 tbsp	*(30 ml)* heavy cream (optional)
	salt and pepper

Lay filets flat on cutting board, roll each and secure with toothpicks. Place in skillet.

Add carrot, mushrooms, celery, shallot, fresh lovage, wine, water and parsley; season well. Cover with waxed paper touching surface and bring to boil over medium heat.

As soon as liquid starts to boil, turn fish rolls over. Reduce heat to low, cover with waxed paper and cook 2 to 3 minutes.

Remove fish rolls from pan and set aside.

Continue cooking liquid in pan 5 minutes over high heat, uncovered.

Meanwhile, melt butter in saucepan over low heat. Mix in flour until well incorporated and continue cooking 1 minute.

Gradually incorporate cooking liquid with vegetables while mixing. Cook sauce 2 to 3 minutes over low heat.

Incorporate cream, if desired, and place fish (with toothpicks removed) in sauce. Simmer 2 minutes to reheat sole. Serve.

1 serving	*202 calories*	*10 g carbohydrate*
18 g protein	*10 g fat*	*2.8 g fiber*

Sole Filets with Garlic Butter and Mushrooms

serves 2

2	sole filets
1 tbsp	(*15 ml*) butter
¼ lb	(*125 g*) fresh mushrooms, cleaned and sliced
1 tbsp	(*15 ml*) garlic butter
1 tbsp	(*15 ml*) chopped fresh parsley
	seasoned flour
	salt and pepper

Dredge fish in flour. Melt regular butter in frying pan. Add fish and cook 2 minutes over medium-high heat.

Turn filets over, season and continue cooking 1 to 2 minutes, depending on size. Transfer cooked fish to hot serving platter.

Return frying pan to stove top and add mushrooms and garlic butter. Sprinkle in parsley and cook 3 to 4 minutes over medium-high heat.

Serve mushrooms with fish.

1 serving	*225 calories*	*9 g carbohydrate*
18 g protein	*13 g fat*	*2.0 g fiber*

Pickerel Filets Forestière

serves 4

1 tbsp	(*15 ml*) butter
1 tbsp	(*15 ml*) vegetable oil
4	pickerel filets
1	shallot, chopped
¼ lb	(*125 g*) fresh mushrooms, cleaned and diced
2	cooked potatoes, peeled and diced
1	lemon, peeled, flesh diced
	salt and pepper

Heat butter and oil in large frying pan over medium-high heat. Add fish (skin side down) and cook 2 minutes.

Turn filets over, season and continue cooking 2 minutes; adjust time depending on size. Transfer fish to hot platter; set aside.

Return frying pan to stove top. Add shallot and vegetables; season well. Cook 3 to 4 minutes over medium-high heat.

Stir in diced lemon and cook 1 minute. Spoon over filets and accompany with baby carrots, if desired.

1 serving	*244 calories*	*17 g carbohydrate*
26 g protein	*8 g fat*	*3.2 g fiber*

Turbot with Capers and Mushrooms

serves 2

2	turbot filets
2 tbsp	(*30 ml*) butter
1 tsp	(*5 ml*) oil
1 tbsp	(*15 ml*) capers
1	apple, cored, peeled and sliced
12	large fresh mushrooms, cleaned and sliced
1 tsp	(*5 ml*) chopped fresh parsley
	seasoned flour
	salt and pepper

Dredge fish in flour. Heat butter and oil in frying pan over medium-high heat. Add fish and cook 2 minutes.

Turn filets over, season and continue cooking 2 minutes; adjust time depending on size. Remove fish to hot platter and set aside.

Add capers, apple and mushrooms to frying pan. Sauté 3 minutes over medium-high heat.

Sprinkle with parsley and serve over fish.

1 serving	*340 calories*	*23 g carbohydrate*
26 g protein	*16 g fat*	*5.5 g fiber*

Haddock Sauté with Tomatoes

serves 2

10 oz	(*280 g*) filet haddock, cut into 1-in. (*2.5-cm*) pieces
1 tbsp	(*15 ml*) vegetable oil
2 tbsp	(*30 ml*) chopped onion
1/3 cup	(*75 ml*) sliced celery
1	garlic clove, smashed and chopped
1 cup	(*250 ml*) coarsely chopped tomatoes
1 tsp	(*5 ml*) oregano
	salt and pepper
	seasoned flour

Dredge fish in flour. Heat oil in frying pan over medium-high heat. Add fish, onion, celery and garlic; cook 3 minutes.

Turn pieces of fish over, season and continue cooking 3 to 4 minutes.

Stir in tomatoes and oregano; season. Cook 3 to 4 minutes over medium-low heat.

Serve over pasta.

1 serving *216 calories* *13 g carbohydrate*
23 g protein *8 g fat* *2.6 g fiber*

Perch Filets with Tomato Fondue

serves 2

3 tbsp	(*45 ml*) olive oil
1 tbsp	(*15 ml*) chopped shallot
¼ cup	(*50 ml*) chopped red onion
3	blanched garlic cloves, chopped
1 tbsp	(*15 ml*) chopped fresh lovage
1 tbsp	(*15 ml*) chopped fresh parsley
28 oz	(*796 ml*) can tomatoes, drained and chopped
2 tbsp	(*30 ml*) tomato paste
2 tbsp	(*30 ml*) teriyaki sauce
1 tbsp	(*15 ml*) chopped fresh ginger
2	perch filets
	salt and pepper
	juice ½ lemon

Begin by preparing tomato fondue. Place 1 tbsp (*15 ml*) oil and shallot in skillet. Add red onion, 1 chopped garlic clove, lovage and parsley; cook 4 to 5 minutes over medium heat.

Stir in tomatoes and season well. Bring to boil and continue cooking 10 minutes over medium heat.

Mix in tomato paste, correct seasoning and mix again. Cook another 3 to 4 minutes.

Meanwhile, place teriyaki sauce, lemon juice, remaining garlic and ginger in small bowl. Add remaining olive oil and mix well.

Brush mixture over both sides of filets and place in metal fish grill. Cook fish about 7 minutes, turning fish grill over 2 to 3 times and basting occasionally. You can use any of the following: barbecue preheated at medium-high, preheated oven at broil or preheated stove-top grill.

When fish is done, serve with tomato fondue, which may be reheated slightly if necessary.

1 serving *435 calories* *25 g carbohydrate*
23 g protein *27 g fat* *4.0 g fiber*

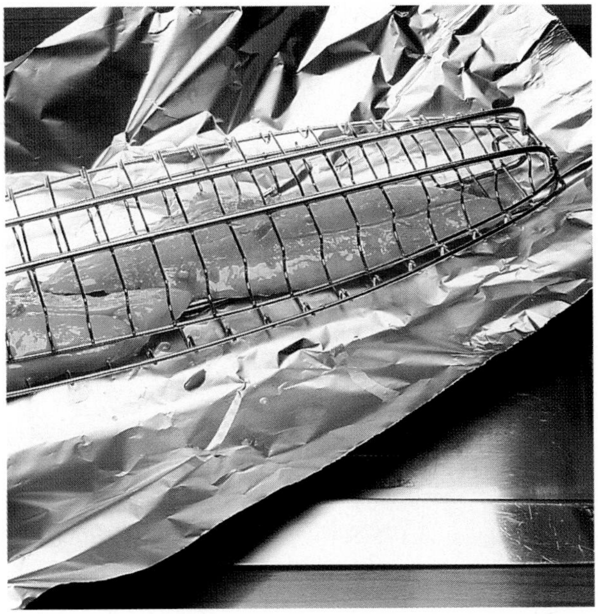

1. A metal fish grill is a worthwhile investment and makes some recipes much easier to prepare. It keeps fish from sticking to the cooking surface.

2. Sauté shallot, red onion, part of garlic, fresh lovage and parsley in oil for 4 to 5 minutes over medium heat.

3. Stir in tomatoes and season well. Bring to boil and continue cooking 10 minutes over medium heat.

4. Mix in tomato paste, correct seasoning and mix again. Cook another 3 to 4 minutes.

Poached Cod in Milk

serves 4

2	12-oz (*340-g*) cod filets, cut into 2
2	shallots, chopped
1 tbsp	(*15 ml*) chopped fresh parsley
4 cups	(*1 L*) hot milk
	salt and pepper

Place fish in buttered baking dish or frying pan. Add shallots and parsley; season well.

Pour in milk and cook over low heat for 4 to 5 minutes. Do not allow liquid to boil.

Turn fish over and continue simmering 4 to 5 minutes, depending on size. Monitor your heat.

Serve with a vegetable.

1 serving 207 calories 0 g carbohydrate
36 g protein 7 g fat 0 g fiber

Cucumber Sautéed Cod Filets

serves 2

1	12-oz (*340-g*) cod filet, cut into 2 pieces
1 tbsp	(*15 ml*) butter
1 tsp	(*5 ml*) vegetable oil
½	cucumber, peeled, seeded and sliced
1	garlic clove, smashed and chopped
1	sprig dill, chopped
	seasoned flour
	salt and pepper
	juice ½ lemon

Dredge fish in flour. Heat butter and oil in large frying pan over medium-high heat. Add cod and cook 3 minutes over medium heat.

Turn fish over; season well. Add cucumber, garlic and dill. Continue cooking 3 minutes; adjust time depending on size.

Remove fish and transfer to hot serving platter. Continue cooking cucumber 2 minutes over high heat.

Sprinkle lemon juice over cucumber and serve with fish.

1 serving	*355 calories*	*17 g carbohydrate*
38 g protein	*15 g fat*	*0.9 g fiber*

Herb-Stuffed Red Snapper

serves 2

1	medium red snapper, cleaned
3	large parsley sprigs
1	green onion, cut into 3
1	sprig tarragon
1 tsp	(*5 ml*) herbes de Provence
	salt and pepper
	oil

Preheat oven to 425 °F (*220 °C*).

Slash outside skin of fish several times and season cavity well.

Place parsley, green onion, tarragon and herbes de Provence inside fish. Set, untied, in oiled roasting pan.

Season outside of fish and brush with oil. Cook in oven 15 minutes or according to size. The fish is cooked when backbone turns white.

Remove from pan, cut off head and tail and filet fish to serve.

1 serving — *196 calories* — *1 g carbohydrate*
30 g protein — *8 g fat* — *0.8 g fiber*

Broiled Snapper and Green Pepper

serves 4

2 tbsp	(*30 ml*) oil
1	garlic clove, smashed and chopped
1 tsp	(*5 ml*) teriyaki sauce
4	red snapper filets, skin side scored
1	green pepper, quartered
	juice ½ lemon
	salt and pepper

Pour oil in bowl. Add lemon juice, garlic, teriyaki sauce and pepper. Mix well.

Brush mixture over both sides of filets and marinate 1 hour.

Place fish and green pepper in baking dish; brush green pepper with leftover marinade. Broil 10 to 12 minutes in preheated oven; adjust time depending on size of filets.

Serve at once.

1 serving	*232 calories*	*2 g carbohydrate*
29 g protein	*12 g fat*	*0.2 g fiber*

Sautéed Red Snapper Filets

serves 2

1	large red snapper filet, cut into 2 pieces
1 tbsp	(*15 ml*) butter
¼ lb	(*125 g*) fresh mushrooms, cleaned and sliced
1	zucchini, sliced
1	small onion, sliced
1	carrot, pared and thinly sliced
1	sprig dill, chopped
	seasoned flour
	salt and pepper
	juice ½ lemon

Score skin side of filets and dredge fish in flour.

Heat butter in frying pan over medium heat. Add fish (skin side down) and season; cook 3 to 4 minutes, partly covered.

Turn fish over and add all vegetables and dill; season well. Continue cooking 3 to 4 minutes.

Turn fish over once more and finish cooking 2 minutes. Transfer fish to hot serving platter.

Cook vegetables another 5 minutes, covered. Sprinkle with lemon juice and serve with red snapper.

1 serving	*380 calories*	*33 g carbohydrate*
35 g protein	*12 g fat*	*6.8 g fiber*

Baked Boston Bluefish

serves 4

1¾ lb	(*800 g*) piece Boston bluefish, boned and butterflied
5	large parsley sprigs
1	green onion, cut in 2 lengthwise
½ tsp	(*2 ml*) herbes de Provence
1	small celery stalk
1 tbsp	(*15 ml*) olive oil
	salt and pepper
	juice 1 lemon

Preheat oven to 425°F (*220°C*).

Oil baking dish and set aside.

With fish opened, place parsley, green onion, herbes de Provence and celery on flesh and season well. Close fish but do not tie.

Place in baking dish and sprinkle fish with oil and lemon juice. Bake 14 minutes in oven. Serve.

1 serving	*234 calories*	*3 g carbohydrate*
33 g protein	*10 g fat*	*0.7 g fiber*

Creamy Salmon Casserole

serves 4

1 tbsp	(*15 ml*) butter
4	small onions, quartered
1 tbsp	(*15 ml*) chopped fresh dill
½ lb	(*250 g*) fresh mushrooms, cleaned and quartered
¼ cup	(*50 ml*) dry white wine
1½ cups	(*375 ml*) white sauce, heated
3 cups	(*750 ml*) leftover cooked salmon, flaked
½ cup	(*125 ml*) grated cheese of your choice
	salt and pepper

Place butter, onions and dill in saucepan. Cook, partly covered, 3 to 4 minutes over low heat.

Add mushrooms and continue cooking 3 to 4 minutes, partly covered, over medium heat.

Pour in wine; cook 2 to 3 minutes, uncovered, over high heat.

Mix in white sauce and cook another 3 to 4 minutes over low heat; season well.

Add salmon, mix and transfer contents to baking dish; sprinkle top with cheese. Broil 4 to 5 minutes in preheated oven until lightly browned and bubbly; then serve.

1 serving	*449 calories*	*17 g carbohydrate*
39 g protein	*25 g fat*	*2.8 g fiber*

1. Place butter, onions and dill in saucepan. Cook, partly covered, 3 to 4 minutes over low heat.

2. Add mushrooms and continue cooking 3 to 4 minutes, partly covered, over medium heat.

3. Increase heat to high and pour in wine; cook 2 to 3 minutes, uncovered.

4. Mix in white sauce and cook another 3 to 4 minutes over low heat; season well.

Dill-Seasoned Salmon Steaks

serves 4

1 tbsp	(*15 ml*) oil
4	salmon steaks, ¾ in. (*2 cm*) thick
1 tbsp	(*15 ml*) butter
2	shallots, finely chopped
1	large sprig dill or fennel, finely chopped
	salt and pepper
	juice ½ lemon

Preheat oven to 400°F (*200°C*).

Heat oil in large frying pan over medium-high heat. When hot, add salmon and cook 2 minutes.

Turn fish over, season well and continue cooking 2 minutes. Transfer pan to oven and finish cooking 12 to 14 minutes. Turn salmon over at halfway point.

Remove fish from pan and keep hot.

Wipe pan clean and add butter. Place on stove top over medium heat. Add shallots and dill and cook about 2 minutes.

Sprinkle in lemon juice and pour sauce over salmon. Serve with potatoes and a fresh green vegetable.

1 serving	*330 calories*	*1 g carbohydrate*
41 g protein	*18 g fat*	*0 g fiber*

Italian Baked Salmon

serves 4

1 tbsp	(*15 ml*) olive oil
4	salmon steaks, ¾ in. (*2 cm*) thick
1	shallot, chopped
1	garlic clove, smashed and chopped
28 oz	(*796 ml*) can tomatoes, drained and chopped
1 tsp	(*5 ml*) oregano
	salt and pepper
	lemon juice

Preheat oven to 400°F (*200°C*).

Heat oil in large frying pan over medium-high heat. Add salmon and cook 2 minutes. Turn fish over, season and continue cooking 2 minutes.

Add shallot and garlic; cook 1 more minute.

Add tomatoes and oregano; correct seasoning. Transfer pan to oven and bake for 12 to 14 minutes. At halfway mark, turn salmon over.

Transfer fish to hot serving platter; set aside.

Return frying pan to stove top over high heat. Sprinkle in lemon juice, cook 1 minute and serve over salmon.

1 serving	*339 calories*	*9 g carbohydrate*
42 g protein	*15 g fat*	*1.7 g fiber*

Salmon Trout Teriyaki

serves 2

2	salmon trout filets
2	green onions, sliced on angle
1 tbsp	(*15 ml*) butter
1 tbsp	(*15 ml*) teriyaki sauce
½ tsp	(*2 ml*) herbes de Provence
	juice 1 lime
	salt and pepper

Place fish in buttered baking dish. Cover with green onions and remaining ingredients.

Broil fish 6 minutes in preheated oven.

Serve with a little tomato fondue,* if desired.

* *See Perch Filets with Tomato Fondue, page 322.*

1 serving	*432 calories*	*5 g carbohydrate*
22 g protein	*36 g fat*	*0.8 g fiber*

Salmon Trout with Mixed Vegetables

serves 2

1	large salmon trout filet
1 tbsp	(*15 ml*) olive oil
1	blanched garlic clove, chopped
1 tsp	(*5 ml*) fennel seeds
1 tsp	(*5 ml*) teriyaki sauce
1 tbsp	(*15 ml*) peanut oil
1	green onion, sliced on angle
½	yellow summer squash, cut into sticks
½	green pepper, cut into sticks
½	zucchini, cut into sticks
8	fresh mushrooms, cleaned and sliced
	juice ½ lime
	few drops Tabasco sauce
	salt and pepper
	juice 1 lemon

Skin fish (if not already done) by slipping knife between flesh and skin. Cut fish into pieces about ½ in. (*1.2 cm*) thick on an angle.

Place pieces in bowl and add olive oil, garlic, fennel seeds, teriyaki sauce, lime juice and Tabasco sauce; season well. Marinate 15 minutes.

Heat peanut oil in frying pan over high heat. Add fish and sauté 3 minutes.

Remove fish and set aside.

Add all vegetables to frying pan, season and cook 4 to 5 minutes over high heat.

Return fish to pan with vegetables; sprinkle with lemon juice. Simmer 1 minute before serving.

1 serving	*569 calories*	*16 g carbohydrate*
25 g protein	*45 g fat*	*5.1 g fiber*

Informal Salmon Stir-Fry

serves 4

4	4½-oz (*130-g*) salmon filets
1 tbsp	(*15 ml*) oil
½ lb	(*250 g*) snow-pea pods, pared
2 cups	(*500 ml*) bean sprouts, washed
1	zucchini, cut into sticks
2 tbsp	(*30 ml*) chopped fresh ginger
	lemon juice
	soy sauce
	salt and pepper

Preheat oven to 400°F (*200°C*).

Place fish on platter and sprinkle with lemon juice and soy sauce; marinate 10 minutes.

Heat oil in large frying pan over medium heat. Add fish and cook 3 minutes. Turn filets over, season and continue cooking 6 to 7 minutes in oven.

Transfer fish to hot serving platter.

Add vegetables and ginger to frying pan; sprinkle with a little more soy sauce. Cook 3 to 4 minutes over high heat.

Season vegetables with pepper only and serve with fish.

1 serving	*359 calories*	*11 g carbohydrate*
45 g protein	*15 g fat*	*5.2 g fiber*

Fresh Salmon Amandine

serves 2

2	salmon steaks, about ½ in. (*1.2 cm*) thick
1 tbsp	(*15 ml*) oil
1 tbsp	(*15 ml*) butter
1 tbsp	(*15 ml*) chopped fresh parsley
1 tbsp	(*15 ml*) slivered almonds
	flour
	salt and pepper
	juice ½ lemon

Preheat oven to 400°F (*200°C*).

Dredge salmon in flour, season and set aside.

Heat oil in frying pan over medium-high heat. Add fish and cook 3 minutes. Turn steaks over, reduce heat to medium and cook another 3 minutes.

Wrap pan handle in foil and transfer to oven; continue cooking 4 to 5 minutes.

Remove fish and transfer to hot serving platter. Set aside.

Add butter, parsley and almonds to frying pan that contained fish; cook 2 minutes over medium heat.

Sprinkle in lemon juice, mix and immediately pour over fish. Serve with spinach.

1 serving	*446 calories*	*12 g carbohydrate*
41 g protein	*26 g fat*	*0.7 g fiber*

Poached Salmon with Egg Sauce

serves 4

WHITE SAUCE: *

3 tbsp	(*45 ml*) butter
3 tbsp	(*45 ml*) flour
2 cups	(*500 ml*) milk
pinch	nutmeg
pinch	cloves
	white pepper

Melt butter in saucepan. When butter starts to bubble, add flour. Mix well, using wooden spoon, and cook 2 minutes over low heat.

Slowly pour in milk while mixing with wooden spoon. Add nutmeg, cloves and pepper. Cook sauce 12 minutes over low heat, stirring 4 times.

POACHED SALMON:

4	salmon steaks, ¾ in. (*2 cm*) thick
2	shallots, sliced
2	sprigs dill
2	small carrots, pared and sliced
2	hard-boiled eggs, chopped
	juice 1 lemon
	salt and pepper

Place salmon in buttered ovenproof baking dish or large frying pan. Add shallots, dill, carrots and lemon juice; season.

Pour in enough cold water to cover fish and bring to boil over medium-high heat. Do not cover dish.

Reduce heat to low and turn fish over; simmer 3 to 4 minutes. When middle bone can be removed easily, fish is cooked.

Carefully remove fish from cooking liquid and transfer to serving plates.

Mix chopped eggs with white sauce and spoon over salmon. Serve.

* *This is a versatile white sauce that can be used in other recipes. For a thinner sauce, simply increase the quantity of milk by 1 cup* (250 ml).

1 serving	*481 calories*	*15 g carbohydrate*
49 g protein	*25 g fat*	*0.8 g fiber*

1. Begin by melting butter in saucepan.

2. When butter starts to bubble, add flour.

3. Cook flour/butter mixture 2 minutes over low heat while mixing with wooden spoon. It is important to cook the flour long enough to eliminate its raw taste.

4. Pour in the milk; when incorporated with the cooked flour, it will begin thickening as it is cooked over low heat.

Broiled Salmon Steaks

serves 2

2	salmon steaks, about ½ in. (*1.2 cm*) thick
2	shallots, chopped
2	slices lemon
2	parsley sprigs
1 tsp	(*5 ml*) olive oil
	few drops lemon juice
	salt and pepper

Preheat oven to 400°F (*200°C*).

Butter small roasting pan. Place salmon steaks in pan and sprinkle with shallots.

Place slice of lemon on each steak and top with remaining ingredients.

Change oven setting to broil and cook 7 minutes or according to size.

Serve with potatoes, if desired.

1 serving	*273 calories*	*0 g carbohydrate*
39 g protein	*13 g fat*	*0.3 g fiber*

Baked Breaded Salmon Filets

serves 4

4	4½-oz (*130-g*) salmon filets, skinned
2	beaten eggs
1 tbsp	(*15 ml*) oil
1 tbsp	(*15 ml*) butter
1	cucumber, peeled, seeded and sliced
½	red pepper, cut into julienne
1	yellow pepper, cut into julienne
	seasoned flour
	seasoned breadcrumbs
	salt and pepper
	grated rind 1 lemon

Preheat oven to 400°F (*200°C*).

Dredge fish in flour, dip in beaten egg and thoroughly coat with breadcrumbs.

Heat oil in large frying pan. Add fish and cook 2 minutes over medium heat. Turn fish over, season and continue cooking 2 minutes.

Transfer to oven and continue cooking fish 10 to 12 minutes.

Before fish is done, place butter and vegetables in saucepan. Add lemon rind, cover and cook 5 minutes.

Season and serve with fish.

1 serving	*424 calories*	*20 g carbohydrate*
41 g protein	*20 g fat*	*1.2 g fiber*

Classic Coquilles Saint-Jacques

serves 4

4 tbsp	(*60 ml*) butter
½ lb	(*250 g*) fresh mushrooms, cleaned and diced large
2	shallots, chopped
1 tbsp	(*15 ml*) chopped fresh parsley
1½ lb	(*750 ml*) scallops
¾ cup	(*175 ml*) dry white wine
1½ cups	(*375 ml*) cold water
¼ tsp	(*1 ml*) fennel seeds
½ tsp	(*2 ml*) herbes de Provence
3 tbsp	(*45 ml*) flour
¼ cup	(*50 ml*) heavy cream
1 cup	(*250 ml*) grated Gruyère cheese
	salt and pepper
	few drops Tabasco sauce
pinch	nutmeg

Place 1 tbsp (*15 ml*) butter, mushrooms, shallots, parsley and scallops in deep skillet. Pour in wine and season; cover with sheet of waxed paper touching surface. Bring to boil over medium heat. Stir and let simmer 2 minutes.

Using slotted spoon, remove scallops and set aside in bowl.

Pour cold water into cooking liquid still in skillet. Add fennel seeds, herbes de Provence and Tasbasco sauce; season well. Cook 5 to 6 minutes over high heat.

Meanwhile, place remaining butter in large saucepan over low heat. When melted, add flour and mix until well incorporated. Cook 2 minutes.

Pour half of cooking liquid from skillet into saucepan containing flour. Mix well.

Pour in remaining cooking liquid and mix well. Incorporate cream and nutmeg; stir and cook sauce 5 to 6 minutes over low heat.

Meanwhile, using slotted spoon, remove scallops from bowl and divide into 4 scallop shells. Pour any juices that have collected in bowl into sauce.

Spoon sauce over scallops in shells (placed on cookie sheet or tray) and top with cheese.

Broil in preheated oven until bubbly. Serve.

1 serving	*615 calories*	*13 g carbohydrate*
53 g protein	*39 g fat*	*1.8 g fiber*

1. Place 1 tbsp (15 ml) butter, mushrooms, shallots, parsley and scallops in deep skillet.

2. Pour in wine and season.

3. Cut out circle of waxed paper and place it on scallops, touching surface. Bring to boil over medium heat.

4. After flour has been cooked, begin adding cooking liquid; it will thicken after simmering over low heat.

Coquilles Saint-Jacques Bretonne

serves 4

3 tbsp	(*45 ml*) butter
2	shallots, chopped
1 cup	(*250 ml*) chopped red onion
3 tbsp	(*45 ml*) chopped fresh parsley
3	blanched garlic cloves, chopped
3 tbsp	(*45 ml*) dry white wine
1½ lb	(*750 g*) scallops, chopped
1 cup	(*250 ml*) dried Italian bread, finely diced
½ tsp	(*2 ml*) tarragon
	salt and pepper

Place 2 tbsp (*30 ml*) butter in skillet. Add shallots, onion, parsley and garlic; cover and cook 10 minutes over low heat.

Pour in wine and cook 3 minutes over high heat.

Stir in scallops and breadcrumbs; add remaining butter. Season and add tarragon. Cook 5 to 6 minutes over medium heat.

Divide mixture into 4 scallop shells set on cookie sheet.

Press mixture lightly with back of a spoon.

Place on middle rack of preheated oven; broil 8 minutes until nicely browned. Serve.

1 serving 308 calories 16 g carbohydrate
34 g protein 12 g fat 0.8 g fiber

1. Place 2 tbsp (30 ml) butter in skillet. Add shallots, onion, parsley and garlic; cover and cook 10 minutes over low heat.

2. After wine has been reduced, add scallops, breadcrumbs and remaining butter. Season and add tarragon.

3. Cook 5 to 6 minutes over medium heat to evaporate liquid and dry out mixture.

4. Divide mixture into 4 scallop shells—use natural shells or dishes, if preferred. Prepare to broil.

Broiled Mussel Coquilles

serves 4

2 tbsp	(*30 ml*) butter
2	blanched garlic cloves, chopped
½ lb	(*250 g*) fresh mushrooms, cleaned and chopped
1	shallot, chopped
1 tbsp	(*15 ml*) chopped fresh parsley
1½ cups	(*375 ml*) cooked chopped mussels
1 cup	(*250 ml*) dried Italian bread, finely diced
1 cup	(*250 ml*) tomato fondue *
	salt and pepper
	fine breadcrumbs
	melted butter

Place butter in skillet. Add garlic, mushrooms, shallot and parsley; season well. Cook 5 minutes over medium heat.

Mix in chopped mussels and diced Italian bread; continue cooking 2 to 3 minutes.

Pour in tomato fondue, mix well, and cook another 2 minutes. Correct seasoning.

Divide mixture into 4 scallop shells and sprinkle with fine breadcrumbs; moisten with a bit of melted butter.

Broil 2 minutes in preheated oven. Serve with fresh sliced bread.

* *See Perch Filets with Tomato Fondue, page 322.*

1 serving	*302 calories*	*21 g carbohydrate*
14 g protein	*18 g fat*	*2.5 g fiber*

Mussels in the Shell with Wine Sauce

serves 4

8½ lb	(*4 kg*) fresh mussels, scrubbed and bearded
2	shallots, finely chopped
2 tbsp	(*30 ml*) chopped fresh parsley
¼ cup	(*50 ml*) dry white wine
1	slice lemon
1 cup	(*250 ml*) light cream, heated
	salt and pepper

Place mussels in large saucepan, being sure to discard any opened shells. Add shallots, parsley, wine and lemon slice. Season with pepper but do not salt.

Cover and cook over medium-high heat until mussels open. Stir once during cooking.

Remove mussels one at a time and transfer to large serving bowl.

Discard lemon slice and return saucepan to stove over high heat; reduce liquid 3 to 4 minutes.

Pour in cream, stir well and cook another 3 to 4 minutes. Correct seasoning and pour sauce over mussels.

1 serving	*385 calories*	*18 g carbohydrate*
49 g protein	*13 g fat*	*0.2 g fiber*

Mussels in Tomato Sauce over Pasta

serves 4

1 tbsp	(*15 ml*) oil
3 tbsp	(*45 ml*) chopped red onion
3	blanched garlic cloves, chopped
2 tbsp	(*30 ml*) chopped fresh parsley
½ tsp	(*2 ml*) tarragon
1½	28-oz (*796-ml*) cans stewed tomatoes, drained and chopped
1	sprig fresh oregano, chopped
3 tbsp	(*45 ml*) tomato paste
2 cups	(*500 ml*) shelled cooked mussels
4	portions cooked pasta, hot
	salt and pepper
pinch	sugar

Place oil, onion, garlic, parsley and tarragon in skillet. Cook 3 minutes over medium heat.

Add tomatoes and fresh oregano; season well. Mix and continue cooking 10 minutes.

Stir in tomato paste and sugar; cook 4 to 5 minutes over low heat.

Mix in mussels and simmer 1 minute over very low heat. Serve at once over hot pasta. If desired, decorate plates with empty mussel shells.

1 serving 387 calories 58 g carbohydrate
23 g protein 7 g fat 3.1 g fiber

1. Cook oil with onion, garlic, parsley and tarragon 3 minutes over medium heat.

2. Add tomatoes and fresh oregano; season well. Mix and continue cooking 10 minutes.

3. Stir in tomato paste and sugar; cook 4 to 5 minutes over low heat.

4. Mix in mussels and simmer 1 minute over very low heat before serving.

Quick Shrimp Sauté with Tomatoes

serves 4

24	medium-large shrimp
1 tbsp	(*15 ml*) vegetable oil
1 tbsp	(*15 ml*) chopped fresh parsley
1 tsp	(*5 ml*) herbes de Provence
2	garlic cloves, smashed and chopped
2	green onions, chopped
¼ cup	(*50 ml*) dry white wine
1½	28-oz (*796-ml*) cans tomatoes, drained and chopped
	salt and pepper
	few drops Tabasco sauce

Peel shrimp, leaving tails intact. Slit backs and remove veins; wash and set aside.

Heat oil in large skillet over high heat. When hot, add shrimp and cook 2 minutes.

Turn shrimp over, season and continue cooking 1 minute.

Add parsley, herbes de Provence, garlic and green onions; cook 2 minutes. Using tongs, remove shrimp and set aside.

With skillet still over high heat, pour in wine and continue cooking 3 minutes.

Mix in tomatoes, season well and sprinkle in Tabasco sauce. Cook 8 to 10 minutes over high heat, stirring several times.

Place shrimp in tomatoes, reheat 1 minute and serve.

1 serving	*266 calories*	*14 g carbohydrate*
39 g protein	*6 g fat*	*3.1 g fiber*

1. Peel shrimp, leaving tails intact. Slit backs using small paring knife and remove veins. Wash shrimp in cold water.

2. Begin sautéing shrimp in hot oil over high heat for 2 minutes. Then turn over, season and cook 1 more minute.

3. Add parsley, herbes de Provence, garlic and green onions; cook 2 minutes.

4. Using tongs, remove shrimp before they become overcooked and set aside.

Pepper Shrimp

serves 4

32	medium-large shrimp
1 tsp	(*5 ml*) herbes de Provence
1 tbsp	(*15 ml*) ground pepper
1 tsp	(*5 ml*) paprika
1 tbsp	(*15 ml*) teriyaki sauce
¼ cup	(*50 ml*) dry white wine
	juice 1 lemon

Without peeling, place shrimp in saucepan. Add herbes de Provence, ground pepper, paprika and lemon juice.

Sprinkle in teriyaki sauce and mix well. Pour in wine, cover and bring to boil over high heat.

As soon as water starts to boil, remove saucepan from heat and drain shrimp. Serve at once (on newspaper if desired) with seafood sauce.

1 serving *230 calories* *4 g carbohydrate*
49 g protein *2 g fat* *0 g fiber*

Broiled Butterflied Shrimp

serves 4

24	large shrimp
1 cup	(*250 ml*) finely chopped cooked red onion
1 tbsp	(*15 ml*) chopped fresh parsley
2	blanched garlic cloves, chopped
3 tbsp	(*45 ml*) soft butter
	few drops Worcestershire sauce
	salt and pepper

Take unpeeled shrimp and cut down along backs to open butterfly-style; remove veins. Arrange on ovenproof platter.

Mix remaining ingredients together in food processor.

Spread mixture over opened shrimp and broil 4 to 5 minutes, depending on size, in preheated oven.

Serve with vegetables.

1 serving	*263 calories*	*4 g carbohydrate*
37 g protein	*11 g fat*	*0.6 g fiber*

Fresh Shrimp with Garlic Purée

serves 4

16–18	garlic cloves, peeled
2 tbsp	(*30 ml*) olive oil
24	medium-large shrimp
3	slices lemon
½ cup	(*125 ml*) dry white wine
1 tsp	(*5 ml*) butter
½ tsp	(*2 ml*) herbes de Provence
1 tsp	(*5 ml*) cornstarch
2 tbsp	(*30 ml*) cold water
½ cup	(*125 ml*) light cream, heated
	few drops lemon juice
	salt and pepper
	few drops hot pepper sauce

Place garlic cloves in small saucepan with enough water to cover. Bring to boil over high heat; continue cooking 8 to 10 minutes over medium heat.

Drain and transfer cloves to mortar; mash with pestle. Transfer purée to fine sieve and force through into bowl. If preferred, use food processor.

Incorporate oil to garlic purée while whisking constantly. Sprinkle with lemon juice, season, mix and set aside.

Place unpeeled shrimp and lemon slices in clean saucepan. Add wine, butter, herbes de Provence and hot pepper sauce. Bring to boil over high heat.

Stir shrimp and continue cooking 1 minute. Remove casserole from stove and let stand several minutes before removing shrimp with tongs.

Leaving saucepan on stove, reduce cooking liquid 2 minutes over high heat.

Mix cornstarch with cold water; stir into liquid. Pour in cream, season and bring to boil. Continue cooking 2 minutes over medium heat.

Peel shrimp, leaving tails intact and serve with sauce. Accompany with garlic purée for dipping.

1 serving	*293 calories*	*7 g carbohydrate*
37 g protein	*13 g fat*	*0 g fiber*

1. Place garlic cloves in small saucepan with enough water to cover. Bring to boil over high heat; continue cooking 8 to 10 minutes over medium heat.

2. Transfer drained cloves to mortar and mash with pestle.

3. Transfer garlic purée to fine sieve and force through into bowl.

4. Cook unpeeled shrimp with lemon slices, wine, butter, herbes de Provence and hot pepper sauce.

King Crab Legs

serves 4

4	large king crab legs
½ cup	(*125 ml*) garlic butter
	breadcrumbs
	pepper

Preheat oven to 400 °F (*200 °C*).

Cut crab legs in half across width; split open lengthwise.

Spread garlic butter over meat and sprinkle with breadcrumbs; place on ovenproof platter. Pepper well.

Change oven setting to broil and place crab legs in oven; broil 5 to 6 minutes.

1 serving	*408 calories*	*9 g carbohydrate*
30 g protein	*28 g fat*	*0.2 g fiber*

GLORIOUS GREENS

The good things of the earth in an explosion of vibrant colors

Mixed Sweet Pepper Salad

serves 4

2 tbsp	(*30 ml*) olive oil
3	slices back bacon, cut into strips
1	small eggplant, peeled and cut into julienne
1	green pepper, cut into julienne
2	red peppers, cut into julienne
2	shallots, chopped
1	garlic clove, smashed and chopped
	salt and pepper
	vinaigrette to taste
	chopped fresh parsley

Heat half of oil in frying pan over high heat. Add bacon and cook 2 to 3 minutes, mixing once during cooking.

Stir in eggplant and cook 4 to 5 minutes over medium heat.

Add remaining vegetables, shallots and garlic; sprinkle in remaining oil. Season, cover and cook 7 to 8 minutes over medium heat. Stir once or twice.

Transfer mixture to serving bowl and toss in vinaigrette to taste. Sprinkle with chopped parsley and other garnishes, if desired, before serving.

1 serving *229 calories* *5 g carbohydrate*
5 g protein *21 g fat* *1.3 g fiber*

Vegetarian Platter

serves 4

4	baking potatoes
2	carrots, pared and sliced on angle
1	zucchini, cut into sticks
½ lb	(*250 g*) green beans, pared
4	onions, cut into 4
1	green pepper, cut into 4
	salt and pepper

Prick potatoes with fork several times and wrap in foil. Bake in preheated oven at 425°F (*220°C*) for 1 hour or until done.

Before potatoes are cooked, place all vegetables in basket of steamer in order in which they are listed. Steam vegetables, removing them as they become cooked, and transfer to bowl of cold water.

When all vegetables are cooked, return to steamer to reheat.

Arrange vegetables and baked potatoes on serving platter and serve with your favorite toppings, such as sour cream, cheese sauce, melted butter, etc.

1 serving *345 calories* *75 g carbohydrate*
9 g protein *1 g fat* *9.4 g fiber*

Caesar Salad Variation

serves 4

2–3	garlic cloves, smashed and chopped
1 tbsp	(*15 ml*) Dijon mustard
1	egg yolk
4–5	anchovy filets, drained and finely chopped
3 tbsp	(*45 ml*) wine vinegar
½ cup	(*125 ml*) olive oil
2	large heads romaine lettuce, washed and dried *
	salt and pepper
	juice 1 lemon
	crumbled cooked bacon
	garlic croutons
	grated Parmesan cheese

Place garlic, mustard and egg yolk in bowl; season well. Add lemon juice, anchovies and vinegar; whisk together.

Incorporate oil in thin stream while whisking constantly. Correct seasoning.

Tear lettuce leaves into small pieces and place in salad bowl. Sprinkle in bacon and croutons. Pour in vinaigrette and toss. Sprinkle with cheese and serve.

* *Washing and drying the lettuce properly is essential. If it is not thoroughly dried, the vinaigrette will not adhere properly and the salad will taste watery.*

1 serving	*408 calories*	*12 g carbohydrate*
9 g protein	*36 g fat*	*1.5 g fiber*

1. Place garlic, mustard and egg yolk in bowl; season well.

2. Add lemon juice, anchovies and vinegar; whisk together.

3. Incorporate oil in thin stream while whisking constantly. Correct seasoning.

4. The vinaigrette should be quite thick.

Julienne Vegetable Salad

serves 4

1	celery stalk
1	large carrot, pared
1	green pepper
1	red pepper
½	zucchini
1	eggplant
1	apple, cored and peeled
1 tbsp	(*15 ml*) chopped fresh parsley
1 tbsp	(*15 ml*) Dijon mustard
1	egg yolk
1 tsp	(*5 ml*) curry powder
3 tbsp	(*45 ml*) wine vinegar
6 tbsp	(*90 ml*) olive oil
	salt and pepper
dash	paprika
	lettuce leaves, washed and dried

Cut all vegetables (leave skin on eggplant) and apple into julienne sticks. It is easier if you square the ends and sides of each vegetable before starting. Try to cut the julienne sticks a uniform size.

Place celery and carrot in salted boiling water. Cover and cook 3 minutes over medium heat.

Add remaining vegetables, season and cover. Continue cooking 2 minutes.

Drain vegetables and rinse under cold water. Drain again and transfer to bowl. Add apple and set aside.

Mix together parsley, mustard, egg yolk, curry powder, paprika, vinegar, salt and pepper in small bowl.

Incorporate oil in thin stream while whisking constantly. If oil is added too quickly, it will be more difficult to incorporate.

Season dressing to taste and pour over salad ingredients. Toss well until evenly coated.

Arrange lettuce leaves on serving platter and add salad. If desired, decorate with hard-boiled egg yolk forced through wire sieve.

1 serving *275 calories* *15 g carbohydrate*
2 g protein *23 g fat* *3.2 g fiber*

Cold Beet Salad

serves 4

6	small fresh beets
1 tbsp	(*15 ml*) chopped fresh parsley
2	shallots, chopped
2	sweet pickled gherkins, chopped
1 tbsp	(*15 ml*) Dijon mustard
2 tbsp	(*30 ml*) wine vinegar
3 tbsp	(*45 ml*) olive oil
	salt and pepper

Cut off tops of beets and discard. Wash beets thoroughly in plenty of cold water, using brush if necessary. Cook in salted boiling water until tender.

When cooked, drain well and set aside until cool enough to handle. Peel and slice beets ¼ in. (*0.65 cm*) thick.

Place slices in bowl. Season, add parsley, shallots and gherkins; set aside.

In smaller bowl, mix together mustard and vinegar. Add olive oil and whisk until incorporated.

Pour vinaigrette over beets, toss and correct seasoning.

Serve on lettuce or spinach leaves.

1 serving	*139 calories*	*9 g carbohydrate*
1 g protein	*11 g fat*	*2.5 g fiber*

The Great Purple Salad

serves 4

6–8	cooked beets, peeled and sliced
2	green onions, sliced
1 tbsp	(*15 ml*) chopped fresh parsley
4	slices corned beef, cut into strips
1 tbsp	(*15 ml*) strong mustard
2 tbsp	(*30 ml*) wine vinegar
3 tbsp	(*45 ml*) olive oil
	salt and pepper
	romaine lettuce leaves, washed and dried

Place beets, onions, parsley and corned beef in bowl. Toss together and season; toss again and set aside.

Place mustard, vinegar, salt and pepper in small bowl; mix together.

Whisk in oil, correct seasoning and pour over salad. Toss until evenly coated.

Decoratively arrange lettuce leaves in glass or attractive serving bowl. Spoon salad on top and serve.

1 serving	*193 calories*	*9 g carbohydrate*
10 g protein	*13 g fat*	*3.5 g fiber*

Jeffrey's Salad

serves 4

½ lb	(*250 g*) green beans, pared and cooked
4	cooked beets, peeled and sliced
2	fresh Italian-type plum tomatoes, sliced
3	anchovy filets, chopped
12	stuffed green olives
2	cooked potatoes, peeled and sliced
2 tbsp	(*30 ml*) capers
1 tbsp	(*15 ml*) Dijon mustard
1 tsp	(*5 ml*) tarragon
1	garlic clove, smashed and chopped
3 tbsp	(*45 ml*) tarragon wine vinegar
½ cup	(*125 ml*) olive oil
1 tbsp	(*15 ml*) lemon juice
2	hard-boiled eggs, sliced
	salt and pepper

Place beans, beets, tomatoes, anchovies, olives, potatoes and capers in large bowl. Toss together and season well.

Place mustard, tarragon, garlic, salt and pepper in small bowl. Add vinegar and whisk together.

Incorporate oil in thin stream while whisking constantly. Add lemon juice and correct seasoning.

Pour dressing over salad and toss. Add eggs, toss again and serve.

1 serving *418 calories* *21 g carbohydrate*
7 g protein *34 g fat* *5.6 g fiber*

Alsatian Salad

serves 4

2	slices ham, ¼ in. (*0.65 cm*) thick, cut into julienne
2	cooked beets, peeled and cut into julienne
2	cooked potatoes, peeled and sliced
1 tbsp	(*15 ml*) chopped fresh parsley
½	red pepper, cut into julienne
2 tbsp	(*30 ml*) mayonnaise
1 tsp	(*5 ml*) olive oil
1	whole chicken breast, cooked, skinned and cut into julienne
	salt and pepper
	juice ½ lemon

Place ham, beets, potatoes, parsley and red pepper in large bowl. Season well and toss together.

Add mayonnaise and sprinkle in lemon juice; mix well.

Sprinkle in olive oil and correct seasoning. Mix again.

Top with chicken and serve.

1 serving *234 calories* *14 g carbohydrate*
22 g protein *10 g fat* *2.1 g fiber*

Cubed Potatoes with Sour Cream

serves 4

2 tbsp	(*30 ml*) melted butter
1	medium onion, finely chopped
4	cooked potatoes, peeled and cubed, still hot
1¼ cups	(*300 ml*) sour cream
	salt and pepper
dash	paprika

Heat butter in large frying pan. Add onion and cover; cook 3 minutes over low heat.

Add potatoes and season. Cook 8 to 10 minutes, uncovered, over medium heat. Stir once or twice.

Add sour cream and gently mix in. Continue cooking 3 minutes over low heat.

Sprinkle with paprika and serve.

1 serving *277 calories* *26 g carbohydrate*
5 g protein *17 g fat* *3.0 g fiber*

Creamy Cucumber Salad

serves 4

1	seedless cucumber, peeled
½	red pepper, sliced
1	small celery stalk, sliced
1	apple, cored, peeled and sliced
½ cup	(*125 ml*) cooked frozen green peas
1 tsp	(*5 ml*) horseradish
3 tbsp	(*45 ml*) sour cream
	salt and pepper
	juice 1 lemon

Cut cucumber into 2 lengthwise and then slice. Place in bowl and season with salt; let stand 15 minutes.

Drain cucumber and transfer to another bowl. Add red pepper, celery, apple and peas.

Sprinkle in lemon juice and season well. Mix in horseradish; then add sour cream and mix until evenly coated.

Correct seasoning. If desired, serve over shredded cabbage and decorate with fresh radishes.

1 serving *86 calories* *15 g carbohydrate*
2 g protein *2 g fat* *3.9 g fiber*

Fresh Tomato Salad

serves 4

4	tomatoes, washed
2	shallots, finely chopped
1 tbsp	(*15 ml*) chopped fresh parsley
2	hard-boiled eggs, chopped
2 tbsp	(*30 ml*) wine vinegar
3 tbsp	(*45 ml*) olive oil
	juice ½ lemon
	salt and pepper

Set tomatoes on cutting board, core side down. Slice in half vertically. Place cut side of tomato on cutting board and slice.

Place slices in bowl with shallots, parsley and eggs.

Sprinkle in vinegar, oil and lemon juice; season generously. Toss, correct seasoning and serve.

1 serving 166 calories 6 g carbohydrate
4 g protein 14 g fat 1.9 g fiber

Pan-Fried Tomato Rounds

serves 4

4	large tomatoes, cored and sliced ¾ in. (*2 cm*) thick
2 tbsp	(*30 ml*) olive oil
3 tbsp	(*45 ml*) soy sauce
2	garlic cloves, smashed and chopped
1 cup	(*250 ml*) flour
3 tbsp	(*45 ml*) melted butter
	salt and pepper
	chopped fresh parsley

Season tomato slices with salt and pepper and place them on large plate.

Mix oil with soy sauce and garlic; pour over tomatoes and let stand 15 minutes.

Turn tomato slices over and let stand another 15 minutes.

Lightly dredge tomato slices in flour. Heat butter in large frying pan and when hot add tomato slices; cook 3 minutes over medium heat.

Turn slices over and continue cooking 3 to 4 minutes or until lightly browned.

Serve sprinkled with fresh parsley.

1 serving	*253 calories*	*21 g carbohydrate*
4 g protein	*17 g fat*	*2.9 g fiber*

Mixed Cucumber Salad

serves 4

1	seedless cucumber, sliced
12	large fresh mushrooms, cleaned
½	red pepper, thinly sliced
1 tbsp	(*15 ml*) chopped fresh parsley
½ cup	(*125 ml*) diced Jarlsberg cheese
¼ cup	(*50 ml*) sliced bamboo shoots
2 tbsp	(*30 ml*) sour cream
1 tbsp	(*15 ml*) olive oil
4 tbsp	(*60 ml*) chopped walnuts
	juice 1 lemon
	paprika to taste
	salt and pepper

Place cucumber in large bowl. Peel off thin skin from mushrooms, starting just beneath the cap, and discard. Slice mushrooms and add to bowl.

Sprinkle in lemon juice. Add red pepper, parsley and paprika; season well.

Add cheese and bamboo shoots; mix well.

Spoon in sour cream and oil; mix well and season to taste.

Sprinkle walnuts over salad and serve.

1 serving	*203 calories*	*10 g carbohydrate*
7 g protein	*15 g fat*	*2.5 g fiber*

Vibrant Rice Salad

serves 4

3	small Italian-type plum tomatoes, cubed
1	yellow banana pepper, seeded and chopped
¼ cup	(*50 ml*) sliced bamboo shoots
1 tsp	(*5 ml*) chopped fresh parsley
2 cups	(*500 ml*) cooked rice
2	hard-boiled eggs, chopped
1 tbsp	(*15 ml*) Dijon mustard
1	garlic clove, smashed and chopped
3 tbsp	(*45 ml*) tarragon wine vinegar
½ cup	(*125 ml*) olive oil
1 tbsp	(*15 ml*) lemon juice
	salt and pepper

Place tomatoes, yellow pepper, bamboo shoots, parsley and rice in bowl; mix well.

Season and add chopped eggs; mix and set aside.

Place mustard and garlic in second bowl; season well. Pour in wine vinegar and whisk well.

Incorporate oil in thin stream while mixing with whisk. Sprinkle in lemon juice, mix well and correct seasoning.

Pour vinaigrette over salad and toss until evenly coated. Serve with fresh lettuce if desired.

1 serving *428 calories* *29 g carbohydrate*
6 g protein *32 g fat* *1.8 g fiber*

Cumin Pasta Salad

serves 4

4 cups	(*1 L*) cooked penne noodles
3	green onions, sliced
1	shallot, chopped
1	carrot, pared and grated
2 tbsp	(*30 ml*) mayonnaise
3 tbsp	(*45 ml*) cottage cheese
1 tsp	(*5 ml*) cumin powder
6	slices crisp-cooked bacon, chopped
1 tsp	(*5 ml*) wine vinegar
	salt and pepper
	juice ½ lemon

Place noodles, green onions, shallot and carrot in large bowl. Season well and mix.

In small bowl, mix together mayonnaise, cottage cheese and cumin powder. Sprinkle in lemon juice and mix again.

Pour dressing over salad, season and mix until completely incorporated.

Add bacon, mix well and sprinkle with vinegar. Mix again and serve.

1 serving	*291 calories*	*38 g carbohydrate*
10 g protein	*11 g fat*	*1.2 g fiber*

Chickpea Salad

serves 4

19 oz	*(540 ml)* can chickpeas, drained
1½ cups	*(375 ml)* cooked cauliflower flowerets
1 tbsp	*(15 ml)* chopped fresh parsley
2 tbsp	*(30 ml)* Dijon mustard
1	shallot, finely chopped
1	garlic clove, smashed and chopped
2 tbsp	*(30 ml)* tarragon wine vinegar
2 tbsp	*(30 ml)* olive oil
	salt and pepper
	lettuce leaves, washed and dried

Place chickpeas, cauliflower, parsley and mustard in bowl; season well.

Add shallot and garlic; mix well. Sprinkle in vinegar and mix again.

Add oil, mix and correct seasoning.

Serve on lettuce leaves.

1 serving *148 calories* *14 g carbohydrate*
5 g protein *8 g fat* *4.2 g fiber*

Mushrooms, Onions and Peas

serves 4

1 tbsp	(*15 ml*) butter
¼ lb	(*125 g*) fresh mushrooms, cleaned and halved
1	onion, cut into 6
¼ tsp	(*1 ml*) tarragon
¼ cup	(*50 ml*) chicken stock, heated
1½ cups	(*375 ml*) cooked frozen green peas
1 tsp	(*5 ml*) cornstarch
2 tbsp	(*30 ml*) cold water
	salt and pepper

Melt butter in deep skillet. Add mushrooms and onion; season well. Cook 3 to 4 minutes over high heat.

Add tarragon and chicken stock; season well and bring to boil. Continue cooking 1 minute.

Stir in peas and cook another minute.

Mix cornstarch with cold water; incorporate into sauce and cook 1 more minute. Serve.

1 serving	*99 calories*	*14 g carbohydrate*
4 g protein	*3 g fat*	*9.0 g fiber*

White Mushrooms

serves 4

2 tbsp	(*30 ml*) butter
1 lb	(*500 g*) fresh mushrooms, cleaned and sliced
1	shallot, finely chopped
1¼ cups	(*300 ml*) white sauce, heated
1 tbsp	(*15 ml*) chopped fresh parsley
	salt and pepper
	few drops lemon juice
dash	paprika

Melt butter in frying pan over medium heat. Add mushrooms and shallot; season well. Cook, partly covered, 8 to 10 minutes.

Pour in white sauce and mix well. Cook 2 to 3 minutes over low heat.

Sprinkle in parsley, lemon juice and paprika; correct seasoning. Mix well and serve at once.

1 serving	*185 calories*	*12 g carbohydrate*
5 g protein	*13 g fat*	*3.3 g fiber*

Mushrooms à l'Orange

serves 4

2 tbsp	(*30 ml*) butter	
1 tbsp	(*15 ml*) olive oil	
1 lb	(*500 g*) large, fresh mushrooms,* cleaned and sliced into 3	
2 tbsp	(*30 ml*) finely chopped orange rind	
1	shallot, finely chopped	
2	garlic cloves, smashed and chopped	
1 tbsp	(*15 ml*) chopped fresh parsley	
1 cup	(*250 ml*) homemade croutons	
	salt and pepper	

Heat butter and oil in frying pan. When hot, add mushrooms and season; cook 2 minutes on each side over high heat.

Stir in orange rind, shallot and garlic. Continue cooking 2 to 3 minutes.

Add parsley and croutons; sprinkle with a little more oil if needed. Cook 2 minutes over high heat and serve at once.

** There are a variety of cultivated mushrooms to choose from. Look for mushrooms that are white and firm. Avoid mushrooms that have caps spreading and starting to separate from the stem—this is an indication of age. Clean mushrooms by brushing with a special brush or rubbing with a clean dish towel or sheet of paper towel.*

1 serving	*162 calories*	*14 g carbohydrate*
4 g protein	*10 g fat*	*3.3 g fiber*

Mixed Vegetables Chinese Style

serves 4

2 tbsp	(*30 ml*) vegetable oil
1	celery stalk, sliced on angle
1	Italian eggplant,* cut into sticks
1	carrot, pared and thinly sliced on angle
½	red pepper, thinly sliced
1	small zucchini, sliced on angle
½	seedless cucumber, sliced on angle
1 cup	(*250 ml*) chicken stock, heated
1 tsp	(*5 ml*) soy sauce
2 tbsp	(*30 ml*) chopped fresh ginger
2 tbsp	(*30 ml*) grated lemon rind
1 tbsp	(*15 ml*) cornstarch
2 tbsp	(*30 ml*) cold water
	salt and pepper

Heat oil in large frying pan over high heat. When very hot, add celery, eggplant and carrot; cook 7 to 8 minutes, mixing occasionally.

Add red pepper, zucchini and cucumber; season well. Continue cooking 5 to 6 minutes over high heat.

Pour in chicken stock and cook 3 to 4 minutes over medium heat.

Mix in soy sauce, ginger and lemon rind; continue cooking 3 to 4 minutes.

Mix cornstarch with cold water; incorporate into sauce and continue cooking 2 minutes.

Serve at once.

* *Italian eggplants are the short purple variety.*

1 serving *115 calories* *11 g carbohydrate*
2 g protein *7 g fat* *3.0 g fiber*

1. Cook celery, eggplant and carrot in hot oil for 7 to 8 minutes. Be sure to mix occasionally.

2. Add red pepper, zucchini and cucumber; season well. Continue cooking 5 to 6 minutes over high heat.

3. Reduce heat to medium and pour in chicken stock; cook 3 to 4 minutes.

4. Mix in soy sauce, ginger and lemon rind; continue cooking 3 to 4 minutes.

Gingered Bok Choy and Greens

serves 4

2	small Italian eggplants, unpeeled
2 tbsp	(*30 ml*) vegetable oil
1	onion, cut into 6
1	bok choy, washed and sliced 1 in. (*2.5 cm*) wide on angle
½	red pepper, sliced
2 tbsp	(*30 ml*) chopped fresh ginger
1½ cups	(*375 ml*) chicken stock, heated
1 tbsp	(*15 ml*) cornstarch
3 tbsp	(*45 ml*) cold water
1 tbsp	(*15 ml*) soy sauce
	salt and pepper

Slice eggplants in half lengthwise; then cut into pieces about 1 in. (*2.5 cm*) long.

Heat oil in large skillet over high heat. Add eggplants and onion; season well. Cook 3 to 4 minutes.

Add bok choy and red pepper; mix well. Sprinkle in ginger and season. Continue cooking 5 to 6 minutes over high heat.

Pour in chicken stock, stir and bring to boil. Correct seasoning.

Mix cornstarch with water; incorporate into sauce. Sprinkle in soy sauce, mix and finish cooking 5 to 6 minutes over low heat.

1 serving *118 calories* *12 g carbohydrate*
4 g protein *6 g fat* *5.9 g fiber*

1. Before beginning the recipe, prepare the ingredients as directed. Be sure to wash the bok choy especially well.

2. Cook eggplants and onion in hot oil for 3 to 4 minutes over high heat.

3. Add remaining vegetables.

4. Add ginger and season well. Continue cooking 5 to 6 minutes, still over high heat.

Brussels Sprouts

serves 4

1½ lb	(*750 g*) Brussels sprouts *
1 tbsp	(*15 ml*) butter
2	slices back bacon, diced
	salt and pepper

Wash Brussels sprouts in plenty of cold water. Using a small knife, trim stems and make an incision in the shape of a cross on the base of each sprout—this will encourage even, rapid cooking.

Place sprouts in salted boiling water and cover. Cook 8 minutes or longer, depending on size. Sprouts should be tender but still a little firm when cooked. They should not be mushy.

When done, place pan under cold running water for several minutes. Drain well.

Heat butter in frying pan. Add bacon and sprouts; cook 3 to 4 minutes over high heat.

Correct seasoning and serve.

* *When choosing fresh Brussels sprouts, look for those with a bright green color and feel for a definite firmness. Avoid discolored sprouts or those with a ragged appearance. Select sprouts of uniform size for ease in cooking.*

1 serving	*137 calories*	*13 g carbohydrate*
10 g protein	*5 g fat*	*5.0 g fiber*

Spinach in White Sauce

serves 4

2	10-oz (*284-g*) bags spinach *
2 cups	(*500 ml*) cold water
1 tbsp	(*15 ml*) butter
1½ cups	(*375 ml*) white sauce, heated
	salt

Fill sink with plenty of cold water and add spinach. Agitate to remove dirt and sand from leaves. Drain and refill; repeat until no trace of grit remains.

Drain spinach well and snip off stems.

Pour cold water into large saucepan and add some salt. Cover and bring to boil.

Add spinach, season with more salt and cover. Cook 3 to 4 minutes over high heat, stirring once during cooking.

Remove spinach from pan and drain well in colander. Press spinach with back of spoon to remove excess water.

Melt butter in large frying pan. Add spinach and cook 1 minute over medium-high heat.

Stir in white sauce and cook 3 minutes. Serve.

* *If available, substitute fresh spinach sold by the bunch. Look for dark green leaves and a very crisp appearance.*

1 serving	*192 calories*	*13 g carbohydrate*
8 g protein	*12 g fat*	*5.5 g fiber*

Baked Leeks with Gruyère

serves 4

½	lemon, cut into 2 pieces
4	leeks
2 tbsp	(*30 ml*) butter
2 tbsp	(*30 ml*) flour
2 cups	(*500 ml*) milk, heated
½ cup	(*125 ml*) grated Gruyère cheese
1 tbsp	(*15 ml*) cornflake crumbs
	salt and white pepper
dash	paprika
pinch	nutmeg

Preheat oven to 400°F (*200°C*).

Fill large saucepan with water and add lemon pieces. Add sprinkling of salt and bring to boil over high heat.

Meanwhile, prepare leeks as directed in the technique.

Add leeks to boiling water, cover and cook 25 to 30 minutes over medium heat. Drain well and set aside.

Melt butter in saucepan. Add flour and mix well; cook 2 minutes over low heat.

Pour in milk and incorporate by mixing well with wooden spoon. Season sauce with salt, pepper, paprika and nutmeg. Cook 8 to 10 minutes over low heat, stirring once or twice during cooking.

Mix in half of cheese and continue cooking 2 to 3 minutes.

Arrange leeks in baking dish. Pour in sauce and top with remaining cheese. Sprinkle with cornflake crumbs and bake 20 minutes.

Serve with a main course.

1 serving	*233 calories*	*19 g carbohydrate*
10 g protein	*13 g fat*	*1.1 g fiber*

1. This picture shows the parts of a fresh leek. Notice that the roots are still intact and that the base (stalk) is white and straight. Begin by rinsing leeks in cold water.

2. Next, cut off and discard the roots and the top green portion of the stalk. (The green leaves can be used for flavoring soups.)

3. Slit the white portion as shown, making sure to leave about ½ in. (1.2 cm) of uncut leek at the base; otherwise it will fall apart. Turn the leek and slit lengthwise once more. This will enable you to wash the leek really well, which is your next step.

4. With all traces of sand and dirt removed, leeks are ready to be cooked. Add them to boiling water with a hint of lemon juice and cook, covered, for 25 to 30 minutes over medium heat.

Broccoli with Old-Fashioned Cheddar Sauce

serves 4

1 tbsp	(*15 ml*) white vinegar
1	head broccoli,* well washed and split from stem into several pieces
2 tbsp	(*30 ml*) butter
2 tbsp	(*30 ml*) flour
2 cups	(*500 ml*) milk, heated
½ cup	(*125 ml*) grated medium-aged Cheddar cheese
	salt and white pepper
dash	paprika
dash	nutmeg

Bring plenty of salted water and vinegar to boil in large saucepan.

Add broccoli, cover and cook 5 minutes over high heat. Depending on size of stalks, time may need adjustment. Cooked broccoli should be tender but still retain a little crispness.

When broccoli is cooked, place saucepan under cold running water to stop cooking process. Drain well and set aside.

Melt butter in small saucepan over low heat. Add flour and mix well; cook 2 minutes.

Pour in milk and incorporate by mixing with wooden spoon. Season sauce with salt, pepper, paprika and nutmeg. Cook 8 to 10 minutes over low heat, stirring several times during cooking.

Stir in cheese and continue cooking 2 to 3 minutes over low heat.

Arrange broccoli on serving platter, top with Cheddar sauce to taste and serve.

* *When choosing a fresh head of broccoli, look for tight green flowerets and sturdy stalks with crisp leaves.*

1 serving *262 calories* *20 g carbohydrate*
14 g protein *14 g fat* *7.3 g fiber*

Sautéed Cauliflower with Croutons

serves 4

¼ cup	(*50 ml*) milk
1	head cauliflower
2 tbsp	(*30 ml*) butter
7–8	fresh mushrooms, cleaned and quartered
1	green onion, sliced
	salt and pepper
	chopped fresh parsley
	homemade croutons

Fill large saucepan with cold water and add sprinkling of salt. Pour in milk and bring to boil.

Meanwhile, cut off most of base from cauliflower and remove tough outer leaves surrounding head. Using small knife, make an incision in the shape of a cross at the base.

Place cauliflower in boiling liquid and cover; cook 8 minutes over medium heat. Depending on size of cauliflower, you may need to adjust time.

When cooked, place saucepan under cold running water for several minutes. Then drain well and set cauliflower on cutting board. Remove the rest of the base and separate into flowerets.

Heat butter in saucepan. Add cauliflower and mushrooms; season well. Cook 3 to 4 minutes over high heat.

Add green onion and chopped parsley to taste; finish cooking 3 to 4 minutes. Serve with croutons.

1 serving	*143 calories*	*15 g carbohydrate*
5 g protein	*7 g fat*	*4.0 g fiber*

Golden Cauliflower

serves 4

¼ cup	(*50 ml*) milk
1	medium head cauliflower
1 tbsp	(*15 ml*) melted butter
1	onion, chopped
1	celery stalk, finely diced
1	garlic clove, smashed and chopped
1 tsp	(*5 ml*) chopped fresh parsley
2 tbsp	(*30 ml*) curry powder
2 cups	(*500 ml*) white sauce, heated
	salt and pepper

Fill large saucepan about ¾ full with hot salted water. Bring to boil.

Meanwhile, prepare cauliflower by cutting off most of base and removing tough outer leaves surrounding head. Using small knife, make an incision in the shape of a cross at the base.

Pour milk into boiling water. When boiling resumes, add cauliflower and cover; cook 10 to 15 minutes, depending on size. Adjust time if needed.

When cooked, drain cauliflower, reserving ½ cup (*125 ml*) of liquid. Set cauliflower aside but keep hot.

Place melted butter in deep skillet over medium heat. When hot, add onion, celery, garlic and parsley; cook 3 to 4 minutes.

Season and add curry powder; mix well and cook 6 to 7 minutes over low heat.

Pour in white sauce and mix very well. Add reserved cooking liquid from cauliflower and season to taste.

Cook sauce 10 minutes over low heat, pour over cauliflower and serve at once.

1 serving	*247 calories*	*20 g carbohydrate*
8 g protein	*15 g fat*	*2.9 g fiber*

1. Cut off most of base and remove tough outer leaves as shown in the background. Make an incision in the shape of a cross at the base. This will promote even, rapid cooking.

2. Cook cauliflower whole in large saucepan containing boiling salted water with milk added. The milk helps the vegetable retain its color.

3. Either after cauliflower is cooked or just before, start preparing curry sauce. Cook onion, celery, garlic and parsley 3 to 4 minutes in hot butter.

4. Add curry powder, mix well, and continue cooking 6 to 7 minutes over low heat.

Spaghetti Squash au Naturel

serves 2

1	spaghetti squash
2 tbsp	(*30 ml*) butter
	freshly ground pepper

Preheat oven to 350°F (*180°C*).

Cut squash in half lengthwise. Remove and discard seeds.

Spread butter over each half and place, flesh side down, on cookie sheet. Bake 1 hour.

Using spoon, loosen flesh into spaghetti-like strands and serve with freshly ground pepper and butter, if desired.

1 serving *217 calories* *23 g carbohydrate*
2 g protein *13 g fat* *4.9 g fiber*

Stuffed Zucchini

serves 4

2	large zucchini
2 tbsp	(*30 ml*) butter
1	onion, chopped
½ lb	(*250 g*) fresh mushrooms, cleaned and finely chopped
2	garlic cloves, smashed and chopped
¼ tsp	(*1 ml*) thyme
½ tsp	(*2 ml*) tarragon
2 tbsp	(*30 ml*) breadcrumbs
	salt and pepper
	melted butter for basting

Preheat oven to 400°F (*200°C*).

Slice each zucchini in half lengthwise. Scoop out most of pulp to make room for stuffing.

Place zucchini in salted boiling water and blanch for 5 to 6 minutes over medium heat. Drain well and set aside.

Heat 2 tbsp (*30 ml*) butter in saucepan. Add onion, mushrooms, garlic and seasonings. Cook 7 to 8 minutes over medium heat.

Stir in breadcrumbs to bind stuffing. Spread mixture into zucchini halves and press stuffed halves together to form whole zucchini again. Tie with kitchen string.

Place stuffed zucchini in baking dish and baste with melted butter. Finish cooking 10 minutes in oven.

Carefully remove string and slice each zucchini into 6 pieces. Serve at once.

1 serving *209 calories* *18 g carbohydrate*
5 g protein *13 g fat* *6.0 g fiber*

Creamy Curried Carrots

serves 4

4	large carrots, pared and thinly sliced
1 tbsp	(*15 ml*) butter
2 tbsp	(*30 ml*) curry powder
½ cup	(*125 ml*) sliced bamboo shoots
1 cup	(*250 ml*) white sauce, heated
pinch	sugar
	salt and pepper

Cook carrots in salted boiling water until tender. Cool under cold running water and drain well.

Heat butter in skillet over medium heat. Add carrots and cook 2 minutes to brown lightly.

Mix in curry powder and continue cooking 2 minutes.

Add bamboo shoots and sugar; cook 3 to 4 minutes over low heat. Season to taste.

Pour in white sauce, stir and simmer 3 to 4 minutes before serving.

Sprinkle with chopped parsley or chives, if desired.

1 serving *181 calories* *21 g carbohydrate*
4 g protein *9 g fat* *1.6 g fiber*

Baked Acorn Squash

serves 4

2	acorn squash, halved
4 tsp	(*20 ml*) butter
1 tbsp	(*15 ml*) brown sugar

Preheat oven to 350°F (*180°C*).

Place squash in roasting pan and drop 1 tsp (*5 ml*) butter in each cavity. Cover with foil and bake 1 hour.

Remove squash from oven and sprinkle with brown sugar. Broil 5 minutes; then serve at once.

1 serving *120 calories* *18 g carbohydrate*
3 g protein *4 g fat* *2.5 g fiber*

Ratatouille Parmesan

serves 4

4 tbsp	(*60 ml*) olive oil
1	large eggplant, cubed with skin
1	onion, finely chopped
2	garlic cloves, smashed and chopped
1 tbsp	(*15 ml*) chopped fresh parsley
½ tsp	(*2 ml*) oregano
¼ tsp	(*1 ml*) thyme
½ tsp	(*2 ml*) basil
¼ tsp	(*1 ml*) crushed chillies
1	zucchini, halved lengthwise and thinly sliced
4	fresh Italian-type plum tomatoes, diced
¼ cup	(*50 ml*) grated Parmesan cheese
	salt and pepper
dash	paprika

Heat 3 tbsp (*45 ml*) of oil in large, deep skillet. When very hot, add eggplant and season well. Cover and cook 15 to 20 minutes over medium-low heat, stirring 2 to 3 times during cooking.

Add onion, garlic and parsley; mix well and correct seasoning. Cover and continue cooking 7 to 8 minutes.

Add seasonings, zucchini, tomatoes and remaining 1 tbsp (*15 ml*) of oil. Mix, cover and cook 35 minutes over medium-low heat.

Add cheese, mix, and finish cooking 7 to 8 minutes, uncovered.

Serve with main course.

1 serving	*220 calories*	*14 g carbohydrate*
5 g protein	*16 g fat*	*5.1 g fiber*

1. Cook eggplant in hot oil for 15 to 20 minutes over medium-low heat. Be sure pan is covered and stir several times during cooking.

2. Add onion, garlic and parsley; mix well and correct seasoning. Cover and continue cooking 7 to 8 minutes.

3. Add seasonings, zucchini, tomatoes and remaining oil. Mix, cover and cook 35 minutes.

4. Mix in cheese and finish cooking 7 to 8 minutes, uncovered.

Helen's Vegetables au Jus

serves 4

5 cups	(*1.2 L*) homemade beef stock
2	potatoes, peeled and halved
4	carrots, pared and cut into 2
½	turnip, peeled and cut into 4
½	head cabbage, cut into 4
3	celery stalks, cut into 2
	salt and pepper
	oil and vinegar to taste
	chopped parsley to taste

Bring beef stock to boil in large saucepan. Add all vegetables and cook over medium heat; season to taste.

Monitor each vegetable—when cooked, remove from beef stock and set aside. Be careful not to overcook.

When all vegetables are done, return to saucepan with beef stock and reheat 2 minutes.

Serve vegetables moistened with a bit of cooking liquid. Add oil and vinegar to taste and garnish with chopped parsley.

1 serving	*236 calories*	*28 g carbohydrate*
4 g protein	*12 g fat*	*4.9 g fiber*

Potato Carrot Purée

serves 4

4	pared carrots, cooked and still hot
4	potatoes, cooked in skins, peeled and still hot
1 tbsp	(*15 ml*) garden mint sauce (commercial)
¼ cup	(*50 ml*) milk, heated
1 tbsp	(*15 ml*) butter
	salt and pepper

Purée cooked vegetables through food mill or potato ricer into bowl.

Add mint sauce and incorporate with wooden spoon.

Pour in milk and mix well. Add butter, season and mix again.

Serve.

1 serving 180 calories 32 g carbohydrate
4 g protein 4 g fat 3.1 g fiber

Castle Potatoes

serves 4

5	potatoes, peeled and washed
3 tbsp	(*45 ml*) butter
2	egg yolks
4 tbsp	(*60 ml*) heavy cream
	salt and pepper
dash	paprika

Cook potatoes in plenty of salted boiling water until done. Drain well and let stand 5 minutes in saucepan to dry.

Purée potatoes using food mill or potato ricer.

Add butter and season; mix thoroughly with wooden spoon.

Incorporate egg yolks; then stir in cream. Add paprika and mix until well combined.

Preheat oven to 400°F (*200°C*).

Spoon potatoes into pastry bag fitted with large star nozzle. Squeeze out mounds of potato on cookie sheet.

Cook 10 to 12 minutes in oven or until lightly browned.

Serve at once with meat or poultry.

1 serving	*277 calories*	*26 g carbohydrate*
5 g protein	*17 g fat*	*3.0 g fiber*

1. Force cooked potatoes through food mill or potato ricer to purée them. If you mash by hand it is very difficult to remove all the lumps.

2. After butter, salt and pepper have been incorporated, add egg yolks and continue mixing with wooden spoon.

3. Add cream and paprika and mix until well combined.

4. Using a pastry bag, squeeze out mounds of potato.

Baked Cabbage with Onions

serves 6

1	cabbage, cut into 4
3 tbsp	(*45 ml*) butter
4	onions, thinly sliced
2 cups	(*500 ml*) sour cream
¼ cup	(*50 ml*) breadcrumbs
2 tbsp	(*30 ml*) melted butter
	salt and pepper
dash	paprika

Place cleaned cabbage in large saucepan containing plenty of boiling salted water. Cover and cook 18 minutes over medium heat. Drain cabbage well and set aside.

Preheat oven to 350°F (*180°C*).

Heat 3 tbsp (*45 ml*) butter in large, deep skillet. When hot, add onions and season; cook 15 to 18 minutes over low heat. Stir several times during cooking.

Add cabbage to skillet and mix in sour cream. Correct seasoning and cover; bake 30 minutes in oven.

Remove cover and sprinkle top with breadcrumbs and melted butter. Change oven setting to broil and brown for 4 minutes.

Serve sprinkled with a dash of paprika.

1 serving	*486 calories*	*34 g carbohydrate*
11 g protein	*34 g fat*	*6.0 g fiber*

Quick Potato Sauté

serves 4

2 tbsp	(*30 ml*) olive oil
1	large onion, thinly sliced
4	large potatoes, cooked in skins
1 tbsp	(*15 ml*) butter
¼ tsp	(*1 ml*) savory
	salt and pepper
	chopped fresh parsley

Heat oil in large skillet over medium heat. Add onion and cover; cook 4 minutes.

Peel potatoes and cut in slices ½ in. (*1.2 cm*) thick. Add to pan with butter and savory; season well.

Cook potatoes 15 minutes over medium-high heat, stirring as needed.

Sprinkle with parsley and serve.

1 serving	*194 calories*	*23 g carbohydrate*
3 g protein	*10 g fat*	*3.0 g fiber*

Ultimate Baked Potatoes

serves 4

4 medium-size baking potatoes scrubbed "ultimate" garnish ideas:

- sour cream and chives
- sour cream and pimento
- strips of back bacon and chopped green onions
- sautéed mushrooms and shallots
- melted butter and crisp crumbled bacon
- grated Parmesan cheese and paprika

Preheat oven to 400°F (*200°C*).

Prick potatoes 2 to 3 times with a wooden skewer to allow steam to escape during cooking. Wrap in foil, prick again and place on oven rack. Bake about 1 hour depending on size.

Just before potatoes are cooked, have ready your choise of "ultimate" garnish.

Remove cooked potatoes, discard foil and slit top in a cross about ¾ in. (*2 cm*) deep. Press sides to open and generously top with garnish.

Serve at once.

1 serving *(with sour cream)* *246 calories* *52 g carbohydrate* *5 g protein* *2 g fat* *3.1 g fiber*

1. If you enjoy eating the skin, remember to wash potatoes well and scrub if necessary. Prick potatoes 2 to 3 times with a wooden skewer to allow steam to escape during cooking.

2. Wrap potatoes in foil. You can purchase potatoes already wrapped in foil, but it is difficult to determine their quality. Remember to prick several times through foil.

3. After potatoes are baked, slit top in a cross about ¾ in. (2 cm) deep.

4. Press sides to open. Remember to discard foil for the final presentation.

Potatoes Provençale

serves 4

4	large potatoes, cooked in skins and still hot
4 tbsp	(*60 ml*) butter
3 tbsp	(*45 ml*) grated Parmesan cheese
1 tsp	(*5 ml*) chervil
1 tbsp	(*15 ml*) heavy cream
	salt and pepper

Peel and cube potatoes. Force through food mill or potato ricer and purée.

Add 3 tbsp (*45 ml*) butter and potatoes and season well. Mix in cheese and then chervil.

Incorporate cream and shape mixture into patties.

Heat remaining butter in large frying pan. Cook potato patties 6 to 7 minutes on each side over medium heat. Season once during cooking. When the first side is well browned, turn patties over.

Serve at once.

1 serving *231 calories* *20 g carbohydrate*
4 g protein *15 g fat* *2.4 g fiber*

French-Fried Potatoes

serves 4

4 large potatoes
salt
peanut oil for frying

Preheat plenty of peanut oil in electric deep-fryer set at 350°F (*180°C*).

Peel potatoes and square ends and sides. Slice potatoes lengthwise into pieces about ¼ in. (*0.65 cm*) thick. Cut into uniform sticks.

Place potato sticks in large bowl and place under cold running water for 2 minutes. Stir potatoes several times to help remove starch.

Drain well and pat dry with a clean dish towel.

Place potato sticks in deep-fryer basket and cook in hot oil for 6 minutes.

Remove basket and set fries aside. Reheat oil to 375°F (*190°C*).

When ready, return fries to hot oil and continue cooking until gloden brown.

Remove from deep-fryer and drain on paper towels. Sprinkle with salt to taste and serve.

1 serving *211 calories* *25 g carbohydrate*
3 g protein *11 g fat* *3.0 g fiber*

Potato Croquettes

serves 4

4	large potatoes, cooked in skins
2 tbsp	(*30 ml*) butter
1	egg yolk
1	egg
¼ tsp	(*1 ml*) nutmeg
½ tsp	(*2 ml*) tarragon
3	beaten eggs
1 cup	(*250 ml*) breadcrumbs
	salt and pepper
	peanut oil for frying

Peel and cube potatoes. Force through food mill or potato ricer and purée.

Add butter to potatoes and season well. Mix to incorporate.

Add egg yolk and 1 whole egg; mix well with wooden spoon. Add nutmeg and tarragon; mix again.

Spread potato mixture flat on dinner plate. Cover with plastic wrap and refrigerate 3 hours.

Preheat plenty of peanut oil in electric deep-fryer set at 375°F (*190°C*).

Shape potato mixture into croquettes (cylindrical-shaped rolls). Dip in beaten egg to coat completely and roll in breadcrumbs.

Deep-fry 3 to 4 minutes.

1 serving *565 calories* *45 g carbohydrate*
13 g protein *37 g fat* *3.5 g fiber*

FOOD FROM OUR NEIGHBORS

Delightful dishes
from
many cultures

French Potato Salad à la Poire (*French*)

serves 4

3	large potatoes, cooked in skins and still hot
8	slices salami, cut into julienne
2	shallots, chopped
2 tbsp	(*30 ml*) chopped fresh parsley
1 tbsp	(*15 ml*) chopped fresh chives
1 tbsp	(*15 ml*) Dijon mustard
3 tbsp	(*45 ml*) wine vinegar
5 tbsp	(*75 ml*) olive oil
3	endives, leaves well cleaned, sliced into 1-in. (*2.5-cm*) pieces
½	pear, peeled and sliced
1 tbsp	(*15 ml*) wine vinegar
2 tbsp	(*30 ml*) olive oil
	salt and pepper
	lemon juice
	romaine lettuce leaves

Cut peeled potatoes into large cubes and place in bowl. Add salami, shallots, parsley and chives; season well.

Place mustard in smaller bowl and season well. Pour in 3 tbsp (*45 ml*) vinegar and 5 tbsp (*75 ml*) oil; whisk together until smooth. Add lemon juice to taste, mix and correct seasoning.

Pour dressing over potatoes in bowl and gently toss to coat evenly. Spoon onto platter and set aside.

Place endives and sliced pear in bowl. Season and sprinkle with a bit of lemon juice. Sprinkle with remaining vinegar and oil; mix well.

Serve endive mixture with potatoes and decorate platter with lettuce leaves.

1 serving	*429 calories*	*25 g carbohydrate*
8 g protein	*33 g fat*	*3.3 g fiber*

Tomato and Feta Plate (*Greek*)

serves 4

2		large ripe tomatoes
¼ lb	(*125 g*)	feta cheese, sliced
¼ cup	(*50 ml*)	chopped feta cheese
1		sprig lovage, coarsely chopped
3 tbsp	(*45 ml*)	wine vinegar
5 tbsp	(*75 ml*)	olive oil
		washed and dried romaine lettuce leaves
		salt and pepper
		juice ¼ lemon

Core tomatoes, cut in half and slice. Arrange lettuce leaves on platter and alternate tomato with slices of feta cheese. Set aside.

Place chopped cheese in bowl and pepper well. Add lovage and vinegar; mix well.

Add oil and lemon juice; mix very well with whisk. Correct seasoning.

Pour dressing over platter and serve.

1 serving	*294 calories*	*8 g carbohydrate*
7 g protein	*26 g fat*	*2.0 g fiber*

Italian Salad (*Italian*)

serves 4

2	tomatoes, cored, halved and sliced
20	pitted black olives
6	stuffed green olives
1	yellow pepper, thinly sliced
1	head romaine lettuce, well washed, dried and in bite-size pieces
½	head cooked broccoli, in flowerets
¼ lb	(*125 g*) cooked green beans
2 tbsp	(*30 ml*) grated Parmesan cheese
1 tbsp	(*15 ml*) Dijon mustard
3 tbsp	(*45 ml*) wine vinegar
7 tbsp	(*105 ml*) olive oil
1 tbsp	(*15 ml*) chopped fresh parsley
½ tsp	(*2 ml*) chopped fresh basil
4	hard-boiled eggs, chopped
	few drops lemon juice
	salt and pepper

Place tomatoes, both types of olives, yellow pepper, lettuce, broccoli and beans in large salad bowl. Set aside.

In smaller bowl place cheese and mustard. Add vinegar and whisk together.

Incorporate oil in thin stream while whisking constantly. Sprinkle in parsley and basil; whisk very well. Add lemon juice and season.

Mix in chopped eggs and pour dressing over salad. Toss until evenly coated and serve. If desired, decorate portions with sliced hard-boiled eggs.

1 serving	*493 calories*	*11 g carbohydrate*
11 g protein	*45 g fat*	*7.8 g fiber*

1. Place cheese and mustard in small bowl.

2. Add vinegar and whisk together.

3. Incorporate oil in thin stream while whisking; then sprinkle in parsley and basil. Whisk very well. Add lemon juice and season.

4. Mix in chopped eggs and prepare to pour over salad.

Gena's Cold Lamb Salad Plate (*Greek*)

serves 4

2 cups	(*500 ml*) leftover cooked sliced lamb
½	yellow pepper, thinly sliced
½	red pepper, thinly sliced
½	green pepper, thinly sliced
½ cup	(*125 ml*) pitted black olives
½	head broccoli, in flowerets, blanched
6	fresh mint leaves, chopped
1	large potato, cooked in skin, peeled and sliced
2 tbsp	(*30 ml*) red wine vinegar
3 tbsp	(*45 ml*) olive oil
½ cup	(*125 ml*) chopped feta cheese
	salt and pepper
	few drops lemon juice

Place lamb in large bowl with peppers and olives; toss and season well. Add broccoli, mint and potato; toss again.

Pepper well and sprinkle with vinegar and oil. Add cheese, toss again and correct seasoning.

Sprinkle with lemon juice and serve on large platter decorated with lettuce leaves and extra slices of cheese, if desired.

1 serving	*407 calories*	*14 g carbohydrate*
27 g protein	*27 g fat*	*6.3 g fiber*

Eggplant Spread (*Greek*)

serves 4–6

2 large eggplants
1 tbsp (*15 ml*) chopped fresh oregano
3 blanched garlic cloves, smashed
4–5 tbsp (*60–75 ml*) olive oil
salt and pepper
assorted crackers and toasted rounds of bread

Preheat oven to 425 °F (*220 °C*).

Score eggplants 3 to 4 times with small knife. Place whole in roasting pan and cook 45 minutes in oven.

Remove eggplants from oven, peel and chop flesh. Place in bowl.

Add oregano and garlic; mix well and season. Incorporate olive oil, whisking constantly.

Serve on crackers and toast.

1 serving	*190 calories*	*21 g carbohydrate*
4 g protein	*10 g fat*	*2.7 g fiber*

Croque-Monsieur aux Oeufs Sauerkraut (*French*)

serves 4

1 tbsp (*15 ml*) olive oil
½ onion, chopped
1 garlic clove, smashed and chopped
2 cups (*500 ml*) sauerkraut, well rinsed
8 thick slices French bread
12 slices Black Forest ham
1½ cups (*375 ml*) grated Swiss cheese
¼ cup (*50 ml*) water
4 beaten eggs
2 tbsp (*30 ml*) butter
extra butter
pepper

Heat oil in skillet. Add onion and garlic; cook 5 to 6 minutes over medium-low heat.

Add sauerkraut, mix and cover; continue cooking 15 to 20 minutes, stirring occasionally.

Meanwhile, spread extra butter over slices of bread. Make 4 sandwiches each containing 3 slices of ham and grated cheese.

Mix water into beaten eggs and pepper well.

Heat butter in large frying pan. Dip sandwiches one at a time in beaten egg mixture to coat well; then place in hot butter.

Cook sandwiches 3 minutes each side over medium heat. Outsides should be nicely browned and cheese inside should be soft if not melted.

Cut sandwiches in half and serve with sauerkraut. A delicious treat before or after an evening show!

1 serving	*578 calories*	*33 g carbohydrate*
35 g protein	*34 g fat*	*2.8 g fiber*

Chunky Avocado Vegetable Dip (*Mexican*)

serves 4

1	cucumber, peeled, seeded and diced small
1	large tmato, skinned, seeded and diced
2	green onions, chopped
½ cup	(*125 ml*) canned refried beans
¼ cup	(*50 ml*) chicken stock
½ tsp	(*2 ml*) Maggi seasoning
1 tbsp	(*15 ml*) chopped seeded jalapeño pepper
1	ripe avocado, peeled and flesh puréed
1 tsp	(*5 ml*) olive oil
	salt and pepper
	juice 1 lemon
	lettuce leaves for decoration

Place cucumber, tomato and green onions in bowl; season well. Set aside.

Heat refried beans with chicken stock in small saucepan. Add to vegetables in bowl and mix well.

Add Maggi seasoning and jalapeño pepper. Mix in avocado and lemon juice until well incorporated.

Sprinkle with olive oil and chill dip 20 minutes.

Serve on bed of lettuce with a variety of dipping chips (nachos) and crackers.

1 serving	*118 calories*	*14 g carbohydrate*
2 g protein	*6 g fat*	*3.6 g fiber*

Avocado Soup (*Mexican*)

serves 4

1	ripe avocado
½ cup	(*125 ml*) whipped cream
2 cups	(*500 ml*) chicken stock
½ tsp	(*2 ml*) Maggi seasoning
	juice ½ lemon
	salt and pepper
	sour cream
	chopped fresh chives
	paprika

Peel avocado and cut flesh into small pieces. Purée in food processor.

Transfer avocado to bowl and whisk in whipped cream. Pour in chicken stock while mixing.

Sprinkle in lemon juice and Maggi seasoning; add salt and pepper to taste.

Chill soup 1 hour.

To serve, garnish portions with dollop of sour cream and sprinkle with chives and paprika.

1 serving 153 calories 7 g carbohydrate
2 g protein 13 g fat 1.2 g fiber

Eggplant with Lima Beans (*Mexican*)

serves 4

1	eggplant, skin pierced
1 tbsp	(*15 ml*) oil
1	onion, chopped
2 tbsp	(*30 ml*) sliced jalapeño pepper
1	garlic clove, smashed and chopped
1	tomato, peeled and chopped
14 oz	(*398 ml*) can lima beans, drained
	salt and pepper

Preheat oven to 400°F (*200°C*).

Place pierced eggplant whole in roasting pan. Bake 45 minutes.

Remove from oven and cube eggplant with skin. Heat oil in large skillet over high heat. Add eggplant, onion, jalapeño pepper and garlic; cook 3 to 4 minutes.

Mix well and add tomato; season. Continue cooking 4 to 5 minutes.

Add lima beans, mix well and correct seasoning. Cook 3 to 4 minutes and serve.

1 serving	*144 calories*	*22 g carbohydrate*
5 g protein	*4 g fat*	*4.5 g fiber*

Mexican Shrimp Dish (*Mexican*)

serves 4

1½ lb	(*750 g*) jumbo shrimp
1 tbsp	(*15 ml*) oil
1	red pepper, cut into large strips
2	green onions, sliced
1 tsp	(*5 ml*) chopped jalapeño pepper
1 cup	(*250 ml*) Mexican piquant sauce
½ cup	(*125 ml*) canned refried beans
½ cup	(*125 ml*) chicken stock, heated
	salt and pepper

Shell shrimp, wash and devein.

Heat oil in large skillet over medium-high heat. Add shrimp and cook 2 minutes.

Add red pepper, green onions and jalapeño pepper; continue cooking 2 to 3 minutes. Correct seasoning.

Remove shrimp and set aside.

Add piquant sauce and refried beans to skillet; mix well and pour in chicken stock. Cook 4 to 5 minutes.

Return shrimp to skillet and simmer 1 minute to reheat.

1 serving	*198 calories*	*13 g carbohydrate*
23 g protein	*6 g fat*	*1.6 g fiber*

1. Add shrimp to hot oil in skillet and cook 2 minutes over medium-high heat.

2. Add red pepper, green onions and chopped jalapeño pepper; continue cooking 2 to 3 minutes. Correct seasoning.

3. Remove shrimp; add piquant sauce to vegetables.

4. Add refried beans and pour in chicken stock. Cook 4 to 5 minutes.

Minced Meat Picadillo (*Mexican*)

serves 4

1 tbsp	(*15 ml*) oil
½ lb	(*250 g*) lean ground beef
1	small onion, chopped
1	green onion, chopped
2	garlic cloves, smashed and chopped
½ cup	(*125 ml*) chopped stuffed green olives
1	small marinated green pepper, seeded and chopped
1 tbsp	(*15 ml*) chopped fresh chives
2 tbsp	(*30 ml*) canned refried beans
½ cup	(*125 ml*) Mexican piquant sauce
½ cup	(*125 ml*) taco sauce
4	tostada shells
1 cup	(*250 ml*) grated Cheddar cheese
	salt and pepper

Heat oil in large frying pan over high heat. Add beef and season; cook 3 to 4 minutes, stirring several times.

Add both types of onions, garlic, olives, green pepper and chives; mix well. Correct seasoning and continue cooking 3 to 4 minutes.

Mix in refried beans and cook another 2 minutes.

Incorporate piquant and taco sauces; let simmer 5 minutes over low heat.

Arrange tostada shells on large ovenproof platter. Spoon meat mixture on each and top with cheese.

Broil until cheese is melted.

1 serving *434 calories* *25 g carbohydrate*
25 g protein *26 g fat* *3.7 g fiber*

Chicken Pepper Tacos (*Mexican*)

serves 4

1 tbsp	(*15 ml*) oil
½	green pepper, cut into julienne
½	red pepper, cut into julienne
½	onion, sliced
2	green onions, chopped
½	zucchini, cut into julienne
2	whole chicken breasts, skinned, boned and cut into strips
3 tbsp	(*45 ml*) canned refried beans
¼ cup	(*50 ml*) chicken stock
2 tbsp	(*30 ml*) taco sauce
4	taco shells
	salt and pepper

Heat oil in large skillet over high heat. Add peppers, both types of onions and zucchini; mix well and season. Cook 4 minutes over medium-high heat.

Add chicken strips to pan, season and continue cooking 7 to 8 minutes. Stir once.

Mix in refried beans, chicken stock and taco sauce; correct seasoning. Cook 2 more minutes; then fill taco shells. Serve at once.

1 serving	*268 calories*	*19 g carbohydrate*
30 g protein	*8 g fat*	*2.1 g fiber*

Chicken Burrito Dinner (*Mexican*)

serves 4

1 tbsp	(*15 ml*) oil
2	whole chicken breasts, skinned, boned and cut into thin strips
1	yellow pepper, cut into julienne
½ cup	(*125 ml*) stuffed green olives, finely chopped
1	large tomato, peeled, seeded and chopped
1	marinated hot green pepper, chopped
¾ cup	(*175 ml*) taco sauce
½ cup	(*125 ml*) canned refried beans
4	soft tortillas
	paprika
	salt and pepper

Heat oil in large skillet over medium-high heat. Add chicken strips and cook 2 to 3 minutes.

Add yellow pepper and olives; season with paprika. Continue cooking 3 to 4 minutes.

Season well and add tomato and marinated chopped pepper; mix well.

Add taco sauce, mix and add refried beans; correct seasoning. Cook 3 to 4 minutes over low heat; serve in tortillas.

1 serving 329 calories 22 g carbohydrate
31 g protein 13 g fat 4.3 g fiber

1. Cook chicken strips in hot oil for 2 to 3 minutes over medium-high heat. Add yellow pepper and olives; season with paprika. Continue cooking 3 to 4 minutes.

2. Season well and add tomato and marinated chopped pepper; mix well.

3. Add taco sauce and mix.

4. Add refried beans, correct seasoning and cook 3 to 4 minutes over low heat.

Green Rice (*Mexican*)

serves 4

1 tbsp	(*15 ml*) vegetable oil
3	green onions, sliced
1	large green pepper, chopped
1 tbsp	(*15 ml*) chopped jalapeño pepper
2	garlic cloves, smashed and chopped
½ cup	(*125 ml*) chopped pitted olives
2 cups	(*500 ml*) cooked white rice, hot
1 tbsp	(*15 ml*) olive oil
1 tbsp	(*15 ml*) chopped fresh parsley
	salt and pepper

Heat vegetable oil in saucepan over medium heat. Add green onions, green and jalapeño peppers, garlic and olives; season well. Cook 4 to 5 minutes.

Transfer contents to food processor; blend until puréed.

Mix green purée with hot rice; season with olive oil and parsley. Correct seasoning, mix again and serve.

1 serving 238 calories 29 g carbohydrate
3 g protein 12 g fat 3.4 g fiber

Pork and Vegetable Strips in Bean Sauce (*Oriental*)

serves 4

1 tbsp	(*15 ml*) oil
2	butterflied pork chops, trimmed of fat and cut into strips
1 tbsp	(*15 ml*) chopped fresh ginger
2	garlic cloves, smashed and chopped
2 tbsp	(*30 ml*) soy sauce
1	red pepper, thinly sliced
1½	yellow peppers, thinly sliced
1	zucchini, thinly sliced
1 cup	(*250 ml*) seedless green grapes
1 cup	(*250 ml*) chicken stock, heated
4 tbsp	(*60 ml*) Chinese bean sauce
1 tbsp	(*15 ml*) cornstarch
3 tbsp	(*45 ml*) cold water
	pepper

Heat oil in wok or skillet over high heat. When hot, add pork, ginger and garlic; cook 2 minutes over medium heat.

Turn pieces over, season with pepper and cook 1 more minute.

Add soy sauce and cook 1 more minute. Remove meat from wok; set aside.

Add vegetables and grapes to wok. Stir-fry 4 minutes over medium-high heat.

Pour in chicken stock and bean sauce; mix well. Bring to boil and cook 1 minute..

Mix cornstarch with cold water; stir into sauce until well incorporated. Cook 2 minutes.

Reheat pork in mixture several seconds and serve at once over rice, if desired.

1 serving	*378 calories*	*18 g carbohydrate*
36 g protein	*18 g fat*	*2.2 g fiber*

Steamed Vegetables (*Oriental*)

serves 4

20	snow pea pods, pared
½	red pepper, sliced into strips
½	zucchini, halved lengthwise and sliced
1	celery stalk, sliced
½	head broccoli, in flowerets
¼ lb	(*125 g*) green beans, pared
	salt and pepper

Place bamboo steamer in wok and pour in enough water to reach bottom of basket.

Add vegetables, placing larger pieces on bottom and season well. Cover basket and steam.

When vegetables are tender (crisp and not overcooked),* remove from basket and serve.

Serve with a variety of dishes, or as is for a truly healthy light meal.

* *Check the vegetables for doneness several times until you become accustomed to the timing.*

1 serving	*44 calories*	*8 g carbohydrate*
3 g protein	*0 g fat*	*4.4 g fiber*

1. An authentic bamboo steamer and a stainless-steel wok are a good investment and will allow you to prepare a wide variety of Oriental dishes. You will find these kitchen utensils handy for other types of cooking too.

2. The principle of vegetable steaming is the same for all vegetables. Begin by placing steamer in wok and pour in enough water to reach bottom of basket. Add desired vegetables, cover basket and steam.

3. Be sure to place the larger pieces of vegetable in bottom of basket, with the thinner strips on top. Season well before covering.

4. When tender but still a little crisp, remove vegetables and serve.

Szechuan Pork with Dipping Sauce (*Oriental*)

serves 4

2	butterflied pork chops, fat trimmed and cut in strips
1 tbsp	(*15 ml*) chopped fresh ginger
2	garlic cloves, smashed and chopped
3	pickled tabasco peppers, finely chopped
1 tsp	(*5 ml*) sesame oil
1 tsp	(*5 ml*) soy sauce
1½ cups	(*375 ml*) chicken stock, heated
2 tbsp	(*30 ml*) bean sauce
1 tbsp	(*15 ml*) plum sauce
½ tsp	(*2 ml*) cornstarch
1 tbsp	(*15 ml*) cold water
1 tbsp	(*15 ml*) vegetable oil
	pepper

Place pork strips in bowl and season with pepper. Add ginger, half of garlic and half of tabasco peppers. Sprinkle with sesame oil and soy sauce; mix well. Pour in ½ cup (*125 ml*) chicken stock and marinate 15 minutes.

Meanwhile, pour bean and plum sauces in small saucepan. Add remaining chicken stock and mix well. Add remaining tabasco peppers and garlic; bring to boil over high heat. Continue cooking 8 to 10 minutes over low heat.

Drain pork, reserving ¼ cup (*50 ml*) liquid; set both aside.

Mix cornstarch with cold water; incorporate to mixture in saucepan. Pour in reserved marinade from meat and cook 1 to 2 minutes over low heat.

Heat vegetable oil in frying pan over high heat. Add pork and cook 3 minutes. Turn strips over, season with pepper and cook another 2 minutes.

Serve at once with dipping sauce and accompany with mild-flavored fruit such as cantaloupe wedges.

1 serving	*335 calories*	*7 g carbohydrate*
34 g protein	*19 g fat*	*0.9 g fiber*

Vegetable Rice (*Oriental*)

serves 4

2 tbsp	(*30 ml*) vegetable oil
1	celery stalk, sliced on angle
½	onion, chopped
½	zucchini, cut into sticks
6	large fresh mushrooms, cleaned and diced
½	red pepper, chopped
20	snow pea pods, pared
1 tbsp	(*15 ml*) chopped fresh ginger
1 tbsp	(*15 ml*) soy sauce
2 cups	(*500 ml*) cooked white rice
	salt and pepper
	few drops sesame oil

Heat vegetable oil in large skillet. Add celery, onion and zucchini; cook 3 to 4 minutes over high heat.

Add mushrooms, red pepper and pea pods; season and sprinkle with sesame oil. Add ginger and mix well; cook 3 to 4 minutes.

Sprinkle in soy sauce and cook 1 more minute.

Mix in rice and finish cooking 3 to 4 minutes. Serve.

1 serving	*216 calories*	*31 g carbohydrate*
5 g protein	*8 g fat*	*5.2 g fiber*

Sake Teriyaki Beef (*Oriental*)

serves 4

1¼ lb	(*625 g*) beef sirloin, very thinly sliced
2 tbsp	(*30 ml*) soy sauce
1 tbsp	(*15 ml*) teriyaki sauce
3 tbsp	(*45 ml*) sake wine
3	garlic cloves, smashed and chopped
1 tbsp	(*15 ml*) brown sugar
2 tbsp	(*30 ml*) peanut oil
	juice ½ lemon
	pepper

Arrange slices of beef on large platter. Sprinkle with soy sauce, teriyaki sauce, lemon juice and sake. Spread garlic over meat and pepper well—do not salt.

Sprinkle with brown sugar, cover and refrigerate 4 hours.

Heat peanut oil in large frying pan over high heat. Add meat and sear 1 minute. Turn slices over and sear 1 more minute.

Serve with rice and soup.

1 serving	*298 calories*	*7 g carbohydrate*
36 g protein	*14 g fat*	*0 g fiber*

Orange Beef Sirloin Stir-Fry (*Oriental*)

serves 4

1¼ lb	(*625 g*) sirloin steak, cut into strips
2	pickled tabasco peppers, chopped
1 tbsp	(*15 ml*) soy sauce
1 tsp	(*5 ml*) sesame oil
2 tsp	(*10 ml*) cornstarch
2 tbsp	(*30 ml*) vegetable oil
½	onion, sliced
1	celery stalk, sliced on angle
1	yellow pepper, thinly sliced
4	water chestnuts, sliced
2 tbsp	(*30 ml*) white vinegar
2 tbsp	(*30 ml*) brown sugar
1 cup	(*250 ml*) orange juice
1 tbsp	(*15 ml*) cold water
	salt and pepper

Place meat in bowl with tabasco peppers; sprinkle with soy sauce and sesame oil. Mix well. Add 1 tsp (*5 ml*) cornstarch and toss; marinate 15 minutes.

Heat 1 tbsp (*15 ml*) vegetable oil in large skillet over high heat. Add meat and sear 1 minute. Turn strips over, season and sear 1 more minute.

Remove meat from pan and set aside.

Add onion and celery to skillet and sprinkle in remaining vegetable oil. Cook 8 to 10 minutes over high heat.

Add yellow pepper and water chestnuts; season and cook 4 minutes over medium-high heat.

Mix in vinegar and brown sugar; cook 3 to 4 minutes over high heat. Add orange juice, mix well and bring to boil.

Mix remaining cornstarch with cold water; incorporate to sauce and season. Cook 2 minutes over low heat.

Place meat with juices in sauce; heat 2 minutes and serve. Decorate with slices of orange.

1 serving	*367 calories*	*21 g carbohydrate*
37 g protein	*15 g fat*	*1.4 g fiber*

Sesame-Seeded Meatballs (*Oriental*)

serves 4

¾ lb	(*375 g*) lean ground beef
2 tbsp	(*30 ml*) brown sugar
1	garlic clove, smashed and chopped
1 tbsp	(*15 ml*) chopped fresh ginger
2 tbsp	(*30 ml*) sesame seeds
1	egg
1 tbsp	(*15 ml*) soy sauce
1 tbsp	(*15 ml*) vegetable oil
	few drops sesame oil
	pepper
	bean sauce

Place beef, brown sugar, garlic, ginger, 1 tbsp (*15 ml*) sesame seeds, egg, soy sauce and sesame oil in bowl of food processor; pepper well and blend until incorporated.

Remove meat and shape mixture into small meatballs.

Heat vegetable oil in large frying pan over high heat. Add meatballs and cook 4 minutes over medium heat. Turn over, pepper well and cook another 4 minutes or until done.

Sprinkle with remaining sesame seeds and cook 1 more minute.

Serve meatballs with an arrangement of garnishes such as sliced oranges, sections pears, etc. Accompany with bean sauce.

1 serving	*264 calories*	*8 g carbohydrate*
22 g protein	*16 g fat*	*0.1 g fiber*

Korean Beef Steak (*Oriental*)

serves 4

1½ lb	(*750 g*) beef sirloin, thinly sliced against the grain
4 tbsp	(*60 ml*) soy sauce
2 tbsp	(*30 ml*) brown sugar
2	garlic cloves, smashed and chopped
2 tbsp	(*30 ml*) peanut oil
	few drops sesame oil
	juice ½ lemon
	sesame seeds

Place meat in bowl and sprinkle with soy sauce and sesame oil. Add brown sugar, lemon juice and garlic; mix well. Chill 3 hours, covered.

Heat peanut oil in wok over high heat. Add meat and sear 1 minute on each side or adjust time depending on thickness.

Remove meat from wok to serving platter and quickly sprinkle with sesame seeds. Serve at once.

1 serving	*501 calories*	*42 g carbohydrate*
45 g protein	*17 g fat*	*0.1 g fiber*

Grilled Pork Tenderloin (*Oriental*)

serves 2

1	pork tenderloin, trimmed of fat
3 tbsp	(*45 ml*) olive oil
2	garlic cloves, smashed and chopped
1 tbsp	(*15 ml*) chopped fresh lovage
1 tsp	(*5 ml*) chopped fresh marjoram
1 tsp	(*5 ml*) chopped fresh rosemary
1	zucchini, cut into 3 lengthwise and again into 3 across width
1 tbsp	(*15 ml*) Dijon mustard
	salt and pepper

Open tenderloin lengthwise butterfly-style. Mix olive oil with garlic and brush some over meat.

Spread fresh seasonings over inside of meat and brush again with oil mixture. Close meat and brush outside with oil. Set aside.

Brush zucchini pieces with oil.

Preheat barbecue grill to high. Cook zucchini 3 to 4 minutes each side.

Reopen tenderloin butterfly-style and place on hot grill. Cook 4 to 5 minutes.

Turn meat over, season and brush with mustard. Cook 4 to 5 minutes.

Turn over once more and cook another 4 to 5 minutes or according to size.

Serve with zucchini.

1 serving	*668 calories*	*7 g carbohydrate*
61 g protein	*44 g fat*	*2.5 g fiber*

Spaghetti Primavera (*Italian*)

serves 4

2 tbsp	(*30 ml*) olive oil
½	head broccoli, well cleaned and in flowerets
½	green pepper, thinly sliced
½	red pepper, thinly sliced
1	zucchini, halved lengthwise and sliced
1	celery stalk, sliced
20	snow pea pods, pared
1	garlic clove, smashed and chopped
4	portions cooked spaghetti, hot
4 tbsp	(*60 ml*) grated Parmesan cheese
	salt and pepper

Heat oil in large frying pan over medium heat. Add broccoli, peppers, zucchini, celery and pea pods; mix well. Add garlic and season well. Cover and cook 4 to 5 minutes.

Mix in spaghetti, correct seasoning and cook, covered, 2 minutes.

Sprinkle in cheese; cover and cook 1 minute. Serve at once.

1 serving	*358 calories*	*54 g carbohydrate*
13 g protein	*10 g fat*	*8.5 g fiber*

Calf Liver Lyonnaise (*French*)

serves 4

2 tbsp	(*30 ml*) butter
2	red onions, thinly sliced
1	garlic clove, smashed and chopped
4	large slices calf liver
	salt and pepper
	seasoned flour
	juice ½ lemon

Melt half of butter in skillet over medium heat. Add onions and garlic; season. Cook 10 to 15 minutes.

Meanwhile, trim fat from liver. Dredge in flour.

Heat remaining butter in frying pan over medium heat. Add liver slices and cook 2½ minutes over medium-low heat.

Turn pieces over, season and continue cooking 2 to 3 minutes or adjust time depending on taste.

Deglaze onions with lemon juice by cooking 1 minute over high heat.

Serve liver with onions.

1 serving — 316 calories — 18 g carbohydrate — 34g protein — 12 g fat — 1.4 g fiber

Wild Mushroom Fantasy (*French*)

serves 4

2 tbsp	(*30 ml*) butter
2	shallots, chopped
2 lb	(*900 g*) white mushrooms, cleaned and quartered
2 cups	(*500 ml*) edible wild mushrooms, cleaned
1 tbsp	(*15 ml*) chopped fresh parsley
1 tbsp	(*15 ml*) chopped fresh chives
3 tbsp	(*45 ml*) dry white wine
1½ tbsp	(*25 ml*) flour
1½ cups	(*375 ml*) hot milk
	salt and pepper
	paprika
	toasted French bread

Melt butter in large skillet over medium-high heat. Add shallots and white mushrooms; cook 5 to 6 minutes.

Add wild mushrooms, parsley and chives; season. Sauté 2 to 3 minutes.

Add wine and continue cooking 3 minutes. Mix in flour and cook 1 minute.

Mix in hot milk and cook 3 to 4 minutes over medium heat.

Sprinkle with paprika and spoon over toasted French bread.

1 serving	*282 calories*	*36 g carbohydrate*
12 g protein	*10 g fat*	*7.5 g fiber*

Strip Steaks Mama Mia (*Italian*)

serves 2

3 tbsp	(*45 ml*) olive oil
1	small eggplant, cubed with skin
1	green pepper, thinly sliced
1	banana pepper, chopped
½	yellow pepper, thinly sliced
1	large tomato, cored and cubed
1 tbsp	(*15 ml*) chopped fresh oregano
1 tsp	(*5 ml*) chopped fresh thyme
2	garlic cloves, smashed and chopped
2	8-oz (*250-g*) strip loin steaks
	salt and pepper

Heat 2 tbsp (*30 ml*) oil in large skillet over high heat. Add eggplant, cover and cook 10 minutes over medium heat.

Mix in peppers, tomato, oregano, thyme and half of garlic; season well. Continue cooking 6 to 7 minutes, partly covered.

Meanwhile, mix remaining oil with leftover garlic; brush over meat.

Preheat barbecue to high.

Cook meat 3 minutes on each side; adjust time depending on thickness. Serve with vegetables.

1 serving	*639 calories*	*14 g carbohydrate*
58 g protein	*39 g fat*	*4.3 g fiber*

Osso Buco (*Italian*)

serves 4

8	veal shanks, 1½ in. (*4 cm*) thick
1½ tbsp	(*25 ml*) oil
1	onion, chopped
3	garlic cloves, smashed and chopped
1 cup	(*250 ml*) dry white wine
28 oz	(*796 ml*) can tomatoes, drained and chopped
2 tbsp	(*30 ml*) tomato paste
½ cup	(*125 ml*) beef gravy, heated
½ tsp	(*2 ml*) oregano
¼ tsp	(*1 ml*) thyme
1	bay leaf, chopped
	seasoned flour
	salt and pepper
pinch	sugar

Preheat oven to 350°F (*180°C*). Dredge veal in flour.

Heat oil in large ovenproof casserole. Sear veal (in two batches) for 3 to 4 minutes on each side over medium-high heat. Season well when turning.

Set seared veal aside. Add onion and garlic to casserole; mix and cook 3 to 4 minutes over medium heat.

Pour in wine and cook 4 minutes over high heat.

Mix in tomatoes, tomato paste and gravy. Add seasonings and sugar; correct seasoning to taste. Bring to boil.

Return veal to casserole. Cover and cook 2 hours in oven.

When veal is cooked, remove from casserole and set aside. Cook sauce over high heat 3 to 4 minutes.

Correct seasoning and pour over veal.

1 serving	*499 calories*	*25 g carbohydrate*
48 g protein	*23 g fat*	*2.8 g fiber*

Veal alla Vista (*Italian*)

serves 4

2 tbsp	(*30 ml*) melted butter	
2	large slices veal shoulder, about 1 in. (*2.5 cm*) thick, cubed	
1	onion, finely chopped	
1	green pepper, diced large	
3	tomatoes, skinned, seeded and diced large	
1 tbsp	(*15 ml*) tomato paste	
½ cup	(*125 ml*) chicken stock, heated	
½ tsp	(*2 ml*) tarragon	
3	green onions, chopped	
	salt and pepper	

Preheat oven to 350°F (*180°C*).

Heat melted butter in frying pan. Add veal and brown on all sides over medium heat. Transfer meat to ovenproof casserole and set aside.

Add chopped white onion and green pepper to frying pan; season well. Cook 4 minutes over medium heat.

Stir in tomatoes, tomato paste and chicken stock; season well. Add tarragon and bring to boil. Cook 3 to 4 minutes over high heat.

Mix well, correct seasoning and pour over veal in casserole. Cover and cook 1 hour in oven.

Top with green onions before serving. Accompany with pasta, if desired.

1 serving	*670 calories*	*10 g carbohydrate*
72 g protein	*38 g fat*	*2.7 g fiber*

Chicken Florence (*Italian*)

serves 4

2 tbsp	(*30 ml*) olive oil
4 lb	(*1.8 kg*) roasting chicken, cleaned, skinned and cut into 8 pieces
1	red onion, chopped
1	garlic clove, smashed and chopped
1	red pepper, cubed
1	green pepper, cubed
1	broccoli stalk, sliced
6	large fresh mushrooms, cleaned and quartered
	seasoned flour
	salt and pepper

Heat oil in large skillet over medium-high heat. Meanwhile, dredge chicken pieces in flour.

When oil is hot, sear chicken 8 minutes on one side. Turn pieces over, season and add onion and garlic. Reduce heat to medium and continue cooking 6 minutes.

Add both peppers, sliced broccoli stalk and mushrooms; correct seasoning. Cover and finish cooking 10 to 12 minutes over low heat.

1 serving	*543 calories*	*22 g carbohydrate*
62 g protein	*23 g fat*	*4.1 g fiber*

Oregano-Seasoned Veal Chops (*Italian*)

serves 2

2	veal chops, about ¾ in. (*2 cm*) thick, trimmed of fat
1 tbsp	(*15 ml*) olive oil
8	large fresh mushrooms, cleaned and sliced
1 tbsp	(*15 ml*) butter
1 tbsp	(*15 ml*) chopped fresh oregano
¼ cup	(*50 ml*) heavy cream
	seasoned flour
	salt and pepper
	juice ½ lemon

Dredge chops in flour. Heat oil in large frying pan over high heat.

When hot, add chops and cook 4 minutes over medium-high heat. Turn chops over, season and continue cooking 5 minutes over medium heat.

Turn over once more and finish cooking 3 minutes or adjust time depending on size. Remove chops to heated platter and set aside.

Add mushrooms to hot frying pan and sprinkle with lemon juice. Add butter and oregano; cook 3 to 4 minutes over high heat.

Stir in cream and correct seasoning; cook 2 to 3 minutes over medium heat.

Pour sauce over veal chops and serve with noodles.

1 serving 498 calories 20 g carbohydrate
28 g protein 34 g fat 3.1 g fiber

1. Choose the freshest meat and produce available.

2. After dredging meat in flour, sear in hot oil 4 minutes over medium-high heat. Continue cooking for about 8 minutes at reduced heat, turning chops over twice. Time will vary according to size of chops and pan—use your judgment.

3. Add mushrooms to hot pan. Sprinkle with lemon juice, add butter and oregano; cook 3 to 4 minutes over high heat.

4. Pour in cream and mix well; correct seasoning. Cook 2 to 3 minutes over medium heat before serving with veal.

White Beans de l'Amour (*French*)

serves 4–6

1 tsp	(*5 ml*) olive oil
1	large red onion, diced large
1	celery stalk, diced large
1	garlic clove, smashed and chopped
1½ cups	(*375 ml*) dry white beans, soaked overnight
28 oz	(*800 ml*) canned tomatoes, with juice
4 cups	(*1 L*) chicken stock, heated
	fresh seasonings to taste: thyme, oregano, basil, parsley
	salt and pepper

Heat oil in large casserole over medium-high heat. Add onion, celery and garlic; cook 5 to 6 minutes.

Add beans and remaining ingredients; mix well. Correct seasoning, cover and bring to boil.

Reduce heat to low and continue cooking, covered, for 3 hours.

1 serving *174 calories* *30 g carbohydrate*
9 g protein *2 g fat* *8.2 g fiber*

Sausages with Gruyère Potatoes (*French*)

serves 2

1 tsp	(*5 ml*) olive oil
2	large veal sausages
½	onion, chopped
1 tbsp	(*15 ml*) peanut oil
2	large potatoes, cooked in skins, peeled and sliced thick
¼ cup	(*50 ml*) grated Gruyère cheese
1 cup	(*250 ml*) leftover tomato sauce or substitute
	salt and pepper

Heat olive oil in frying pan. Add sausages and cook 3 to 4 minutes over medium heat. Turn over, season and continue cooking 3 minutes.

Add onion and cook with sausages for 25 to 30 minutes, depending on size, over medium-low heat. Turn sausages several times.

Meanwhile, heat peanut oil in skillet over medium-high heat. Add potatoes, season and cook 16 to 18 minutes. Turn slices over often.

Add grated cheese and cook 3 more minutes over medium heat.

Mix tomato sauce into pan containing sausages and cook 4 to 5 minutes.

Serve at once with potatoes.

1 serving	*691 calories*	*48 g carbohydrate*
28 g protein	*43 g fat*	*4.5 g fiber*

Veal Shanks Lizanne (*French*)

serves 4

4	veal shanks, about 1 in. (*2.5 cm*) thick, trimmed of fat
1 tbsp	(*15 ml*) oil
1	large red onion, in small wedges
2	garlic cloves, smashed and chopped
2 cups	(*500 ml*) dry red wine
2	tomatoes, cored and cut in wedges
2 tbsp	(*30 ml*) tomato paste
1	sprig thyme, chopped
1	sprig oregano, chopped
1	sprig lovage, chopped
1 tbsp	(*15 ml*) butter
½ lb	(*250 g*) fresh mushrooms, cleaned and quartered
	seasoned flour
	salt and pepper

Preheat oven to 350°F (*180°C*). Dredge meat in flour.

Heat oil in large deep skillet over high heat. Add veal and sear 8 minutes on each side over medium heat.

Add onion and garlic; cook 3 to 4 minutes.

Pour in wine, add tomatoes and tomato paste; season well. Add fresh chopped herbs, cover and cook 1½ hours in oven.

Just before end of cooking time, melt butter in frying pan. Sauté mushrooms 3 minutes; season well.

Add mushrooms to veal, cover and continue cooking 1½ hours in oven. Serve.

1 serving	*319 calories*	*20 g carbohydrate*
26 g protein	*15 g fat*	*4.0 g fiber*

1. Dredge veal in seasoned flour. This will help the searing process.

2. Begin by searing first side for 8 minutes. During this time, do not disturb the meat.

3. Turn shanks over to sear second side.

4. Add onion and garlic; continue cooking 3 to 4 minutes.

Souvlaki (*Greek*)

serves 4

1½ lb	(*750 g*) cubed lamb from the leg
4 tbsp	(*60 ml*) olive oil
2 tbsp	(*30 ml*) chopped fresh mint
2	garlic cloves, smashed and chopped
3	green onions, cut into 2-in. (*5-cm*) lengths
	salt and pepper
	juice 1 lemon

Place lamb, oil, pepper and lemon juice in bowl. Add mint and garlic; season again and mix. Cover with sheet of plastic wrap and marinate 3 hours in refrigerator.

Alternate lamb and green onion on metal skewers. Broil in preheated oven or on preheated grill 3 to 4 minutes on each side over high heat.

Serve on pita bread, if desired.

1 serving *392 calories* *4 g carbohydrate*
40 g protein *24 g fat* *0.6 g fiber*

Scallop Skewers (*Greek*)

serves 4

1½ lb	(*750 g*) medium-size scallops
2 tbsp	(*30 ml*) olive oil
1	garlic clove, smashed and chopped
1 tbsp	(*15 ml*) chopped fresh oregano
	juice ½ lemon
	white pepper

Place scallops in bowl with all ingredients; mix and cover with plastic wrap. Refrigerate 2 to 3 hours.

Thread scallops on wet wooden skewers. Place on preheated grill or in preheated oven at broil. Cook 1 minute on each side over high heat.

Serve with fresh vegetables and lemon.

1 serving *213 calories* *1 g carbohydrate*
32 g protein *9 g fat* *0 g fiber*

Herbed Lamb Chops (*Greek*)

serves 4

8	¾-in. (*2-cm*) thick lamb chops
2	garlic cloves, peeled and cut into pieces
8	parsley sprigs
8	oregano sprigs
8	thyme sprigs
2	garlic cloves, smashed and chopped
1 tbsp	(*15 ml*) chopped fresh parsley
1 tsp	(*5 ml*) chopped fresh rosemary
3 tbsp	(*45 ml*) olive oil
	juice 1 lemon
	salt and pepper

Preheat barbecue to high.

Trim excess fat from chops and discard. Insert garlic pieces in meat.

Tuck fresh herbs in fold of each chop and carefully thread on skewers. Set aside.

Place chopped garlic, parsley, rosemary and lemon juice in small bowl; mix well. Incorporate oil using whisk and season.

Brush over both sides of chops and pepper meat well—do not salt. Cook on preheated barbecue 3 minutes.

Turn skewers over; cook another 3 to 4 minutes depending on taste. Remove from skewers before serving.

1 serving	*309 calories*	*3 g carbohydrate*
27 g protein	*21 g fat*	*0.1 g fiber*

1. Trim excess fat from chops.

2. Tuck fresh herbs in the fold of each chop; then carefully thread on skewers. This technique will make chops easier to handle during barbecuing.

3. Baste chops on both sides with garlic herb marinade.

4. Pepper well but do not salt.

Paprika Chicken Stew (*Hungarian*)

serves 4–6

4 lb	(*1.8 kg*) chicken, cleaned
1 tbsp	(*15 ml*) olive oil
1 tbsp	(*15 ml*) butter
1	red onion, cubed
1½ tbsp	(*25 ml*) paprika
28 oz	(*800 ml*) canned tomatoes, with juice
2	blanched garlic cloves, smashed
1	sprig lovage, chopped
1	green pepper, cubed and sautéed
	seasoned flour
	salt and pepper

Preheat oven to 350°F (*180°C*).

Cut chicken into 8 pieces as shown on facing page. Skin and dredge meat in seasoned flour.

Heat oil in large ovenproof casserole over high heat. Add chicken pieces and sear 4 minutes over medium-high heat.

Add butter to pan, turn chicken pieces over and continue searing 4 minutes.

Add onion and paprika; cook another 6 to 7 minutes. Add tomatoes with juice and garlic; mix well.

Add lovage, season and bring to boil. Cover and finish cooking 30 minutes in oven.

Add sautéed green pepper to casserole; cover and resume cooking for 15 minutes.

1 serving	*367 calories*	*17 g carbohydrate*
41 g protein	*15 g fat*	*2.0 g fiber*

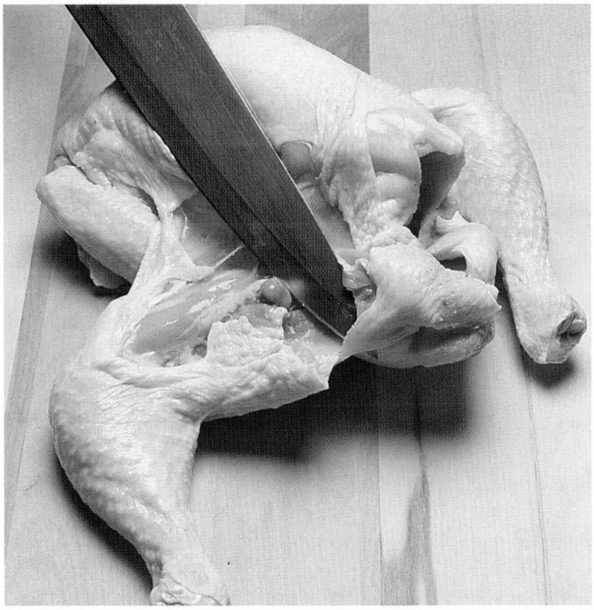

1. Begin cutting chicken by removing legs from body. Once detached, cut each into 2 pieces at the joint.

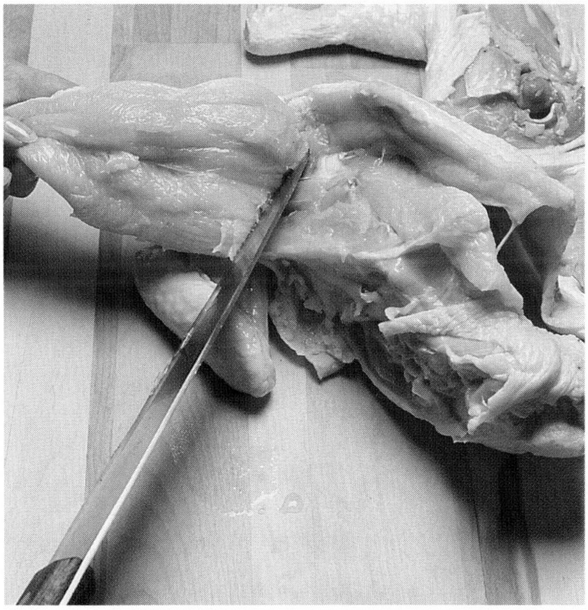

2. Remove breasts without the bone and set aside. Finish by cutting off wings, being sure to snip off tips. You should have 8 pieces.

3. Skin chicken pieces, dredge in flour and sear in hot oil 4 minutes on each side. This will seal in the juices.

4. Add onion and paprika; cook another 6 to 7 minutes before adding remaining ingredients.

Hungarian Veal on a Bun (*Hungarian*)

serves 4

3 tbsp	(*45 ml*) butter
2	small onions, cut in wedges
1 tbsp	(*15 ml*) paprika
3 tbsp	(*45 ml*) flour
3 cups	(*750 ml*) chicken stock, heated
1	red pepper, cubed
2 cups	(*500 ml*) leftover, cooked veal, sliced, trimmed of fat
½	cucumber, peeled and sliced
	salt and pepper
	English muffins, toasted

Melt 2 tbsp (*30 ml*) butter in saucepan over medium heat. Add onions; cover and cook 4 minutes.

Sprinkle in paprika and flour; mix very well. Cook, uncovered, 2 to 3 minutes over low heat.

Pour in chicken stock, mix well and season. Bring to boil and cook sauce 12 minutes over medium-low heat.

Before sauce is done, melt remaining butter in frying pan. Add red pepper, veal and cucumber; sauté 3 minutes over medium-high heat.

Transfer veal mixture to sauce and simmer 2 to 3 minutes.

Serve over toasted English muffins.

1 serving	*436 calories*	*37 g carbohydrate*
27 g protein	*20 g fat*	*1.8 g fiber*

Sour Cream Meatloaf (*Hungarian*)

serves 6–8

1 lb	(*500 g*) lean ground beef
½ lb	(*250 g*) lean ground pork
1	small onion, grated
¾ cup	(*175 ml*) coarse breadcrumbs
1 cup	(*250 ml*) milk
½ tsp	(*2 ml*) ground cloves
1 tsp	(*5 ml*) basil
½ tsp	(*2 ml*) marjoram
1	egg, slightly beaten
3 tbsp	(*45 ml*) sour cream
1 tbsp	(*15 ml*) flour
½ cup	(*125 ml*) chicken stock
	salt and pepper
	paprika

Preheat oven to 350°F (*180°C*).

Place both meats and onion in large bowl. Mix and season well.

Soak breadcrumbs in milk for 10 minutes, and then add to meat; incorporate well. Sprinkle in cloves, basil and marjoram; mix well.

Mix in beaten egg and pack mixture into buttered 9½ × 5½ in. (*24 × 14 cm*) loaf pan. Set in roasting pan with 1 in. (*2.5 cm*) hot water and cook 30 minutes in oven.

Mix sour cream, flour and chicken stock together. Pour mixture over meatloaf still in pan and season well; sprinkle with paprika.

Return to oven and continue baking 15 minutes. Serve with a sauce, if desired.

1 serving	*226 calories*	*11 g carbohydrate*
23 g protein	*10 g fat*	*0.6 g fiber*

Hungarian Veal Cutlets (*Hungarian*)

serves 4

4	5-oz (*140-g*) veal cutlets, flattened thin
2	beaten eggs
2 cups	(*500 ml*) seasoned breadcrumbs
1 tbsp	(*15 ml*) oil
1 tbsp	(*15 ml*) butter
	juice 1½ lemons
	salt and pepper

Preheat oven to 375 °F (*190 °C*).

Place cutlets in dish and squeeze in lemon juice; marinate, covered, 1 hour in refrigerator.

Dip veal in beaten eggs; then dredge in breadcrumbs. Redip veal in eggs and finish with final coating of breadcrumbs. Season well.

Heat oil and butter in large frying pan. Add cutlets and brown 2 to 3 minutes over medium heat.

Turn cutlets over, season and transfer to oven; cook 8 minutes.

Serve with sour cream and your choice of fresh vegetable.

1 serving	*567 calories*	*42 g carbohydrate*
39 g protein	*27 g fat*	*1.8 g fiber*

HAPPY ENDINGS

Irresistible sweets, cakes, pies and pastries—pure pleasure!

Flambéed Peaches

serves 6

3 tbsp (*45 ml*) syrup*
6 peaches, peeled and halved
2 tbsp (*30 ml*) Jazz peach flavored vodka
1 tsp (*5 ml*) cornstarch
2 tbsp (*30 ml*) cold water
1 cup (*250 ml*) strawberries, washed and hulled

Heat syrup in large frying pan over medium heat. Add peaches and cook 2 minutes on each side. Pour in vodka and continue cooking 2 minutes. Flambé.

Remove peaches and set aside.

Mix cornstarch with cold water; stir into sauce until incorporated. Cook 1 minute.

Return peaches to pan, add strawberries and cook 1 more minute. Serve warm.

* *See Rainbow Tartlets, page 488.*

1 serving	*80 calories*	*19 g carbohydrate*
1 g protein	*0 g fat*	*1.8 g fiber*

Fresh Fruit Bite

serves 2

2	slices muskmelon
1	cactus pear, halved
2	large wedges papaya
½	grapefruit
1	pear, halved and hollowed
4	thin slices mango
1	apricot, halved and pitted
	fresh strawberries for decoration
	ricotta cheese (optional)

These quantities are ample for two and can be stretched to serve more diners, depending on your menu. The most important thing is to choose fresh fruit—if one kind is not available, substitute something that is.

Second, the arrangement of the fruit will be a deciding factor in how appealing your presentation is; use the picture for guidance.

1 serving *161 calories* *36 g carbohydrate*
2 g protein *1 g fat* *4.3 g fiber*

Mixed Fruit Compote

serves 8–10

12	peaches, peeled and sectioned
3 tbsp	(*45 ml*) syrup*
2 tbsp	(*30 ml*) Jazz peach flavored vodka
1	mango, peeled, sliced and diced
1	papaya, cubed
1½ cups	(*375 ml*) whole strawberries, washed and hulled
2	kiwis, peeled and sliced
1 tbsp	(*15 ml*) cornstarch
2 tbsp	(*30 ml*) cold water

Place peaches and syrup in large skillet. Add vodka and cook 3 to 4 minutes over medium heat.

Mix in mango; continue cooking 3 to 4 minutes.

Add remaining fruit, cover and cook another 3 to 4 minutes.

Mix cornstarch with cold water; stir into fruit until well incorporated. Simmer 2 to 3 minutes.

Serve warm.

* *See Rainbow Tartlets, page 488.*

1 serving 116 calories 28 g carbohydrate
1 g protein 0 g fat 2.6 g fiber

1. Place peaches with syrup in large skillet.

2. Pour in Jazz vodka and cook 3 to 4 minutes over medium heat.

3. Add mango; mix and continue cooking 3 to 4 minutes.

4. Add remaining fruit, cover and cook 3 to 4 minutes more.

Honeymooners' Heaven

serves 2

1½ cups	(*375 ml*) fresh raspberries, washed
¼ cup	(*50 ml*) syrup *
1 tsp	(*5 ml*) orange liqueur
12	strawberries, washed and hulled
½ cup	(*125 ml*) crème anglaise **
1	large scoop vanilla ice cream
	whipped cream
	blackberries

Force raspberries through fine sieve into small saucepan. Add syrup and liqueur; mix well. Bring to boil; continue cooking 1 to 2 minutes. Cool before using.

To assemble sundae, begin by choosing a very large glass that can hold at least 3 cups (*750 ml*) water.

Place most of strawberries in bottom of glass. Ladle in some of raspberry sauce and crème anglaise.

Add scoop of ice cream, surround with remaining strawberries and drizzle in remaining raspberry sauce and crème anglaise.

Decorate with whipped cream and blackberries. Serve with two very long spoons.

* *See Rainbow Tartlets, page 488.*
** *See Dessert on Broadway, page 463.*

1 serving	*506 calories*	*78 g carbohydrate*
8 g protein	*18 g fat*	*3.2 g fiber*

Dessert on Broadway

serves 4

CRÈME ANGLAISE:

4	large egg yolks
½ cup	(*125 ml*) powdered fruit sugar
1 cup	(*250 ml*) hot scalded milk, still hot
¼ tsp	(*1 ml*) vanilla

Have ready saucepan half-filled with hot water.

Using electric hand beater, mix egg yolks and sugar in large stainless-steel bowl until light and frothy.

Slowly incorporate milk with vanilla while whisking. Place bowl over saucepan on stove with heat set at low. Cook cream until thick enough to coat back of a spoon. You must whisk constantly!

Remove bowl from saucepan and whisk a little more to cool. Then set aside to finish cooling; cover with waxed paper so that it touches surface. For best consistency, refrigerate 6 hours before using.

ASSEMBLY:

3 cups	(*750 ml*) fresh raspberries, washed
2 tbsp	(*30 ml*) syrup*
4	slices white cake, preferably square, about ½ in. (*1.2 cm*) thick
4	scoops vanilla ice cream
1 cup	(*250 ml*) blackberries, washed
	confectioners' sugar

Place half of raspberries in food processor; blend to purée. Transfer to small saucepan and mix in syrup; bring to boil and continue cooking 2 minutes. Remove, strain and set aside to cool.

When ready to serve, arrange ingredients on counter.

Begin by placing slice of cake on each of 4 plates.** Ladle crème anglaise and raspberry purée onto opposite sides of cake. Set scoop of ice cream on cake and decorate with remaining berries. Sift confectioners' sugar lightly over each plate and serve at once.

1 serving	*550 calories*	*88 g carbohydrate*
9 g protein	*18 g fat*	*6.6 g fiber*

* *See Rainbow Tartlets, page 488.*

** *Choose large (preferably glass) plates for a pretty presentation.*

The Ultimate Trifle

serves 8–12

1	Génoise cake,* cut into ½-in. (*1.2-cm*) thick square pieces
2 cups	(*500 ml*) halved fresh strawberries
1 cup	(*250 ml*) mixed berries (in season)
1	recipe crème anglaise**
1 cup	(*250 ml*) heavy cream, whipped
	vodka
	whole strawberries for decoration

This trifle takes some imagination on your part. You can reduce the quantities for a smaller group or add and substitute at will. The following is the basic assembly procedure.

Choose an attractive trifle bowl. Have all your ingredients ready on counter.

Begin by placing one third of cake squares in bottom of bowl. Follow with sprinkling of vodka, one-third of halved strawberries and same amount of mixed berries.

Ladle in some of crème anglaise and add dollops of whipped cream.

Repeat twice and finish with a topping of whole strawberries. Chill slightly to firm cream (if you can resist waiting) or serve at once. No calorie counting, please!

* *See Basic Génoise Cake, page 500.*
** *See Dessert on Broadway, page 463.*

1 serving *325 calories* *37 g carbohydrate*
6 g protein *16 g fat* *2.1 g fiber*

Ladies' Luncheon Strawberry Maria

serves 4

3 cups	(*750 ml*) fresh strawberries, washed and hulled
1/3 cup	(*75 ml*) powdered fruit sugar
4 tbsp	(*60 ml*) Tia Maria
2 tbsp	(*30 ml*) orange juice
1 tsp	(*5 ml*) lemon juice

Place all ingredients in bowl, toss lightly and marinate 2 to 3 hours at room temperature.

Dish out into glass bowls and decorate with freshly whipped cream and additional berries of your choice. Serve with strong coffee.

1 serving	*128 calories*	*27 g carbohydrate*
1 g protein	*0 g fat*	*2.6 g fiber*

Baked Peach Halves

serves 4

6	peaches, halved and peeled
3 tbsp	(*45 ml*) syrup*
¼ cup	(*50 ml*) water
⅓ cup	(*75 ml*) brown sugar
½ cup	(*125 ml*) all-purpose flour
1 tbsp	(*15 ml*) cinnamon
⅓ cup	(*75 ml*) butter, softened

Preheat oven to 350°F (*180°C*).

Place peaches, cut side up, in one layer in large baking dish. Sprinkle each first with syrup, then with water.

Mix brown sugar and flour together in small bowl. Add cinnamon and mix.

Cream in butter using finger tips. Sprinkle mixture in hollows of peach halves and bake 20 minutes. Do not cover.

* *See Rainbow Tartlets, page 488.*

1 serving *363 calories* *54 g carbohydrate*
3 g protein *15 g fat* *2.4 g fiber*

Peaches à la Saint-Germain

serves 4

4	ripe peaches, halved and peeled
3 tbsp	(*45 ml*) syrup*
3 tbsp	(*45 ml*) Cointreau liqueur
1 cup	(*250 ml*) puréed raspberries
	ice cream
	blanched sliced almonds
	confectioners' sugar

Place peaches, syrup, liqueur and raspberries in frying pan; cover and cook 5 minutes over low heat.

Remove peaches from sauce and set aside to cool. Continue cooking sauce 3 minutes over high heat. Remove and cool.

To serve dessert, arrange peaches with ice cream on serving platter or individual plates.

Top with fruit sauce and garnish with almonds and decorate with confectioners' sugar.

* *See Rainbow Tartlets, page 488.*

1 serving 318 calories 52 g carbohydrate
5 g protein 10 g fat 4.9 g fiber

Caramel Custard

serves 6

½ cup	(*125 ml*) granulated sugar
¼ cup	(*50 ml*) cold water
⅓ cup	(*75 ml*) cold water
½ cup	(*125 ml*) granulated sugar
4	large eggs
2	large egg yolks
1 tsp	(*5 ml*) vanilla
2 cups	(*500 ml*) scalded milk, still hot

Preheat oven to 350°F (*180°C*).

Place ½ cup (*125 ml*) sugar and ¼ cup (*50 ml*) water in small saucepan. Set over medium-high heat to caramelize sugar. Stir once at the beginning to help sugar melt but do not stir again. You can brush sides of saucepan with a little more cold water to prevent loose granules from burning.

When sugar is at caramel stage, quickly add ⅓ cup (*75 ml*) cold water and continue cooking 30 seconds.

Immediately pour into 6 custard dishes, rotating each to coat evenly. Set dishes aside in roasting pan.

Begin making custard by placing remaining measure of sugar in large stainless-steel bowl. Add all eggs and vanilla.

Incorporate ingredients well by mixing gently with whisk. Try to avoid foaming.

Slowly pour in milk while whisking; when incorporated, strain custard before pouring into dishes.

Add enough hot water to roasting pan to measure 1 in. (*2.5 cm*) and place in oven; bake for 45 minutes.

Cool custard on counter; then refrigerate until thoroughly chilled.

To serve, run knife around inside edge of molds and invert each on dessert plate.

1 serving	*251 calories*	*39 g carbohydrate*
8 g protein	*7 g fat*	*0 g fiber*

1. Once the sugar/water mixture starts to change color it will caramelize quite quickly, so keep a sharp eye on it to avoid burning. This mixture is just about ready for the next step, which is …

2. … adding 1/3 cup (75 ml) cold water. It might be wise to stand back a little while doing this. Without stirring, continue cooking caramel 30 seconds before pouring into custard dishes.

3. It is important to rotate each dish immediately after you have poured in caramel, as the sugar will start to set very quickly.

4. While caramel is hardening in dishes, begin making custard.

Chocolate Custard Caramel

serves 6

½ cup	(*125 ml*) granulated sugar
¼ cup	(*50 ml*) cold water
⅓ cup	(*75 ml*) cold water
½ cup	(*125 ml*) granulated sugar
4	large eggs
2	egg yolks
1 tsp	(*5 ml*) Tia Maria
2 oz	(*60 g*) semisweet chocolate, melted
2 cups	(*500 ml*) scalded milk, still hot

Preheat oven to 350°F (*180°C*).

The caramel is optional for this recipe—the custard will be tasty without it. Place ½ cup (*125 ml*) sugar and ¼ cup (*50 ml*) water in small saucepan. Set over medium-high heat to caramelize sugar, stirring once at beginning to help melt sugar.

When sugar is at caramel stage,* quickly add ⅓ cup (*75 ml*) cold water and cook 30 seconds more.

Immediately pour into custard dishes, rotating each to coat evenly. Set dishes aside in roasting pan.

To make custard, place remaining sugar, all eggs and Tia Maria in stainless-steel bowl. Whisk until thoroughly incorporated but not foaming.

Place melted chocolate in another stainless-steel bowl and whisk in hot milk.

Incorporate chocolate milk to egg mixture, whisking constantly. Pass mixture through fine sieve and pour into custard dishes.

Add enough hot water to roasting pan to measure 1 in. (*2.5 cm*) and place in oven; bake for 45 minutes.

Cool on counter; then refrigerate until thoroughly chilled.

To serve, run knife around inside edge of molds and invert each on dessert plate. If made without caramel, decorate with whipped cream.

1 serving   312 calories   42 g carbohydrate
9 g protein   12 g fat   0.2 g fiber

* *See pictures of Caramel Custard, page 469.*

Raspberry Custard

serves 6

1¼ cups	*(300 ml)* fresh raspberries, washed
2 tbsp	*(30 ml)* liqueur of your choice
2 tbsp	*(30 ml)* powdered fruit sugar
4	large eggs
2	large egg yolks
½ cup	*(125 ml)* granulated sugar
2 cups	*(500 ml)* scalded milk, still hot

Preheat oven to 350°F *(180°C)*.

Marinate raspberries in liqueur and powdered fruit sugar for 10 minutes.

Meanwhile, place all eggs in large stainless-steel bowl. Incorporate granulated sugar while whisking gently, being careful that mixture does not foam.

Slowly pour in milk while whisking until incorporated. Strain custard.

Divide raspberries into 6 custard dishes and place in roasting pan. Pour in custard and add enough hot water to pan to measure 1 in. *(2.5 cm)*. Bake 45 minutes in oven.

Cool on counter; then refrigerate until thoroughly chilled.

To serve, run knife around inside edge of mold and invert onto plate. You can ladle a little crème anglaise * into bottom of plates, if desired, and perhaps top with more berries.

* *See Dessert on Broadway, page 463.*

1 serving	*235 calories*	*26 g carbohydrate*
8 g protein	*11 g fat*	*1.9 g fiber*

Decadent Chocolate Mousse

serves 4–6

4		large eggs, separated
¼ cup	(*50 ml*)	powdered fruit sugar, sifted
2 oz	(*60 g*)	unsweetened chocolate
1 cup	(*250 ml*)	heavy cream, whipped

Place egg yolks in stainless-steel bowl and add sugar. Using whisk, mix together and set bowl over saucepan half-filled with simmering water.

Cook over low heat while whisking constantly to prevent eggs from cooking—mixture should thicken in about 2 to 3 minutes

Remove saucepan from heat; with bowl still on saucepan, continue whisking for about 5 minutes.

Place chocolate in another stainless-steel bowl; melt over saucepan half-filled with hot water set over medium heat. Cool chocolate in bowl on counter.

Mix melted chocolate into egg mixture until well incorporated; set aside.

Beat egg whites until they form soft peaks; set aside.

Fold whipped cream into chocolate mixture.

Using spatula, begin folding beaten whites into mixture. They should be well incorporated, but you can leave a trace of white for a marbled effect.

Spoon mousse into individual glass dishes and chill 2 to 3 hours before serving.

1 serving	*275 calories*	*11 g carbohydrate*
6 g protein	*23 g fat*	*0.2 g fiber*

1. Place egg yolks and sugar in stainless-steel bowl.

2. With bowl set over saucepan half-filled with simmering water, cook mixture over low heat while whisking constantly.

3. Incorporate cooled chocolate to egg mixture.

4. Beat whites until they form soft peaks.

Chocolate Filling Cream

5 oz	(*140 g*) semisweet chocolate
4	egg yolks
¾ cup	(*175 ml*) confectioners' sugar
⅓ cup	(*75 ml*) heavy cream
1 cup	(*250 ml*) unsalted butter, softened

Melt chocolate in stainless-steel bowl placed over saucepan half-filled with hot water set over low heat.

Remove bowl and add egg yolks, sugar and cream. Place bowl over saucepan again and beat mixture while cooking for 6 to 7 minutes. Water in saucepan should be simmering.

Remove and place in refrigerator to cool.

When cooled, whisk in butter until thick and smooth.

1 recipe	*3488 calories*	*128 g carbohydrate*
24 g protein	*320 g fat*	*3.2 g fiber*

Butter Cream Frosting

1 cup	(*250 ml*)	unsalted butter, room temperature
1¼ cups	(*300 ml*)	confectioners' sugar
2		egg yolks
		liqueur to taste

Cream butter and beat until light and fluffy.

Sift confectioners' sugar and gradually add to butter while mixing with electric hand beater at low speed.

Beat in first egg yolk. Add second yolk and beat again until smooth.

Add liqueur to taste and beat once more. Use as a frosting or filling for layer cakes.

1 recipe	*2544 calories*	*160 g carbohydrate*
8 g protein	*208 g fat*	*0 g fiber*

Country Rice Pudding

serves 6

3 cups	(*750 ml*)	water
¾ cup	(*175 ml*)	long-grain rice, rinsed
3½ cups	(*875 ml*)	hot milk
⅓ cup	(*75 ml*)	granulated sugar
¼ cup	(*50 ml*)	golden seedless raisins
¼ cup	(*50 ml*)	sultana raisins
1		egg
2		egg yolks
¼ cup	(*50 ml*)	heavy cream
pinch		salt
		grated rind 1 orange
		grated rind 1 lemon

Preheat oven to 350°F (*180°C*). Butter 8-cup (*2-L*) soufflé mold and sprinkle sides and bottom with brown sugar; set aside.

Bring water with pinch of salt to boil in saucepan over high heat. Add rice, stir to loosen and cook, covered, 10 minutes over medium heat.

Drain well and set rice aside to cool.

Mix hot milk with sugar. Stir in rice, raisins and fruit rinds. Pour into prepared mold and bake 1 hour.

Mix all eggs with cream in a bowl. Remove soufflé mold from oven and incorporate egg mixture to pudding.

Return to oven and resume cooking 15 minutes.

Serve pudding warm or cold.

1 serving	*292 calories*	*46 g carbohydrate*
9 g protein	*8 g fat*	*1.1 g fiber*

1. Add rinsed rice to boiling salted water. Cook, covered, 10 minutes over medium heat.

2. Mix hot milk with sugar.

3. It is important to drain rice well before adding it to milk mixture.

4. After 1 hour of cooking, incorporate egg mixture to pudding and resume cooking 15 minutes.

Bananas in Their Skins

serves 4

4	ripe bananas
2 tbsp	(*30 ml*) syrup *
3 tbsp	(*45 ml*) jam of your choice
2 tbsp	(*30 ml*) Tia Maria
	Italian meringue **

Preheat oven to 400°F (*200°C*).

Slash skins lengthwise once and remove bananas. Set skins aside.

Place bananas in baking dish and score each several times. Brush with syrup and jam. Sprinkle with Tia Maria. Bake 6 to 7 minutes.

Carefully replace bananas in their skins and decorate with Italian meringue piped through pastry bag. Place in ovenproof platter or pan and bake until golden brown. The skins will become quite dark.

* *See Rainbow Tartlets, page 488.*
** *See Italian Meringue Crunch Cookies, page 479.*

1 serving	*425 calories*	*99 g carbohydrate*
5 g protein	*1 g fat*	*4.1 g fiber*

Italian Meringue Crunch Cookies

serves

1 cup	(*250 ml*) powdered fruit sugar
4	large egg whites (with no trace of yolks)
½ tsp	(*2 ml*) vanilla
	cocoa for dusting

Preheat oven to 200°F (*100°C*). Butter and flour cookie sheets; set aside.

Sift sugar into stainless-steel bowl. Place over saucepan half-filled with hot water over low heat.

Add egg whites and vanilla to bowl. With water simmering, begin beating mixture at low speed. When it starts to take shape, increase speed to medium and continue beating steadily.

Just before meringue starts to peak, increase speed to high and continue beating. Test meringue by turning bowl upside-down. Egg whites should remain firmly in place.

Remove bowl from saucepan and continue to beat at high speed until meringue is cold.

Spoon some of meringue into pastry bag fitted with plain nozzle. Squeeze out different shapes (fingers, mushroom caps, etc.) onto cookie sheets.

Use soup spoon to drop lumps of meringue on some cookies, which will give uneven textures.

Place cookie sheets in oven and bake 3 hours.

Remove to cool on counter and sprinkle with cocoa.

1 recipe *1008 calories* *228 g carbohydrate*
24 g protein *0 g fat* *0 g fiber*

Pastry Cream

2 tbsp	(*30 ml*) Cointreau liqueur
1 tsp	(*5 ml*) vanilla
3	large eggs
2	large egg yolks
1 cup	(*250 ml*) granulated sugar
½ cup	(*125 ml*) sifted all-purpose flour
2 cups	(*500 ml*) scalded milk, still hot
1 tbsp	(*15 ml*) unsalted butter

Place liqueur, vanilla, all eggs and sugar in large stainless-steel bowl. Beat with electric hand beater at high speed until light and fluffy—about 1½ minutes.

Sift flour over mixture and incorporate with wooden spoon.

Pour in milk while whisking; then transfer cream to heavy bottomed saucepan.

Cook over medium heat while mixing constantly with whisk or wooden spoon. Cream will become very thick, forming ribbons.

Transfer cream to bowl, quickly whisk in butter, and let cool before covering with waxed paper. Refrigerate until use (up to 2 days).

1 recipe *1800 calories* *294 g carbohydrate*
48 g protein *48 g fat* *2.4 g fiber*

Paradise Islands

serves 4

4	egg whites
½ cup	(*125 ml*) powdered fruit sugar
2 cups	(*500 ml*) milk
	crème anglaise *

Beat egg whites until firm, then add sugar and continue beating 1 minute.

Pour milk into large, deep saucepan and bring to boiling point. Reduce heat to allow milk to simmer.

Dip ice-cream scoop into meringue and gently drop mounds in simmering milk. Depending on the size of your pan, you may have to do this in several batches to avoid crowding. Poach meringues for 1 to 2 minutes on each side.

Using slotted spoon, remove meringues to paper towels to drain.

Ladle a small amount of crème anglaise into bottom of dessert plate. Set meringues on top and serve. If desired, decorate with caramel.

* *See Dessert on Broadway, page 463.*

1 serving *331 calories* *58 g carbohydrate*
9 g protein *7 g fat* *0 g fiber*

Icy Strawberry Soufflé

serves 4–6

3 cups	(*750 ml*) fresh strawberries, washed and hulled
1	small envelope unflavored gelatine
⅓ cup	(*75 ml*) hot water
5	large eggs, separated
½ cup	(*125 ml*) granulated sugar
1 cup	(*250 ml*) heavy cream, whipped

Prepare mold as directed in technique; set aside.

Place strawberries in food processor and purée; set aside.

Sprinkle gelatine into small bowl with hot water, mix and set aside.

Place egg yolks and granulated sugar in stainless-steel bowl. Whisk together and place over saucepan half-filled with hot water set over low heat. Cook about 2 to 3 minutes, whisking constantly.

Remove bowl from pan and whisk in gelatine mixture. Quickly whisk in puréed berries and chill until mixture starts to solidify around edges.

While mixture is chilling, beat egg whites until stiff; set aside.

Remove bowl from refrigerator and gently whisk in whipped cream. Then, using spatula, fold in beaten whites.

Pour into prepared mold and freeze 6 to 8 hours.

1 serving	*308 calories*	*25 g carbohydrate*
7 g protein	*20 g fat*	*1.8 g fiber*

1. Choose a 4-cup (1-L) straight-sided mold. Using two thicknesses of foil, make a collar long enough to wrap around mold. It should be at least 4 in. (10 cm) high. Tape securely to mold as shown in picture.

2. Place whole berries in bowl of food processor and prepare to purée.

3. Whisk puréed berries into egg mixture until well incorporated. Chill.

4. After whipped cream has been incorporated, gently fold in beaten egg whites before transferring mixture to prepared mold for freezing.

Poached Pears au Chocolat

serves 4

4	pears, cored from bottom and peeled
¼ cup	(*50 ml*) syrup *
½ cup	(*125 ml*) water
1 cup	(*250 ml*) confectioners' sugar
2 oz	(*60 g*) bitter chocolate
1 tsp	(*5 ml*) vanilla
3 tbsp	(*45 ml*) milk
1	egg yolk
4	crepes **

Place pears in saucepan. Pour syrup over pears and add water; cover and cook 3 to 4 minutes over medium heat.

Turn pears over; cover and continue cooking 3 to 4 minutes.

Remove pears from saucepan and set aside.

Place sugar, chocolate, vanilla and milk in stainless-steel bowl. Place over saucepan half-filled with hot water and melt over low heat.

Mix well and remove bowl from saucepan. Mix in egg yolk and let stand several minutes.

Meanwhile, partly wrap pears in crepes (a little syrup will held hold crepe) and place on dishes.

When chocolate is tepid, ladle over pears and serve.

* *See Rainbow Tartlets, page 488.*
** *See Sunrise-Filled Crepes, page 485.*

1 serving	*566 calories*	*92 g carbohydrate*
9 g protein	*18 g fat*	*3.9 g fiber*

Sunrise-Filled Crepes

serves 4

CREPE BATTER:

3 tbsp (*45 ml*) granulated sugar
1 cup (*250 ml*) all-purpose flour
3 large eggs
1 cup (*250 ml*) milk
½ cup (*125 ml*) warm water
3 tbsp (*45 ml*) melted butter, lukewarm
pinch salt

Place sugar, flour, salt, eggs and milk in large bowl; mix together using whisk until well incorporated.

Whisk in warm water. Add melted butter and whisk again.

Pour batter through sieve into clean bowl and refrigerate 1 hour.

Make crepes. (Refer to Allumettes, page 99, for directions, if needed.)

FILLING:

1 cup (*250 ml*) strawberries, washed and hulled
1 cup (*250 ml*) raspberries, washed
2 tbsp (*30 ml*) syrup *
1 tbsp (*15 ml*) liqueur of your choice
1 cup (*250 ml*) whipped cream

Place strawberries and raspberries in bowl and add syrup and liqueur; marinate 10 minutes.

Gently mix whipped cream with berries.

Have 8 crepes ready (you can easily freeze the rest); spread berry filling over each crepe. Fold over lengthwise and serve at once.

* *See Rainbow Tartlets, page 488.*

1 serving	*494 calories*	*54 g carbohydrate*
11 g protein	*26 g fat*	*4.4 g fiber*

Quick Raspberry Crepes

serves 4

3 cups (*750 ml*) raspberries, washed
2 tbsp (*30 ml*) syrup *
1 tsp (*5 ml*) cornstarch
2 tbsp (*30 ml*) cold water
4 crepes **
4 scoops frozen raspberry yogurt
few drops lemon juice

Purée raspberries in food processor.

Transfer berries to small saucepan with syrup and lemon juice; mix well. Bring to boil, and then simmer 8 to 10 minutes. Stir occasionally.

Mix cornstarch with cold water; incorporate to fruit and cook 1 minute.

Pour fruit sauce into bowl and set aside to cool.

When ready to serve, arrange opened crepes on plates. Spread some of fruit sauce over each and set a scoop of frozen yogurt in middle. Wrap crepe around yogurt and garnish with remaining sauce.

Serve at once.

* *See Rainbow Tartlets, page 488.*
** *See Sunrise-Filled Crepes, page 485.*

1 serving	*353 calories*	*59 g carbohydrate*
9 g protein	*9 g fat*	*7.8 g fiber*

Strawberry Cream Pie

serves 6

2 cups	(*500 ml*) fresh strawberries, washed and hulled
2 tbsp	(*30 ml*) sugar
1 cup	(*250 ml*) pastry cream * or whipped cream
1	precooked sweet dough ** shell in 19-in. (*23-cm*) loose-bottomed tart pan
	juice 1 orange

Place strawberries, sugar and orange juice in saucepan. Cover and cook 2 minutes over medium-high heat. Remove from heat and set aside to cool.

Spread pastry cream or whipped cream in bottom of sweet dough crust.

Neatly arrange berries so that they are standing up in cream. Pour juice from saucepan over berries and chill 1 hour before serving.

* *See Pastry Cream, page 480.*
** *See Cream-Filled Fruit Flan, page 495.*

1 serving	*357 calories*	*53 g carbohydrate*
7 g protein	*13 g fat*	*1.9 g fiber*

Rainbow Tartlets

serves 4–6

SYRUP:

2 cups (*500 ml*) granulated sugar
1 cup (*250 ml*) cold water

Place sugar and water in small saucepan. Set over medium heat, stir gently and boil until temperature reaches 212°F (*100°C*).

Remove syrup from heat, let cool and store in glass jar. Use as a glaze for fruit-topped desserts.

ASSEMBLY:

sweet dough *
pastry cream **
sliced fresh peaches (canned may be substituted; drained)
sliced kiwi
halved strawberries
beaten egg

Bring prepared dough to room temperature; use half for this recipe. Store leftover dough in refrigerator.

Roll out dough on floured surface using floured rolling pin and line desired number of tartlet pans. Trim off excess dough while leaving sides higher than edges of pan. Pinch edges with fingertips and chill 30 minutes.

Preheat oven to 400°F (*200°C*).

Prick bottom and sides of dough with fork and brush with beaten egg. Precook in oven about 8 to 10 minutes or until cooked and brown in color. Cool.

Arrange tartlets on serving platter and spoon some pastry cream in bottom of each. Artfully arrange fruit on top and glaze with syrup.

Chill before serving.

* *See Cream-Filled Fruit Flan, page 495.*
** *See Pastry Cream, page 480.*

1 serving	*423 calories*	*64 g carbohydrate*
8 g protein	*15 g fat*	*1.6 g fiber*

Raspberry Peach Tartlets

serves 4

2	ripe peaches, halved and peeled
2 tbsp	(*30 ml*) syrup *
2 tbsp	(*30 ml*) Jazz peach flavored vodka
1 cup	(*250 ml*) raspberries, washed
	sweet dough ** (for tartlet shells)
	chocolate sauce ***

Bake tartlet shells 8 to 10 minutes in oven preheated at 400 °F (*200 °C*).

Place 4 precooked cooled tartlets on serving platter and fill bottoms with chocolate sauce. Set aside.

Place peaches in saucepan with syrup and vodka. Cover and poach 3 to 4 minutes. Turn once during cooking.

Using slotted spoon, transfer peaches to plate; set aside to cool.

Add raspberries to syrup in saucepan and cook 2 minutes over medium heat. Do not cover.

Transfer sauce to food processor and purée; let cool.

To assemble dessert, place peach half (cut side down) in tartlet on chocolate sauce.

Spoon raspberry sauce over and serve.

* *See Rainbow Tartlets, page 488.*
** *See Cream-Filled Fruit Flan, page 495.*
*** *See Poached Pears au Chocolat, page 484.*

1 serving	*625 calories*	*92 g carbohydrate*
8 g protein	*25 g fat*	*4.4 g fiber*

Fresh Blueberry Pie

serves 6–8

4 cups	(*1 L*) fresh blueberries, washed
3 tbsp	(*45 ml*) granulated sugar
3 tbsp	(*45 ml*) brown sugar
1 tbsp	(*15 ml*) grated orange rind
1 tbsp	(*15 ml*) grated lemon rind
2 tbsp	(*30 ml*) sifted cornstarch
1 tbsp	(*15 ml*) butter
	pie dough *
	beaten egg

Preheat oven to 400°F (*200°C*).

Roll out half of dough and line 9-in. (*23-cm*) pie plate.

Place berries, both types of sugar, both rinds and cornstarch in bowl; toss together and pack into pie shell. Dot with butter.

Roll out other half of dough. Moisten edges of pie shell with water and carefully lay pie crust on top. Pinch edges shut and make several slits with small knife in upper crust.

Brush dough with beaten egg and place in oven; bake 40 to 45 minutes.

* *See All-American Apple Pie, page 491.*

1 serving	*387 calories*	*49 g carbohydrate*
5 g protein	*19 g fat*	*6.8 g fiber*

All-American Apple Pie

serves 6–8

PIE DOUGH:

2 cups	(*500 ml*) sifted all-purpose flour
⅔ cup	(*150 ml*) shortening, room temperature
¼ cup	(*50 ml*) chilled water
1 tbsp	(*15 ml*) chilled water
pinch	salt

Resift flour with salt into large bowl. Add shortening and, using pastry blender, incorporate until mixture resembles oatmeal.

Add both measures of chilled water and form dough into ball. Wrap in waxed paper and refrigerate 1 hour.

Before using, remove dough and let stand 1 hour at room temperature.

Cut dough in half. Flour board and rolling pin; roll out half of dough and line 9-in. (*23-cm*) pie plate. Set aside.

FILLING:

7	baking apples, peeled, cored and sliced
3 tbsp	(*45 ml*) granulated sugar
3 tbsp	(*45 ml*) brown sugar
1 tsp	(*5 ml*) cinnamon
2 tbsp	(*30 ml*) sifted cornstarch
1 tbsp	(*15 ml*) grated lemon rind
1 tbsp	(*15 ml*) lemon juice
1 tbsp	(*15 ml*) butter
	beaten egg

Preheat oven to 400°F (*200°C*).

Place apples, both types of sugar, cinnamon, cornstarch, lemon rind and lemon juice in bowl; toss together and pack into prepared pie shell. Dot apples with butter.

Roll out other half of dough. Moisten edges of pie shell with water and carefully lay pie crust on top. Pinch edges shut and make several slits with small knife in upper crust.

Brush dough with beaten egg and place in oven; bake 40 to 45 minutes. Serve pie plain, with cheese or with vanilla ice cream.

1 serving	*415 calories*	*56 g carbohydrate*
5 g protein	*19 g fat*	*3.6 g fiber*

Old-Fashioned Apple Crumb Pie

serves 6

2 tbsp	(*30 ml*) all-purpose flour
1 tsp	(*5 ml*) cinnamon
½ cup	(*125 ml*) brown sugar
6	large cooking apples, cored, peeled and sliced
⅓ cup	(*75 ml*) all-purpose flour
⅓ cup	(*75 ml*) butter, softened
⅓ cup	(*75 ml*) brown sugar
	few drops lemon juice
	pie dough

Preheat oven to 400°F (*200°C*). Have ready 9-in. (*23-cm*) pie plate lined with dough.

Mix 2 tbsp (*30 ml*) flour, cinnamon and ½ cup (*125 ml*) brown sugar together in bowl. Add apples and lemon juice and toss until evenly coated.

Pack apples into pie shell. Mix remaining ingredients together and sprinkle over top.

Bake 15 minutes in oven; then reduce heat to 375°F (*190°C*) and continue baking 35 minutes.

1 serving	*470 calories*	*74 g carbohydrate*
3 g protein	*18 g fat*	*4.1 g fiber*

Peach-Filled Puffs with Chantilly Cream

serves 6

3 tbsp	(*45 ml*) syrup *
4 tbsp	(*60 ml*) water
2 tbsp	(*30 ml*) Lamb's light rum
3	ripe peaches, halved and peeled
1½ cups	(*375 ml*) heavy cream, cold
1 tsp	(*5 ml*) vanilla
¼ cup	(*50 ml*) sifted confectioners' sugar
6	cream puffs **

Place syrup, water, rum and peach halves in saucepan; cook 3 minutes at boil. Remove from heat and let fruit cool in syrup.

Drain peaches well and slice; set aside.

Pour cream and vanilla into stainless-steel bowl. Beat at medium speed until soft peaks form.

Add half of confectioners' sugar; beat 45 seconds at high speed. Gently fold in remaining sugar.

Slice off tops of cream puffs. Spoon Chantilly cream into pastry bag fitted with star nozzle and fill bottoms of puffs.

Arrange peach slices on cream and reassemble puffs. You may serve at once, if desired, or chill several hours until use.

* *See Rainbow Tartlets, page 488.*
** *See Chocolate Éclairs, page 496.*

1 serving	*491 calories*	*35 g carbohydrate*
9 g protein	*35 g fat*	*1.4 g fiber*

Blueberry and Peach Open Pie

serves 6

3 cups	(*750 ml*) fresh blueberries, washed and stemmed
2	peaches, peeled and sliced
1 tbsp	(*15 ml*) grated lemon rind
1 tbsp	(*15 ml*) grated orange rind
1 tbsp	(*15 ml*) grated lime rind
1 tbsp	(*15 ml*) cornstarch
3 tbsp	(*45 ml*) granulated sugar
1	precooked sweet dough * shell in 9-in. (*23-cm*) loose-bottomed tart pan

Place all pie ingredients in saucepan. Cover and cook 5 to 6 minutes over medium-high heat. Remove and let cool.

Pour into sweet dough crust and chill 30 minutes before serving. If desired, decorate with whipped cream.

* *See Cream-Filled Fruit Flan, page 495.*

1 serving	*298 calories*	*48 g carbohydrate*
4 g protein	*10 g fat*	*6.7 g fiber*

Cream-Filled Fruit Flan

serves 4–6

SWEET DOUGH:

(for tartlets, tarts and various desserts)

1¾ cups	(*425 ml*)	sifted all-purpose flour
¼ lb	(*125 g*)	unsalted butter, softened
⅔ cup	(*150 ml*)	granulated sugar
¼ tsp	(*1 ml*)	vanilla
1		large egg
2 tbsp	(*30 ml*)	cold water
pinch		salt
		beaten egg

Mound flour on cutting board and sprinkle in salt. Make well in middle of flour and add all of butter. Using fingertips, incorporate until mixture resembles oatmeal.

Form another well in middle and add sugar, vanilla, egg and water. Incorporate until mixture becomes dough-like and forms ball.

Knead dough 2 or 3 times only, to incorporate fully. Wrap in clean cloth and let rest 1 hour in bottom of refrigerator.

Remember to remove dough from refrigerator 1 hour before using.

For this fruit flan use half of dough. Remaining dough can be kept for several days in refrigerator.

Using floured rolling pin, roll out dough on floured surface until about ⅛ in. (*0.30 cm*) thick. Drape dough over rolling pin and carefully unroll over medium-size flan ring or springform pie plate. Gently line pan and trim off excess dough, leaving sides higher than edges of pan. Pinch edges with fingertips and chill 30 minutes.

Preheat oven to 400°F (*200°C*).

Prick bottom and sides of dough with fork. Cut out circle of waxed paper to fit bottom and place on dough.

(*continued on page 496*)

Cover with baking weights or dried beans. Place in oven and precook until just brown.

Remove from oven and take out weights and paper; brush all over with beaten egg. Return to oven and continue precooking about 10 minutes.

Cool before filling.

FILLING:

½ cup	(*125 ml*) apricot jelly or jam
2 tbsp	(*30 ml*) syrup *
	pastry cream **
	sliced fresh peaches (canned can be substituted; drained)
	sliced kiwi
	halved strawberries

Place apricot jelly and syrup in small saucepan; cook 2 minutes over medium heat. Strain through sieve and set aside until tepid.

Spread pastry cream in bottom of precooked shell. Arrange fruit neatly by type, starting from outside.

Brush tepid glaze mixture over fruit and chill 1 hour before serving.

* *See Rainbow Tartlets, page 488.*
** *See Pastry Cream, page 480.*

1 serving	*474 calories*	*80 g carbohydrate*
7 g protein	*14 g fat*	*1.8 g fiber*

Chocolate Éclairs

serves 4–6

CREAM PUFF DOUGH:

1 cup	(*250 ml*) water
4 tbsp	(*60 ml*) unsalted butter, cut into pieces
¼ tsp	(*1 ml*) salt
1 cup	(*250 ml*) all-purpose flour
4	large eggs
	beaten egg

Preheat oven to 375°F (*190°C*). Lightly butter and flour 2 cookie sheets; set aside.

Place water, butter and salt in heavy-bottomed saucepan. Bring to boil and cook 2 minutes until butter is completely melted. Remove pan from heat.

Add all of flour, mixing rapidly with wooden spoon.

Return saucepan to stove over low heat. Dry dough 3 to 4 minutes, stirring constantly with wooden spoon. The dough should not adhere to your fingers when pinched.

Transfer dough to bowl and let cool 4 to 5 minutes. Add 4 eggs, one at a time, mixing well between additions. The dough must regain its original texture before the next egg is added.

Spoon dough into pastry bag fitted with plain nozzle. Squeeze out desired shapes onto prepared cookie sheets, leaving enough space between each for rising.

Brush tops with beaten egg and smooth tails with fork; set aside 20 minutes.

Place cookie sheets in middle of oven and bake 35 minutes. Turn oven off, set door ajar and let dry 1 hour before filling.

ASSEMBLY:

4 oz	(*125 g*) unsweetened chocolate
4 tbsp	(*60 ml*) water
⅓ cup	(*75 ml*) granulated sugar
	whipped cream

Place chocolate in stainless-steel bowl; melt over saucepan containing warm water set over low heat.

Transfer chocolate to small saucepan and add water and sugar; bring to boiling point.

Remove saucepan from heat and let cool to lukewarm; beat mixture to thicken.

Carefully slice éclairs in half lengthwise and fill bottoms with whipped cream. You can use a variety of other creams such as Chocolate Filling Cream (see page 474).

Dip tops in chocolate and assemble; chill until set.

1 serving	*602 calories*	*36 g carbohydrate*
11 g protein	*46 g fat*	*1.3 g fiber*

Chocolate Bread

serves 6–8

4 oz	(*125 g*) semisweet chocolate
½ cup	(*125 ml*) powdered fruit sugar
¼ lb	(*125 g*) butter, softened
3	large eggs
½ cup	(*125 ml*) sifted cake flour
¼ cup	(*50 ml*) chopped walnuts (optional)
2 tbsp	(*30 ml*) blanched sliced almonds
2	egg whites, beaten stiff

Preheat oven to 350°F (*180°C*). Lightly butter and flour 5 × 9 in. (*13 × 23 cm*) loaf pan that is about 2½ in. (*6 cm*) deep; set aside.

Place chocolate in stainless-steel bowl and set in oven to melt.

Remove bowl; add sugar and butter. Mix well with whisk.

Add whole eggs, one at a time, whisking well between additions.

Sift flour over batter and incorporate with wooden spoon.

Stir in nuts and fold in egg whites. Transfer batter to prepared loaf pan and rap bottom against cutting board to settle batter.

Bake 40 minutes in oven or until cake is done.

Remove from oven, cool slightly in pan, and unmold onto wire rack to finish cooling.

Slice as you would a loaf of bread and serve with milk. A midnight snack if there ever was one!

1 serving	*362 calories*	*25 g carbohydrate*
7 g protein	*26 g fat*	*0.9 g fiber*

Nutty Chocolate Quatre-Quarts

serves 6–8

4 oz	(*125 g*) semisweet chocolate
⅓ cup	(*75 ml*) granulated sugar
2 tbsp	(*30 ml*) Tia Maria
¾ cup	(*175 ml*) melted butter
4	large egg yolks
½ cup	(*125 ml*) sifted cake flour
½ cup	(*125 ml*) chopped nuts
4	large egg whites, beaten stiff

Preheat oven to 350°F (*180°C*). Butter and flour 8-in. (*20-cm*) square cake pan; set aside.

Place chocolate, sugar and Tia Maria in stainless-steel bowl placed over saucepan half-filled with hot water. Melt over low heat.

Remove from heat and whisk in melted butter.

Add egg yolks, one at a time, beating very well between additions with electric hand beater.

Sift flour over batter and incorporate with wooden spoon. Fold in nuts.

Fold in egg whites until most trace of white is gone.

Pour batter into prepared cake pan and bake 30 to 35 minutes or until cake is done.

Cool slightly in pan before unmolding onto wire rack. When completely cooled, cut into squares and serve. Although this is a rich-tasting cake, you will find it very light.

1 serving	*422 calories*	*22 g carbohydrate*
7 g protein	*34 g fat*	*1.1 g fiber*

Basic Génoise Cake

serves 6–8

¾ cup	(*175 ml*) granulated sugar
5	large eggs
1¼ cups	(*300 ml*) sifted cake flour
¼ cup	(*50 ml*) clarified butter, tepid
	Tia Maria
	pastry cream *
	chocolate flakes

Preheat oven to 350°F (*180°C*). Lightly butter and flour 8½-in. (*22-cm*) springform cake pan.

Place sugar in stainless-steel bowl set over saucepan half-filled with hot water. Add eggs. Over low heat with water simmering, whisk for 4 to 5 minutes. Use electric hand beater if desired.

Mixture should become quite thick and expand in volume. When cream forms ribbons, transfer bowl to counter. Sift 1 cup (*250 ml*) of flour over bowl; fold in using spatula until all traces are gone.

Sift in rest of flour and fold using spatula. Gradually add butter while folding. All traces of butter must be incorporated.

Pour batter into cake pan and bake in middle of oven 35 to 40 minutes or until cake is done.

Let stand 5 minutes; then unmold and finish cooling on wire rack.

When cold, slice off layer. Sprinkle Tia Maria over bottom layer and cover with pastry cream. Replace top layer, sprinkle with more liqueur and ice outside of cake with remaining cream. Top with chocolate flakes and chill 2 hours.

* *See Pastry Cream, page 480.*

1 serving	*428 calories*	*57 g carbohydrate*
10 g protein	*16 g fat*	*1.0 g fiber*

1. Whisk sugar and eggs together in stainless-steel bowl set over saucepan with simmering water. Continue for 4 to 5 minutes—do not stop stirring.

2. The sugar and egg mixture will become considerably thicker and expand greatly in volume. Also, when it is folded with a spatula it will form ribbons—at this point, remove bowl to counter.

3. Even though flour is sifted, resift it when adding it to batter. Incorporate flour in 2 measures.

4. Incorporate butter in thin stream while continuing to fold with spatula—all trace of yellow must be gone. If needed, use wooden spoon to finish incorporating.

Vanilla Quatre-Quarts

serves 6–8

4		large eggs
¾ cup		(*175 ml*) granulated sugar
½ tsp		(*2 ml*) vanilla
¾ cup		(*175 ml*) sifted cake flour
¼ cup		(*50 ml*) clarified butter, tepid

Preheat oven to 350°F (*180°C*). Butter and flour 8-in. (*20-cm*) square cake pan; set aside.

Beat eggs with sugar and vanilla using electric hand beater. Continue for 3 to 4 minutes or until foamy.

Sift flour over mixture and incorporate with spatula.

Incorporate butter with spatula. Pour batter into prepared cake pan and bake 30 minutes or until cake is done.

Cool slightly in pan before unmolding onto wire rack. When completely cooled, cut into squares and serve. This cake is a delicious treat for school lunches.

1 serving	*200 calories*	*28 g carbohydrate*
4 g protein	*8 g fat*	*0.4 g fiber*

Almond Vodka Cake

serves 6

¾ cup	(*175 ml*) granulated sugar
5	large eggs, separated
¼ tsp	(*1 ml*) vanilla
3 tbsp	(*45 ml*) Jazz peach flavored vodka
1¾ cups	(*425 ml*) powdered almonds
1 cup	(*250 ml*) sifted cake flour
¼ cup	(*50 ml*) melted clarified butter

Preheat oven to 350°F (*180°C*). Butter and flour 8½-in. (*22-cm*) springform cake pan; set aside.

Place sugar, egg yolks, vanilla and vodka in large bowl; beat with electric hand beater until light and frothy.

Beat egg whites until stiff; set aside.

Sift half of powdered almonds and half of flour; add half of beaten whites to sugar/yolk mixture in large bowl. Fold to incorporate using spatula.

Add remaining almonds, flour and whites using same procedure.

Incorporate butter in thin stream while folding constantly until well incorporated.

Pour batter into cake pan and bake 30 to 35 minutes or until cake is done.

Cool slightly on counter before unmolding, and then let stand on wire cake rack until cold.

This cake can be served plain or dressed up a bit, depending on the occasion. Use your imagination.

1 serving	*543 calories*	*51 g carbohydrate*
15 g protein	*31 g fat*	*1.7 g fiber*

Super-Rich Double Cheesecake

serves 10–12

2	8-oz (*250-g*) packages cream cheese, room temperature
2 cups	(*500 ml*) ricotta cheese, room temperature
½ cup	(*125 ml*) granulated sugar
3	large eggs
3	egg yolks
2 tbsp	(*30 ml*) Jazz peach flavored vodka
1 cup	(*250 ml*) whipped cream
3 cups	(*750 ml*) raspberries, washed
2 tbsp	(*30 ml*) syrup *
1 tsp	(*5 ml*) cornstarch
2 tbsp	(*30 ml*) cold water
	graham crumb crust **
	finely grated rind 1 orange and 1 lemon
pinch	nutmeg
	few drops lemon juice

Preheat oven to 325 °F (*160 °C*).

Place cream cheese in bowl of mixer; cream until soft. Add ricotta cheese and continue mixing until incorporated. Mix in fruit rinds.

Add sugar and nutmeg to bowl; mix to incorporate, scraping sides of bowl with spatula if needed.

Add whole eggs, mix thoroughly and scrape down sides as needed. Continue blending until batter is smooth.

Add egg yolks and vodka; mix again.

Spoon in whipped cream and blend once more.

Pour batter into prepared crust, smoothing top with spatula. Bake in middle of oven for 1½ hours. Remove from oven and let cool. Chill 6 to 8 hours in cake pan before serving.

At some point before serving, make fruit topping. Purée raspberries in food processor; transfer to small saucepan.

Add syrup and lemon juice, mix well and bring to boil. Simmer 8 to 10 minutes, stirring occasionally.

Mix cornstarch with cold water; stir into mixture and cook 1 more minute. Pour fruit topping into bowl and set aside to cool. Chill before spreading over cake.

If desired, decorate with whipped cream piped through pastry bag.

** See Rainbow Tartlets, page 488.*

*** Prepare graham crumb crust according to directions on package. Use 9-in. (23-cm) springform cake pan. Cook as directed.*

1 serving	*440 calories*	*27 g carbohydrate*
11 g protein	*32 g fat*	*2.5 g fiber*

1. Cream both cheeses with fruit rinds in bowl of electric mixer.

2. Add sugar and nutmeg; mix to incorporate, scraping sides of bowl with spatula if needed.

3. Add whole eggs, mix very well and scrape down sides as needed. Continue beating until batter is smooth.

4. Add egg yolks and vodka.

Strawberry Layer Cake

serves 10–12

3 cups	(*750 ml*) fresh strawberries, halved
2 tbsp	(*30 ml*) powdered fruit sugar
2 tbsp	(*30 ml*) orange juice
2	Génoise cakes *
	Grand Marnier liqueur
	whipped cream

Marinate strawberries in sugar and orange juice for 30 minutes.

When ready to assemble dessert, begin by slicing Génoise cakes into 2 layers, for a total of 4 layers.

Set first layer on cake plate and soak with liqueur. Spread a layer of whipped cream over cake and arrange a layer of strawberries.

Repeat above procedure for remaining layers, ending with final topping of strawberries artistically arranged for a pretty presentation.

If desired, choose another fruit to garnish top of cake and use leftover whipped cream piped through pastry bag to decorate sides, as shown in picture.

* *See Basic Génoise Cake, page 500. For this recipe use 10-in.* (26-cm) *springform cake pans. Remember to make 2!*

1 serving	*475 calories*	*54 g carbohydrate*
9 g protein	*23 g fat*	*1.8 g fiber*

INDEX

indicates use of a microwave oven.

RECIPE INDEX

indicates use of a microwave oven.